GCSE OCR 21st Century
Physics
The Revision Guide

This book is for anyone doing **GCSE OCR 21st Century Physics**.

GCSE Science is all about **understanding how science works**.
And not only that — understanding it well enough to be able to **question** what you hear on TV and read in the papers.

But you can't do that without a fair chunk of **background knowledge**. Hmm, tricky.

Happily this CGP book includes all the **science facts** you need to learn, and shows you how they work in the **real world**. And in true CGP style, we've explained it all as **clearly and concisely** as possible.

It's also got some daft bits in to try and make the whole experience at least vaguely entertaining for you.

What CGP is all about

Our sole aim here at CGP is to produce the highest quality books — carefully written, immaculately presented and dangerously close to being funny.

Then we work our socks off to get them out to you — at the cheapest possible prices.

Contents

Ideas About Science

Module P1 — The Earth in the Universe

Module P2 — Radiation and Life

Module P3 — Sustainable Energy

Module P4 — Explaining Motion

Module P5 — Electric Circuits

Module P6 — Radioactive Materials

Module P7 — Studying the Universe

Controlled Assessment

Published by CGP

From original material by Richard Parsons.

Editors:
Helena Hayes, Helen Ronan, Lyn Setchell, Jane Towle, Julie Wakeling, Dawn Wright.

Contributors:
Mark A Edwards, Moira Steven, Paul Warren, Andy Williams.

ISBN: 978 1 84762 636 3

With thanks to Mark A Edwards, Ian Francis and Glenn Rogers for the proofreading.

With thanks to Jan Greenway for the copyright research.

With thanks to iStockphoto for permission to reproduce the photograph used on page 12.

Graph to show trend in atmospheric CO_2 concentration and global temperature on page 24 based on data by EPICA Community Members 2004 and Siegenthaler et al 2005.

Data used to construct table on page 67 from World Nuclear Association: www.world-nuclear.org

With thanks to Science Photo Library for permission to reproduce the images used on pages 87 and 88.

Groovy website: www.cgpbooks.co.uk

Printed by Elanders Ltd, Newcastle upon Tyne.
Jolly bits of clipart from CorelDRAW®

The Scientific Process

This section isn't about how to 'do' science — but it does show you the way most scientists work, and how scientists try to find decent explanations for things that happen. It's pretty important stuff.

Scientists Come Up With Hypotheses — Then Test Them

1) Scientists try to explain things. Everything.
2) They start by observing or thinking about something they don't understand — it could be anything, e.g. planets in the sky, a person suffering from an illness, what matter is made of... anything.
3) They then try to come up with a hypothesis:
   - A hypothesis isn't just a summary of their observations (e.g. alpha particles can't penetrate paper).
   - It's an explanation for it (e.g. alpha particles can't penetrate paper because of their large size).
   - Observations made by scientists are just that — observations. They don't show what the hypothesis should be. In order to come up with a decent explanation for their observations, scientists need to use their imagination.
   - A good hypothesis should account for all of the observations made and any other available data (i.e. what's already been observed). If it doesn't, it's not really a very good explanation.
4) The next step is to test whether the hypothesis might be right or not. This involves making a prediction based on the hypothesis and testing it by gathering evidence (i.e. data) from investigations.
5) If evidence from experiments backs up a prediction, it increases confidence in the hypothesis — in other words, people are more likely to believe that the hypothesis is true. It doesn't prove a hypothesis is correct though — evidence could still be found that disagrees with it.
6) If the experimental evidence doesn't fit with the hypothesis, then either those results or the hypothesis must be wrong — this decreases confidence in the hypothesis.
7) Sometimes a hypothesis will account for all the data and still turn out to be wrong — that's why every hypothesis needs to be tested further (see next page).

Different Scientists Can Come Up With Different Explanations

Observations can pretty much always be explained in more than one way. Which can make the scientific process a little tricky...

1) Different scientists can make the same observations and come up with different explanations for them — and both these explanations might be perfectly good ones.
2) This is because you need to interpret what you're observing to come up with an explanation, and different people often interpret things in different ways.
3) Sometimes a scientist's personal background will influence the way he or she thinks. For example, a trained geneticist might lean towards a genetic explanation for a particular disease, but someone else might think it's more about the environment.
4) In these situations, it's important to test the explanations as much as possible — to see which one is most likely to be true (or whether it's a combination of both).

Science is a "real-world" subject...

Science isn't just about explaining things that people are curious about. If scientists can explain something that happens in the world, then maybe they can predict what will happen in the future. They might even be able to control future events. This could make life a bit better in some way, either for themselves or for other people.

The Scientific Process

The scientific process can be quite long... which is why there's another page on it. I bet you just can't wait to see how it ends up. Enjoy.

Several Scientists Will Test a Hypothesis

1) The scientific process depends on 'peer review'. This means that scientific explanations are judged by other scientists who work in the same field.

2) Traditionally, new scientific explanations are announced in peer-reviewed journals, or at scientific conferences.

A peer-reviewed journal is one where other scientists check results and scientific explanations before the journal is published. They check that people have been 'scientific' about what they're saying (e.g. that experiments have been done in a sensible way). But this doesn't mean that the findings are correct, just that they're not wrong in any obvious kind of way.

3) Once other scientists have found out about a hypothesis (through a journal or conference), they'll start to base their own predictions on it and carry out their own experiments. This allows them to test and critically evaluate the new hypothesis.

4) When other scientists test the new hypothesis they will also try to reproduce the earlier results. Results that can't be reproduced by another scientist aren't very reliable (they're hard to trust) — and scientists tend to be pretty sceptical about them.

5) There's very little confidence in new claims that haven't been evaluated by other scientists in this way.

If Evidence Supports a Hypothesis, It's Accepted — for Now

1) If a hypothesis survives the peer review process, then scientists start to have a lot of confidence in it and accept it as a theory. Our currently accepted theories have been tested many, many times over the years and survived.

2) Once scientists have gone through this process and accepted a theory, they take a lot of persuading to drop it — even if some new data appears that can't be explained using the existing theory.

3) Until a better, more plausible explanation is found (one that can explain both the old and new data), the tried and tested theory is likely to stick around — because it already explains loads of other observations really well. And remember, scientists are always sceptical about new data until it's been proved to be reliable (see above).

That's my theory and I'm sticking to it...

So there you have it. The scientific process in a nutshell. A two-page nutshell. More of a coconut shell really... Never mind. The point is, these two pages contain everything you need to know about how scientists go from making an observation, to coming up with a nice, neat explanation. And in case you were thinking this has no relevance to you, you'll need to know it for your controlled assessment (see p. 90-93) and for your exams.

Data

This page is all about what scientists do with data and why it's so important...

Scientists Need Reliable Data, Not Opinion, to Justify an Explanation

1) The only scientific way to test a hypothesis is to gather reliable data.
2) Reliable data is data that has been repeated by a scientist lots of times or reproduced by other scientists in independent experiments.
3) Opinions are not reliable data — they can't be reproduced in an experiment by other scientists, so they can't be used to support a hypothesis.

Measurements Will Always Vary to Some Extent

1) If you take a lot of measurements of the same thing, you won't always get the same result.
2) This could be for lots of reasons, e.g. the conditions you're taking your measurements in change, or you've made a mistake when measuring (human error).
3) Because measurements of the same thing always vary, no individual measurement can be relied upon to give you the true value of the quantity you're measuring.

Repeating Measurements Helps You to Estimate the True Value

1) To get a good estimate of the true value, scientists must repeat their measurements.
2) Repeated measurements will have a range of values — some values will be higher than the true value and some will be lower. This means it's likely that the true value lies somewhere within this range.
3) The true value can then be estimated by calculating the mean (the average value — add up all the repeated results and divide by the total number of results).
4) Because individual results vary, the mean result is more likely to be close to the true value. This is because it accounts for the variations (both higher and lower) of several repeats — which should roughly cancel each other out.
5) Measurements that are obviously outside the range of repeated results are called outliers — they're usually a sign that something has gone wrong. If possible, a scientist will check the measurement — and if they've got a good reason to doubt its accuracy, they'll ignore it.

EXAMPLE: This table shows the results of an experiment to measure the density of gold — the measurement was repeated 8 times:

1) The result of test 3 is very different from the others. It's an outlier. It's likely that an error occurred when the measurement was taken, so it can be ignored.
2) The table suggests that the true value of the density of gold is in the range of 19.1 – 19.5 g/cm^3, where most of the measurements lie.
3) A mean (average) gives you the best estimate of the true value. In this case it works out at 19.3 g/cm^3.

Test	Density of gold (g/cm^3)
1	19.3
2	19.4
3	12.8
4	19.1
5	19.3
6	19.2
7	19.5
8	19.2

Working out averages — it's just mean...

Data is the cornerstone of science — it's used to test every hypothesis, so it really is pretty blummin' important. What a shame then, that estimating the true value and spotting outliers isn't just a bit more fun... sigh...

Correlation and Cause

Correlation and cause come up a lot in science, so it's important that you understand the difference.

A Correlation is a Relationship Between Two Factors

1) Scientists often think about scientific processes as a load of different factors which might affect an outcome. For example, if the outcome is getting skin cancer, it might be affected by factors such as where a person lives, occupation, genes, etc.
2) They collect data and use it to look for relationships between a factor and an outcome.
3) If an outcome happens when a factor is there, but not when it isn't there, scientists say there's a correlation — i.e. the outcome is related to the factor.
4) If an outcome increases or decreases as a factor increases or decreases, they're also said to be correlated.

A Correlation Doesn't Prove One Thing Causes Another

Just because there's a correlation between a factor and an outcome, it doesn't mean that the factor causes the outcome. There might be another, hidden factor that's affecting them both. Here's an example:

1) Primary school children with bigger feet tend to be better at maths.
   There's a correlation between the factor (big feet) and the outcome (better maths skills).
2) But it'd be crazy to say that having big feet causes you to be better at maths (and even weirder to say that being good at maths causes bigger feet...).
3) There's another (hidden) factor involved — their age. Older children are usually better at maths. They also usually have bigger feet. Age affects both their maths skills and the size of their feet.

Sometimes a correlation is just when a factor makes an outcome more likely, but not inevitable. E.g. if you spend a lot of time in the sun, it increases your risk of getting skin cancer, but doesn't mean you will get it.

Scientists Need to Do Fair Tests

1) A scientist might notice a correlation between a factor and an outcome and hypothesise that the factor causes the outcome. To check this, they must then look for evidence by doing a scientific study.
2) To make their study a fair test, the scientist must control all the other factors that might influence the outcome. This will make sure that the only factor affecting the outcome is the one being studied (see page 90).
3) Scientists can't usually test the whole population that they're studying (e.g. everyone who lives near a nuclear power plant) so they compare samples instead. A sample is just a portion of the population.
4) There are two ways that scientists can make sure their study is a fair test when comparing samples:
   - The samples can be matched in every way apart from the factor that they're investigating.
   - The samples can be chosen at random — then it's equally likely that all samples will be affected by other factors in the same way.
5) The larger the sample size used in a study, the more confident a scientist can be about their hypothesis. E.g. scientists wouldn't have much confidence in the findings of a study linking nuclear power plants to cancer if only a few people who live near nuclear power plants had been surveyed.
6) Scientists don't usually accept that a factor causes an outcome unless they can work out a plausible mechanism that links the two things. E.g. there's a higher rate of skin cancer in people that spend a lot of time in the sun than people who don't — the factor (exposure to sunlight) and the outcome (cancer) are correlated. Sunlight contains cancer-causing radiation that's absorbed by skin — this is the mechanism.

All sheep die — Elvis died, so he must have been a sheep...

You read about correlations in the media all the time. Reporters often make the mistake of thinking that if two things are correlated then one must cause the other. However, you can't, can't, can't just think this. Got that?

Risk

By reading this page you are agreeing to the risk of a paper cut or severe drowsiness that could affect your ability to operate heavy machinery... Think carefully — the choice is yours.

Nothing is Completely Risk-Free

1) Everything that you do has a risk attached to it.
2) Some risks seem pretty obvious, or we've known about them for a while, like the risk of getting cancer if you work with radiation, or of having a car accident when you're travelling in a car.
3) New technology arising from scientific advances can bring new risks, e.g. some scientists believe that using a mobile phone a lot may be harmful.
4) You can estimate the size of a risk based on how many times something has happened in a big sample (e.g. 100 000 people) over a given period (say, a year). For example, you could assess the risk of a driver crashing their car by recording how many people in a group of 100 000 drivers crashed their cars in a one year period.
5) To make a decision about an activity that involves a risk, we need to take into account the chance of the risk happening and how serious the consequences would be if it did. So if an activity involves a risk that's very likely to happen, with serious consequences if it does, that activity is considered high risk.

People Make Their Own Decisions About Risk

1) Not all risks have the same consequences, e.g. if you chop veg with a sharp knife you risk cutting your finger, but if you go scuba-diving you risk death. You're much more likely to cut your finger during half an hour of chopping than to die during half an hour of scuba-diving. But most people are happier to accept a higher probability of an accident if the consequences are short-lived and fairly minor.
2) People also tend to be more willing to accept a risk if they're choosing to do something (e.g. go scuba diving), rather than if they're having the risk imposed on them (e.g. having a nuclear power station built next door).
3) People's perception of risk (how risky they think something is) isn't always accurate. They tend to view familiar activities as low-risk and unfamiliar activities as high-risk — even if that's not the case. For example, cycling on roads is often high-risk, but many people are happy to do it because it's a familiar activity. Air travel is actually pretty safe, but a lot of people perceive it as high-risk.
4) People also tend to over-estimate the risk of things whose effect lasts a long time, or is invisible, e.g. ionising radiation.

We have to Choose Acceptable Levels of Risk

1) Activities have different benefits and risks for different groups of people. For example, in building and running a new nuclear power station:

- Construction companies benefit from years of work in building the power station.
- Local people benefit from new jobs — but risk suffering from higher radiation exposure.
- The national population benefits from a reliable source of electricity — but some people may be at risk.
- There's a global benefit because nuclear power contributes a lot less to climate change than burning fossil fuels — but there's a global risk too, from a major accident like the Chernobyl disaster.

2) To make a decision about a course of action (e.g. whether or not to build a new nuclear power station) we need to weigh up the benefits and risks involved for everyone.
3) Governments and public bodies are often the ones who have to choose on behalf of other people whether the risks for a particular course of action are acceptable. Sometimes their decisions can be controversial, especially if the people who are most at risk are not the ones that benefit.

Not revising — an unacceptable exam risk...

All activities pose some sort of risk, it's just a question of deciding whether that risk is worth it in the long run.

Science — Benefits and Costs

Science can give us amazing things — cures for diseases, space travel, heated toilet seats... But sometimes, these things come at a cost.

Scientific Technology Usually Has Benefits and Costs

Scientists have created loads of new technologies that could improve our lives. With nuclear technology, for example, benefits include:

1) Being able to generate huge amounts of electrical energy.
2) Releasing less greenhouse gases into the atmosphere (compared to fossil fuels) when generating electricity.

However, it's not all good news. Sometimes new technology can have unintended or undesired impacts on our quality of life or the environment. For example:

1) Working with radioactive isotopes can increase people's risks of getting certain types of cancer.
2) Nuclear reactors are fairly safe but when accidents happen they can have long-lasting effects for large numbers of people, as well as the environment.
3) Nuclear waste is hard to get rid of and can be damaging to the environment.
4) When a nuclear power station is shut down, it takes a long time before the land can be used safely for anything else.

When developing new technologies, the benefits should always be weighed against the costs.

Human Activities Impact on the Environment

1) Even when we don't mean to, human beings have a huge effect on our surroundings. Science can help us to identify some of the unintentional impacts our activities have on the environment. For example, the main impacts of massive human population growth are:

- We're using more land — we need land to build houses, grow crops and farm animals. To get it we often have to cut down forests and take over grassland.
- We're using more non-renewable resources — these are resources (such as fuels) that will eventually run out, e.g. oil, coal and natural gas.
- We're polluting more — more people means more rubbish, sewage, cars and industry, which can seriously damage the environment.

2) Scientists can also help us to minimise the effects of our activities and make the way we live more sustainable — i.e. less damaging to the environment, so that we don't use up resources for future generations. For example:

- Developing techniques for improving crop yield should mean we can grow more crops in a smaller area — so less land gets taken up by agriculture.
- Developing technology which generates electricity from renewable energy sources (e.g. wind power, solar power) should help reduce the need for us to use coal, oil and natural gas as fuels — so they'll last longer.

Revision benefits include passing your exams...

The car is a good example of an advance in scientific technology that has improved our quality of life, but had an unintentional negative impact on the environment. Science is now helping us to reduce this negative effect though, by developing cleaner and more renewable energy sources for cars to run on. Excellent.

Science and Ethics

Science can often raise important issues to do with ethics — whether something is morally right or wrong...

Some Questions Are Unanswerable by Science

1) There are some questions that all the experiments in the world won't help us answer — the "Should we be doing this at all?" type questions.
2) Take space exploration. It's possible to do it — but does that mean we should?
3) Different people have different opinions. For example...

Some people say it's a good idea... it increases our knowledge about the Universe, we develop new technologies that can be useful on Earth too, it inspires young people to take an interest in science, etc.

Other people say it's a bad idea... the vast sums of money it costs should be spent on more urgent problems, like providing clean drinking water and curing diseases in poor countries. Others say that we should concentrate research efforts on understanding our own planet better first.

4) This question of whether something is morally right or wrong can't be answered by more experiments — there is no "right" or "wrong" answer.
5) The best we can do is get a consensus from society — a judgement that most people are more or less happy to live by. Science can provide more information to help people make this judgement, and the judgement might change over time. But in the end it's up to people and their conscience.

There Are Two Key Arguments About Ethical Dilemmas

1. Some people think that certain actions are always unnatural or wrong. This means that, whatever the possible benefits, they feel those actions are unacceptable.

2. Some people may say that the right decision is the one that brings the greatest benefit to the greatest number of people.

The Law is Sometimes Involved Too

The law is involved in regulating some areas of scientific research, for example:

1) Animal research is regulated. For example, in the UK, scientists researching on vertebrates must have a licence and they must show that the likely benefits of the research outweigh any animal suffering.
2) Genetic manipulation is also regulated. In Britain, genetic manipulation of human body cells is allowed, but the modification of reproductive cells (sperm and egg cells) isn't.
3) There are regulations about the effect of research on the environment, e.g. pollution is monitored.
4) All sites carrying out nuclear research have to abide by strict health and safety laws.

Hmmm, tricky...

As you can see, science isn't just about knowing your facts. You need to think about the ethical issues of new technology — as well as the kinds of arguments people consider to make decisions about what should be done.

The Solar System

The first topic to get your teeth into and what a topic to start on — the Earth in the Universe, snazzy.

Planets Reflect Sunlight and Orbit the Sun in Ellipses

The Solar System consists of a star (the Sun) and lots of stuff orbiting it:

1) There are eight planets orbiting the Sun in almost circular paths (ellipses).
2) Closest to the Sun are the inner planets — Mercury, Venus, Earth and Mars.
3) Then the asteroid belt — see below.
4) Then the outer planets, much further away — Jupiter, Saturn, Uranus and Neptune.

There are also various other things — dwarf planets, comets, dust and so on... all in orbit around the Sun. Planets often have moons orbiting them — they're usually much smaller and found close to the planet. These also count as part of the Solar System.

Stars and Planets are Very Different from Each Other

1) You can see some planets with the naked eye. They look like stars, but they're totally different.
2) Stars are huge (the Sun's diameter is over 100 times bigger than the Earth's), very hot and very far away. They give out lots of light — which is why you can see them even though they're far away.
3) Planets are smaller and they just reflect sunlight falling on them. The planets in the Solar System are also much much closer to us than any star (except the Sun).

The Solar System is About 5 Thousand Million Years Old — We Think

1) The Solar System was formed over a very long period from big clouds of dust and gas.
2) For some reason (maybe a nearby star exploding), one cloud started to get squeezed slightly.
3) Once the particles had moved a bit closer to each other, gravity took over. It pulled things closer and closer together until the whole cloud started to collapse in on itself.
4) At the centre of the collapse, particles came together to form a protostar. When the temperature got high enough, a process called fusion started — hydrogen nuclei joined together to make helium.
5) Fusion gives out massive amounts of heat and light, so... a star, our Sun, was born. (The Sun and other stars' energy comes from the fusion of hydrogen nuclei.)
6) All of the chemical elements in the clouds with heavier atoms than helium and hydrogen were also formed in the stars by the fusion of different nuclei.
7) Around the Sun, material from the cloud containing hydrogen, helium and heavier elements started to clump together and these clumps became planets. (So the Sun and planets are similar ages.)
8) The oldest rocks on Earth are actually meteorites (rocks from space that crashed into Earth — we think they were formed not long after the birth of the Solar System). These are about 4500 million years old — so we know the Solar System is at least that old.

Asteroids and Comets are Smaller Than Most Planets

1) Asteroids and comets are made of stuff left over from the formation of the Solar System.
2) The rocks between Mars and Jupiter didn't form a planet, but stayed as smallish lumps of rubble and rock — these are asteroids.
3) Comets are balls of rock, dust and ice which orbit the Sun in very elongated ellipses, often in different planes from the planets. The Sun is near one end of the orbit.
4) As a comet approaches the Sun, its ice melts, leaving a bright tail of gas and debris which can be millions of kilometres long. This is what we see from Earth.

Asteroids... my dad had those — very nasty...

So one minute there was a big cloud of dust... the next there were planets... well, it took a bit longer actually.

Beyond the Solar System

There's all sorts of exciting stuff out there. The whole Solar System is just part of one galaxy. And there are billions upon billions of galaxies. Yup, the Universe is big — huge in fact...

We're in the Milky Way Galaxy

1) Our Sun is one of thousands of millions of stars which form the Milky Way galaxy — about 1 in 100 000 000 000 (or 10^{11}) if you had to write it out.
2) The Sun is about halfway along one of the spiral arms of the Milky Way.
3) The distance between neighbouring stars in a galaxy is usually millions of times greater than the distance between planets in the Solar System.

The Whole Universe Has More Than a Thousand Million Galaxies

1) Every galaxy is made up of thousands of millions of stars, and the Universe is made up of thousands of millions of galaxies — that's a lot of stars.
2) Galaxies themselves are often millions of times further apart than the stars are within a galaxy.
3) So even the slowest among you will have worked out that the Universe is mostly empty space and is really really BIG.

Distances in Space Can Be Measured Using Light Years

1) Once you get outside our Solar System, the distances between stars and between galaxies are so enormous that kilometres seem too pathetically small for measuring them.
2) For example, the closest star to us (after the Sun) is about 40 000 000 000 000 kilometres away (give or take a few hundred billion kilometres). Numbers like that soon get out of hand.
3) So we use light years instead. A light year is the distance that light travels through a vacuum (like space) in one year. Simple as that.
4) Light travels really fast — 300 000 km/s. So 1 light year is equal to about 9 460 000 000 000 km.
5) Just remember — a light year is a measure of DISTANCE (not time).

You Need to Know Some Relative Sizes, Distances and Ages

You need to know the relative sizes and distances of some different stuff in space — this just means the size in relation to the size of something else, e.g. the Earth's diameter is smaller than the Sun's:

SMALLEST
- Diameter of the Earth
- Diameter of the Sun
- Diameter of the Earth's orbit
- Diameter of the Solar System
- Distance from the Sun to the nearest star
- Diameter of the Milky Way
- Distance from the Milky Way to the nearest galaxy

LARGEST

1) The Sun's diameter is about 100 times bigger than the diameter of the Earth.
2) The diameter of the Milky Way is about 600 billion times the diameter of the Sun. Yup... it's pretty big.
3) The Milky Way and its nearest galaxy are about 600 000 times further apart then the Sun and its nearest star.

You need to know some ages too:

Different stuff in space	Age (million years)
Earth	5000
Sun	5000
Universe	14 000

The Earth and the Sun are a similar age. But the Universe is about 3 times older.

You may think it's a long way down the street to the chip shop...

...but that's nothing compared to distances in space. Space is also less tasty (and even worse for your health).

Looking into Space

We can't travel to stars to study them — it'd take 'a while' (thousands of years, at the very least). All we can realistically do is measure the radiation coming from them.

Radiation Can Tell Us a Lot About Stars and Galaxies

1) We can tell a lot about a star by studying the electromagnetic radiation it emits (e.g. light, X-rays, radio waves — see page 18). For example, the colour that a star appears is actually a pretty good guide to its surface temperature.
2) To work out how far away a star is, you can use various methods.
3) For 'nearby' stars, you can use parallax. Astronomers take pictures of the sky six months apart (when Earth is at opposite sides of its orbit).

Parallax is when something appears to move when you look at it from different places (e.g. hold your finger at arm's length and look at it first through your left eye, then your right — it seems to move against the background).

Earth
The Sun
Apparent movement of nearby star (compared to the really far away stars).
Nearby star
Slightly further away star
Apparent movement of far away star.

4) The apparent movement of a star between the two photos lets you work out how far away it is. Stars further away appear to move less (the really distant stars don't appear to move at all — the movement is too small to detect).
5) Another way to get an idea of the distance to a star is to measure its brightness.
6) Unfortunately, a star that looks very bright to us here on Earth could be either:
   a) quite close to Earth but not actually that bright, or b) a long way away and very bright indeed.
7) However, astronomers know how much radiation certain types of star actually emit, and so by examining how bright they look from Earth, they can tell how far away those stars must be.

The Atmosphere and Light Pollution Cause Some Problems

1) If you're trying to detect light, Earth's atmosphere can be a bit of a pain — it absorbs quite a bit of the light coming from space before it can reach us.
2) And light pollution (light thrown upwards from streetlamps, etc.) makes it hard to see dim objects.
3) That's why scientists put the Hubble Space Telescope in space — where you don't get these problems.

We See Stars and Galaxies as They Were in the Past

1) Electromagnetic radiation (including light) travels pretty fast — in a vacuum it goes at about 300 000 km per second. (Something travelling at that speed would go right around the Earth in about 0.13 seconds.)
2) Since the Sun is about 150 million km away from Earth, the radiation from the Sun that reaches us must have left about 8 minutes before we actually see it.
3) That means that when we look at the Sun, we see it as it was about 8 minutes ago. So if it suddenly exploded (but, fingers crossed, it won't for a while), we wouldn't know anything about it for about 8 minutes.
4) Since the nearest star to us after the Sun is about 4.2 light years away, light from it takes 4.2 years to reach us. This means we see it as it was 4.2 years ago.
5) When we look at other stars, this effect is even more extreme. For example, we see the North Star as it was during the time of William Shakespeare (it's about 430 light years away).

Constant stars, in them I read such art...

(From a Shakespeare Sonnet)

A bit of culture there. Now then... measuring the distance to a star is very hard (especially ones that are really far away) — scientists have to make certain assumptions about the star and about the space between it and Earth. What this means is that there's a degree of uncertainty in those measurements. So if someone says they know to the nearest kilometre how far away a star in a distant galaxy is, they're lying.

The Life of the Universe

You've been around for at least 14 years now. Well the Universe has been around a billion times longer...

Distant Galaxies are Moving Away from Us

1) When a galaxy is moving away from us the wavelength of the light from it changes — the light becomes redder. This is called red shift.
2) By seeing how much the light has been red-shifted, you can work out how quickly it's moving away. The greater the red shift, the faster it's moving away.
3) And from observations of different red-shifts of different galaxies we know that:

> The more distant the galaxy, the faster it moves away from us.

4) This provides evidence that the whole Universe is expanding.

The Big Bang Theory — the Universe Is Expanding

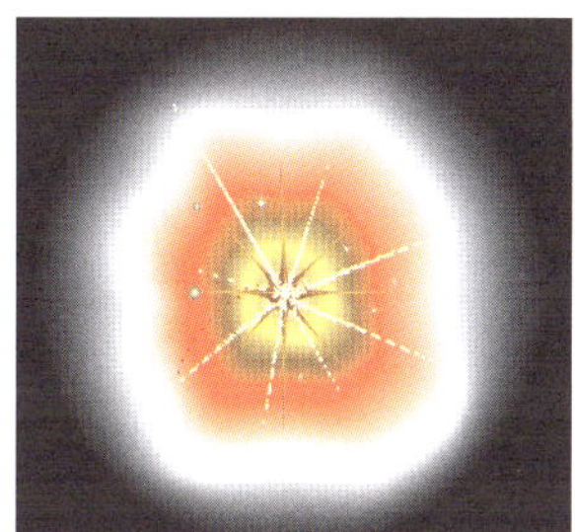

1) Right now, all the galaxies seem to be moving apart at great speed from a single point — see above. But something must have got them going. That 'something' was probably a big explosion — the Big Bang...
2) According to this theory, all the matter and energy in the Universe must have been compressed into a very small space. Then it exploded and started expanding, and the expansion is still going on now.
3) The age of the Universe can be estimated from the current rate of expansion. We think the Big Bang probably happened about 14 thousand million years ago.
4) But... it's difficult to estimate this because it's hard to tell how much the expansion has slowed down since the Big Bang.

We Don't Know How (or If) the Universe Will End...

1) The Universe's ultimate fate depends on how fast it's expanding and the total mass there is in it.
2) But these things are hard to measure, so determining the fate of the Universe is difficult.
3) To calculate how fast it's moving, you need to measure large distances, but the Universe is huge, so it's hard to accurately measure the distances involved.
4) You also need to accurately observe the motion of objects (e.g. galaxies). This is difficult because they're far away, you have to make lots of assumptions about their motion, and pollution gets in the way (p.10).
5) It's also tricky to measure how much mass there is because most of it appears to be invisible — it doesn't glow like a star. Astronomers can only detect this dark matter by the way it affects the movement of the things we can see.
6) The amount of dark matter in the Universe (as well as what it actually is) is one of the great unanswered questions in science. And it matters (no pun intended), because it will dictate the future of the Universe.
7) This is because all the mass everywhere is attracted together by gravity. The more mass there is, the greater this pull, and the greater the slowing down of the Universe's expansion.

- If there's enough mass compared to how fast the galaxies are currently moving, the Universe will eventually stop expanding — and then begin contracting. This would end in a Big Crunch.
- If there's not enough mass in the Universe to stop the expansion, it could expand forever, with the Universe becoming more and more spread out into eternity.

In the beginning, there was... well, it's so hard to tell...

In fact (and this is a bit weird, I admit), according to recent observations, the Universe seems to be expanding faster and faster, not slowing down at all. What's going on there? We have no idea. But it shows how new evidence (if confirmed by other observations) makes scientists rethink their theories.

The Changing Earth

There are some really dull things in our Solar System. For example, asteroids don't do much except go round and round the Sun. The Earth, however, is different...

The Earth is an Active Planet

1) It's kind of tempting to think that the Earth is a steady, unchanging place that'll always look pretty much as it does now.
2) But no... in a few tens of millions of years, Earth's going to look a lot different.
3) Mountains that are enormous today won't be nearly so grand. And the map of the world will be very different — whole continents will have moved. Weird.
4) This isn't anything new — Earth's been changing for thousands of millions of years.

Rocks Provide a Record of Changes in the Earth

Rocks change over the years, and provide clues about the history of the Earth.

1) Look at the Grand Canyon, for example. Over time, the Colorado River has eroded (worn away) the rock, leaving an impressive slash through the middle of Arizona.

2) Erosion goes on everywhere. We see it happening, for example, when cliffs are worn away by the sea. But other processes must be happening as well. If not, all the mountains would have been worn down by now... Earth would be perfectly smooth.
3) So something must be making new rock. And evidence is pretty easy to find — e.g. when lava from volcanoes sets, it forms brand new rock.
4) Fossils also provide evidence that rock is constantly forming. The animals and plants couldn't have dug themselves into the middle of rocks — the rocks must have built up around them.
5) The age of the Earth can be estimated from rocks — the oldest rocks found so far that were made on Earth are about 4 thousand million (4 000 000 000) years or so old. So the Earth must have been around for at least that long. Wowzers.

Fossils are traces of animals and plants from long ago. They're most commonly found in rocks.

Rocks are Being Constantly Recycled

In fact, evidence suggests rocks are constantly changing and being recycled — in the 'rock cycle'.

1) Particles eroded from existing rock (e.g. by water flowing over them) get washed into the sea and settle as sediment. Over time, these sediments get crushed together to form sedimentary rocks.
2) These can get pushed to the surface, or they can descend into the heat and pressure inside the Earth. If they descend, the structure of the rock can change completely as it gets heated and crushed. Sometimes the rock actually melts (but will solidify into new rock if it cools, e.g. near Earth's surface).

3) When any of these rocks are pushed up to reach the surface, the cycle starts again — they gradually get worn down and carried off to the sea again... and so on.
4) The rock cycle needs some very powerful forces to push rock up or down as described — but there's very good evidence that this is what happens. For example, some rock formations show rock that's been squeezed so hard it's just folded.

If you want to see the Rocky Mountains, don't leave it too long...

Erosion will eventually wear down the Rockies — in millions of years they won't be there. Shame. There's more about what causes the forces responsible for all the pushing up and down of rock on page 14. And there's more evidence about how and why Earth changes on page 13. It's all exciting stuff.

Wegener's Theory of Continental Drift

Now we know that some of the changes we see on Earth are caused by continental drift — but someone had to come up with the theory first...

Observations About the Earth Hadn't Been Explained

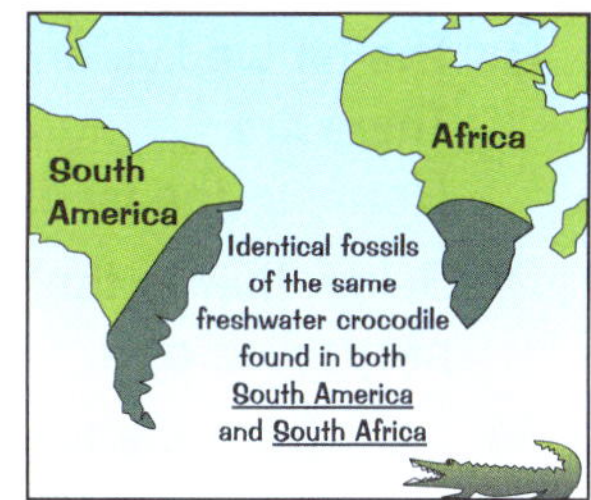

1) For years, fossils of very similar plants and animals had been found on opposite sides of the Atlantic Ocean. Most people thought this was because the continents had been linked by 'land bridges', which had sunk or been covered by water as the Earth cooled. But not everyone was convinced, even back then.
2) Other things about the Earth also puzzled people — like why the coastlines of Africa and South America matched so well. And why fossils from sea creatures had been found high in the Alps.

Explaining These Observations Needed a Leap of Imagination

What was needed was a scientist with a bit of insight... a smidgeon of creativity... a touch of genius...

1) Alfred Wegener hypothesised that Africa and South America had previously been one continent which had then split. He started to look for more evidence to back up his hypothesis. He found it...
2) There were matching layers in the rocks on different continents, and similar fossils in both South America and South Africa.

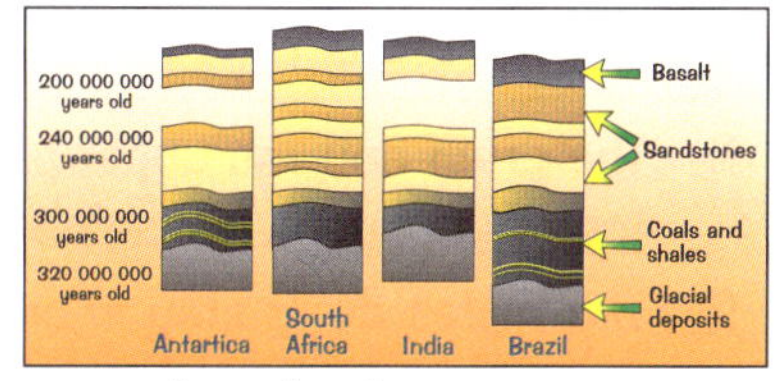

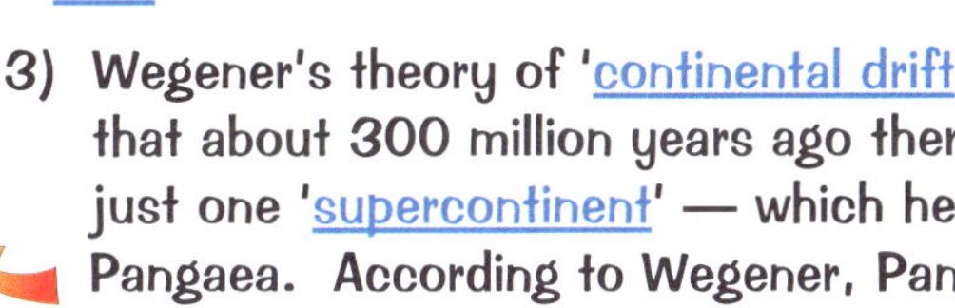

3) Wegener's theory of 'continental drift' supposed that about 300 million years ago there had been just one 'supercontinent' — which he called Pangaea. According to Wegener, Pangaea broke into smaller chunks... and these chunks (our modern-day continents) are still slowly 'drifting' apart.

The Theory Wasn't Accepted at First — for a Variety of Reasons

1) Wegener's theory explained things that couldn't be explained by the 'land bridge' theory — like mountain building, which Wegener said happened as continents smashed into each other. But it was a big change, and the reaction from other scientists was hostile.
2) The main problem was that Wegener's explanation of how the 'drifting' happened wasn't convincing (and the movement wasn't detectable). Wegener claimed the continents' movement could be caused by tidal forces and the Earth's rotation — but other geologists showed that this was impossible.
3) Also, it probably didn't help that Wegener wasn't a 'proper' geologist — he was a meteorologist.

Eventually, the Evidence Became Overwhelming

1) In the 1950s, scientists investigated the Mid-Atlantic ridge, which runs the whole length of the Atlantic.
2) They found evidence that magma (molten rock) rises up through the sea floor, solidifies and forms underwater mountains that are roughly symmetrical either side of the ridge. The evidence suggested that the sea floor was spreading — by a few cm per year.
3) Even better evidence that the continents are moving apart came from the magnetic orientation of the rocks. As the liquid magma erupts out of the gap, iron particles in the rocks tend to align themselves with the Earth's magnetic field — and as it cools they set in position. Now then... every half million years or so the Earth's magnetic field swaps direction — and the rock on either side of the ridge has bands of alternate magnetic polarity, symmetrical about the ridge.
4) This was convincing evidence that new sea floor was being created... and continents were moving apart.

I told you so — but no one ever believes me...

Wegener wasn't right about everything, but his main idea was correct. Nowadays, we know that it's not just the continents that move, but whole tectonic plates (including oceans) — see the next page.

The Structure of the Earth

We can tell a lot about what goes on deep inside the Earth by looking at what happens on the surface.

The Earth Has a Crust, Mantle and Core

The Earth is almost spherical and it has a layered structure, a bit like a Scotch egg. Or a peach.

1) The bit we live on, the crust, is very thin (about 20 km). There are two types of crust — continental crust (forming the land), and oceanic crust (under oceans).
2) Below that is the mantle. The mantle has all the properties of a solid, except that it can flow very slowly.
3) Heat from the core and heat from radioactive decay in the mantle causes the mantle to flow in convection currents.
4) At the centre of the Earth is the core, which we think is made of mainly iron and nickel.

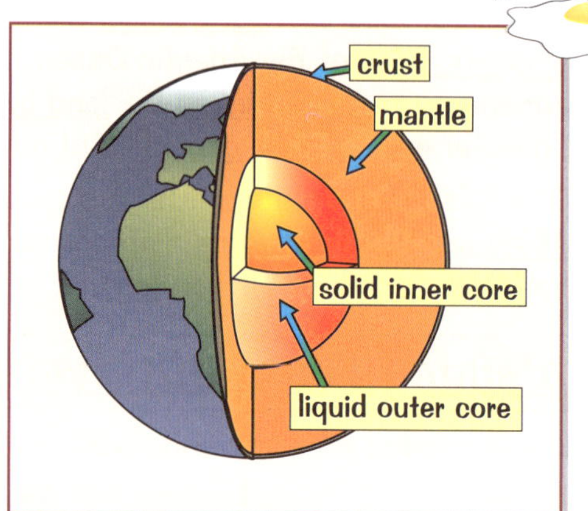

The Earth's Surface is Made Up of Tectonic Plates

1) The crust and the upper part of the mantle are cracked into a number of large pieces called tectonic plates. These plates are a bit like big rafts that 'float' on the mantle.
2) The plates don't stay in one place though — convection currents in the mantle, caused by heating in the core and mantle, cause the plates to drift.
3) It's movements in the mantle that cause the sea floor to spread — see previous page.
4) The map below shows the edges of the plates as they are now, and the directions they're moving in (red arrows).
5) Most of the plates are moving at speeds of a few cm per year relative to each other.
6) Tectonic plates can stay put for a while, and then occasionally, the plates move very suddenly, causing an earthquake. Earthquakes happen more often nearer the edges of plates.

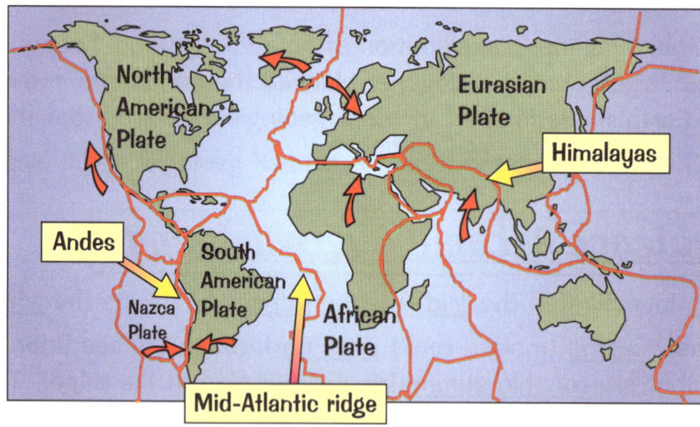

7) Volcanoes often form at the boundaries between two tectonic plates too — where plates meet, magma is produced, which can rise up, forming volcanoes.
8) As plates crash into each other, mountains are formed. For example, the Himalayas are where India is crashing into the Eurasian plate — the Himalayas are still growing by a centimetre or two per year as India keeps moving northwards. Similar collisions created the Alps and the Pyrenees.
9) These processes also contribute to the rock cycle — pushing rock down, or up to Earth's surface. Where the plates collide, one often gets pushed underneath the other.

Learn about plate tectonics — but don't get carried away...

Oh, big wow — the plates move a few cm every year... who cares. Unfortunately for us, that's what causes earthquakes and volcanoes. If you have got here without realising that — it's time to read the page again.

Seismic Waves

You can't drill very far into the crust of the Earth (only about 12 km), so scientists use seismic waves produced by earthquakes to investigate the Earth's inner structure.

Earthquakes Cause Different Types of Seismic Waves

1) When there's an earthquake, it produces wave motions (shock waves) which travel on the surface and inside the Earth. We record these seismic waves all over the surface of the planet using seismographs.
2) Seismologists measure the time it takes for the shock waves to reach each seismograph.
3) They also note which parts of the Earth don't receive the shock waves at all.
4) There are two different types of seismic waves that travel through the Earth — P-waves and S-waves.

P-Waves Travel Through Solids and Liquids

1) P-waves travel through solids and liquids.
2) They travel faster than S-waves.
3) P-waves are longitudinal (see next page).

P-waves refract as density changes

No P-waves reach here

P-waves pass through core and are detected here

S-Waves Only Travel Through Solids

1) S-waves only travel through Solids.
2) They are Slower than P-waves.
3) S-waves are transverse (see next page).

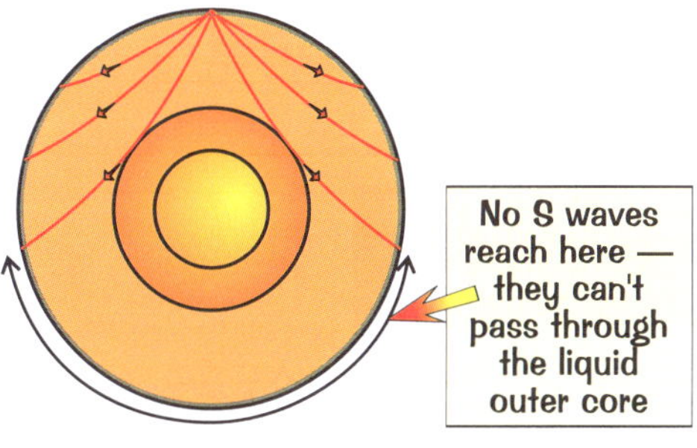

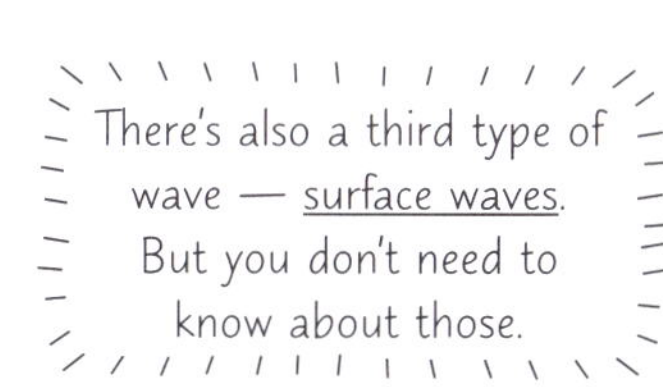

The Waves Curve with Increasing Depth

1) When seismic waves reach a boundary between different layers of the Earth, some waves will be reflected.
2) The waves also change speed as the properties (e.g. density) of the mantle and core change. This change in speed causes the waves to change direction — which is refraction.
3) Most of the time the waves change speed gradually, resulting in a curved path. But when the properties change suddenly, the wave speed changes abruptly, and the path has a kink.

The Seismograph Results Tell Us What's Down There

1) About halfway through the Earth, P-waves change direction abruptly. This indicates that there's a sudden change in properties — as you go from the mantle to the core.
2) The fact that S-waves are not detected in the core's shadow tells us that the outer core is liquid — S waves only pass through Solids.
3) P-waves seem to travel slightly faster through the middle of the core, which strongly suggests that there's a solid inner core.
4) Note that S-waves do travel through the mantle, which shows that it's solid. It only melts to form magma in small 'hot spots'.

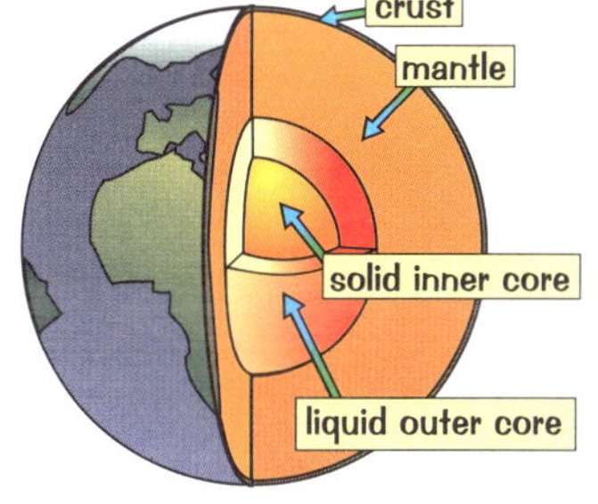

What's that coming straight through the core? Is it a P-wave, is it a P-wave?

You need to remember that P-waves are longitudinal and S-waves are transverse. You might find it helpful to think of them as Push-waves and Shake-waves. Gosh — what a useful little trick. You can thank me later...

Waves — The Basics

Now it's time for the exciting science behind the wave machine at the swimming baths...

Waves Have Amplitude, Wavelength, Frequency and Speed

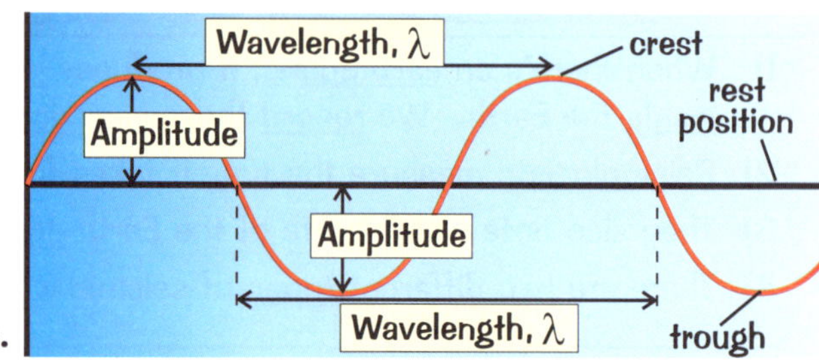

1) All waves are basically just disturbances that are caused by a vibrating source.
2) They carry and transfer energy in the direction that the wave travels, but do not transfer matter.
3) The amplitude is the distance from the rest position to the crest or trough (NOT from a trough to a crest). The bigger the amplitude, the more energy the wave has.
4) The wavelength is the length of a full cycle of the wave, e.g. from crest to crest.
5) Frequency is the number of complete waves passing a certain point per second OR the number of waves produced by a source each second. Frequency is measured in hertz (Hz). 1 Hz is 1 wave per second.
6) The speed is, well, how fast it goes.
7) You can work out the distance a wave has travelled, how long it took or the speed it was going by using the formula:

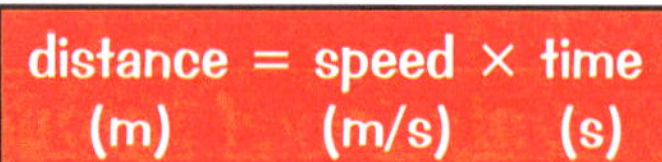

distance (m) = speed (m/s) × time (s)

Waves Can Be Transverse or Longitudinal

Most waves are TRANSVERSE: E.g. light and all other EM waves, waves on strings, S-waves (see previous page).

In TRANSVERSE waves the vibrations are at 90° to the DIRECTION OF TRAVEL of the wave.

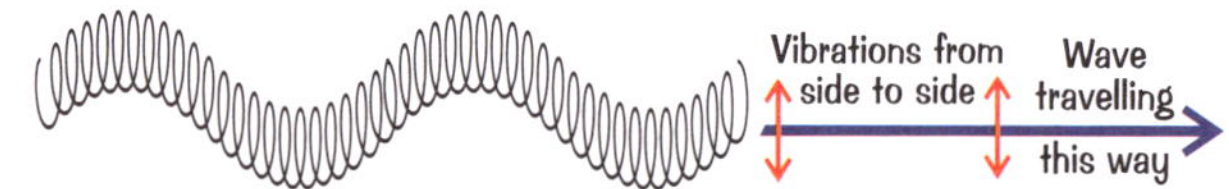

But some are LONGITUDINAL: E.g. sound and ultrasound, P-waves (see previous page).

In LONGITUDINAL waves the vibrations are along the SAME DIRECTION as the wave is travelling.

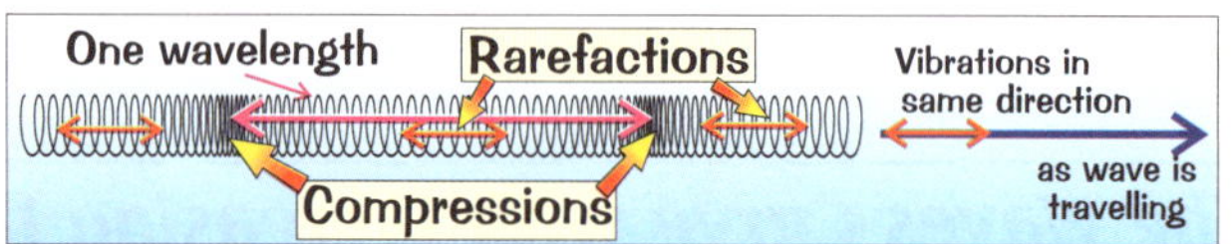

Wave Speed = Frequency × Wavelength

You need to learn this equation — and practise using it.

Speed (m/s) = Frequency (Hz) × Wavelength (m)

OR $v = f\lambda$

Speed (v is for velocity)
Frequency
Wavelength (that's the Greek letter 'lambda')

EXAMPLE: A radio wave has a frequency of 92.2×10^6 Hz. Find its wavelength. (The speed of all EM waves is 3×10^8 m/s.)

ANSWER: You're trying to find λ using f and v, so you've got to rearrange the equation. So $\lambda = v \div f = 3 \times 10^8 \div 9.22 \times 10^7 = 3.25$ m.

v / f × λ

Flick to the inside front cover for more on formula triangles.

1) The speed of a wave is usually independent of the frequency or amplitude of the wave.
2) For example, the speed of sound waves in air is constant — always the same.
3) When the speed of a wave is constant the wavelength is inversely proportional to the frequency. This means that waves with lower frequencies have longer wavelengths, and waves with higher frequencies have shorter wavelengths.

Lambda nsak — waves & lentils...

Try this: A sound wave travelling in a solid has a frequency of 19 kHz and a wavelength of 12.5 cm. Find its speed.*

*Answer on page 96.

Revision Summary for Module P1

And that's the first section done — but it's not quite over yet. Try these questions, and if there's something you don't know, go back and learn it. Even if it's all that tricky business about the origins of the Universe. And don't miss any questions out — you don't get a choice about what comes up on the exam so you need to be sure that you've learnt it all.

1) How many planets are in the Solar System?
2) Other than planets, name three things that orbit the Sun.
3) Approximately how old is the Solar System?
4) What is the source of the Sun's energy?
5) What are comets made of?
6) Roughly how many stars make up the Milky Way?
7) What is a light year?
8) Roughly how many times larger is the diameter of the Milky Way than the diameter of the Sun?
9) Briefly describe parallax and how it's used to measure the distance of nearby stars.
10) Explain why we see stars and galaxies as they were in the past.
11) What is red shift?
12) Explain the evidence that shows that the Universe is expanding.
13) Name the process that wears mountains down.
14) Briefly explain Wegener's theory of continental drift.
15) Give three reasons why Wegener's theory was rejected at first.
16) How fast are some sea floors spreading each year?
17) Briefly explain the changes you see in the magnetic orientation of sea floor rocks.
18) Draw a labelled diagram of the Earth showing the crust, mantle and core.
19) What causes tectonic plates to drift?
20) Where do most earthquakes and volcanoes occur?
21) How are the Himalayas being formed?
22) Name the two types of seismic waves caused by earthquakes, and state whether each type is a transverse or longitudinal wave.
23) What type of seismic wave cannot pass through liquids?
24) Draw a labelled diagram of a wave showing the amplitude and wavelength.
25) What is the formula that relates wave speed, frequency and wavelength?
26)*A radio wave has a wavelength of 3 m. Find its frequency. (The speed of all EM waves is 3×10^8 m/s.)
27)*Eva is building a sandcastle. She estimates that 1 wave passes her sandcastle every 2 seconds, and that the crests of the waves are 90 cm apart. Calculate the speed, in metres per second, of the waves passing Eva's sandcastle.

*Answers on page 96.

Electromagnetic Radiation

Light, X-rays and microwaves are all the same kind of thing, just quite different. Right, that's clear then.

Light is a Type of Electromagnetic Radiation

1) Light is a type of electromagnetic radiation (EM radiation).
2) Radiation is just a transfer of energy. E.g. sunlight is a transfer of energy from the Sun to the Earth.
3) Visible light (the colours of the rainbow, from red to violet — it can be written as red visible light violet) is just radiation that our eyes can detect. Radiation that's further along in the 'red' direction is called infrared. Similarly, radiation that's further along in the 'violet' direction is called ultraviolet.
4) There are seven types of radiation altogether, making up the electromagnetic spectrum —

Electromagnetic Radiation Transfers Energy in 'Packets'

1) All types of electromagnetic radiation transfer energy. For example, you can feel the warmth of the Sun because heat energy is travelling through space as infrared radiation.
2) This energy is delivered as photons. A photon is a tiny 'droplet' or 'packet' of energy (imagine droplets of water from a very 'fine' shower — but made of energy rather than water).
3) Sometimes it is more useful to think of light as a wave (e.g. when talking about reflection and things like that). But when you need to think of the energy transferred by electromagnetic radiation it's sometimes easier to think about photons.

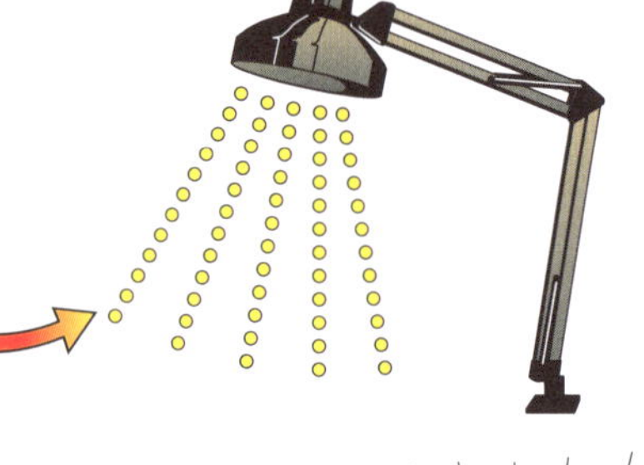

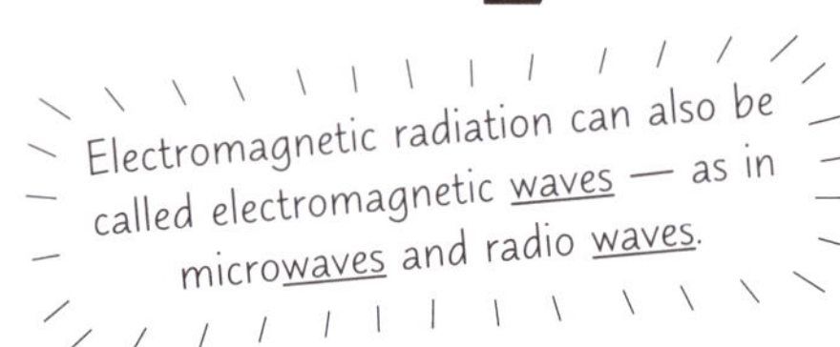

Some Types of EM Radiation Transfer More Energy Than Others

1) Each photon carries a tiny quantity of energy, but not all photons have the same amount of energy. The amount of energy carried by a photon depends on the frequency of the radiation.
2) The frequency, and so photon energy, increases as you go along the electromagnetic spectrum. Radio wave photons have the lowest frequency and the least energy, and gamma ray photons have the highest frequency and the most energy:

The Royal Mail — they're good at transferring packets...

Remember that EM radiation is just the transfer of energy, as photons. Visible light is just electromagnetic radiation that we can see — and very pretty it is too. There's nothing special about it though — other creatures 'see' other parts of the spectrum — bees see ultraviolet, for instance.

EM Radiation and Energy

All sorts of objects emit EM radiation. You're emitting some infrared radiation at this very moment.

EM Radiation is Emitted from a Source...

1) Many objects emit electromagnetic radiation, e.g. the Sun, radio transmitters, mobile phones, etc. Any object that emits radiation is called a source.
2) The frequency of thermal (heat) radiation emitted from an object increases with temperature.
3) Once emitted, all types of EM radiation can travel through space (a vacuum). In a vacuum, all EM radiation travels at the same speed — the 'speed of light'.
4) The speed of light in a vacuum is about 300 000 km/s or 3.0×10^8 m/s.

...And Transmitted, Reflected or Absorbed Somewhere Else

1) When radiation is emitted from a source, it spreads out until it reaches some matter (a substance — like air, glass, walls...). Three things can then happen:
   - The radiation might be transmitted — just keep going, like light passes through glass.
   - It could be reflected — bounce back, like light reflected from a mirror.
   - Or the radiation could be absorbed — like a sunbather absorbing UV rays from the Sun.
2) What happens depends on what the substance is like and the type of radiation.
3) Two or three of these things can happen at the same time. E.g. when sunlight shines on glass a lot of the light is transmitted, but some of it is reflected — so you can check your hair in shop windows.
4) Radiation may be absorbed by objects a long way from the source, e.g. when a parked car warms up in the sunshine:

   Infrared radiation is emitted from the Sun and travels 150 000 000 km through space, to Earth. Some of it is then absorbed or reflected by the atmosphere — but some of it reaches the car and warms it up.
5) Objects that absorb radiation are called detectors — our eyes are light detectors for instance.

Intensity Decreases as Distance from the Source Increases

1) When radiation is absorbed by matter, the photons transfer their energy to the matter.
2) The energy 'deposited' by a beam of photons depends on how many photons there are and the energy of each photon. (Total energy = number of photons × energy of each photon.)
3) The intensity (or strength) of radiation means how much energy arrives at each square metre of surface per second.
4) The units of intensity are W/m^2 — watts per square metre.
5) The intensity of a beam of radiation decreases with distance from the source because:
   - The beam spreads out.
   - The beam gets partially absorbed as it travels.
6) For example, as infrared radiation from the Sun travels through space and the atmosphere, it spreads out and some is absorbed or reflected back by the atmosphere. So the radiation is less intense on Earth that it would be, say, on the planet Mercury (which is closer to the Sun and has no atmosphere).

The same area here gets fewer 'hits'...
...than here
1 m
1 m
1 m
1 m
1 m
1 m
SOURCE

Intensity decreases with distance from ketchup...

Remember, different types of EM radiation behave differently. E.g. radio is transmitted through brick walls but light isn't. The other thing to remember from this page is the stuff about intensity. As you get further from the source, intensity decreases. That's why it's cold on Pluto — it's so far from the Sun.

Ionisation

Generally, high-energy EM radiation is more harmful than low-energy radiation. Here's why.

Some EM Radiation Causes Ionisation

1) All substances are made of atoms and molecules.
2) When a photon hits an atom or molecule, it sometimes has enough energy to remove an electron and change the atom or molecule.
3) This process is called ionisation:

Before ionisation

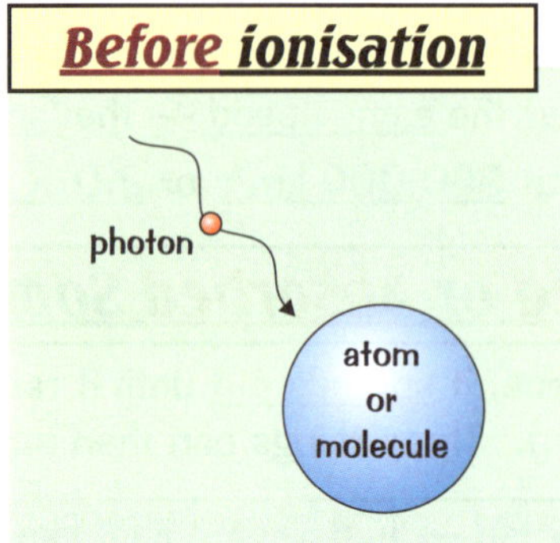

After ionisation

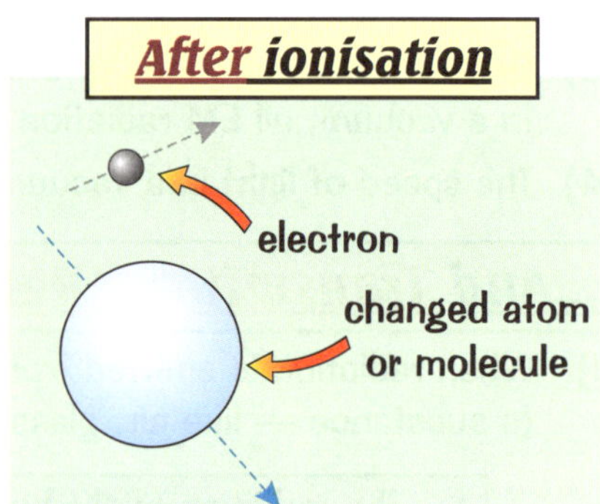

4) The changed atoms or molecules can go on to initiate (start) other chemical reactions.
5) It takes a lot of energy to remove an electron from an atom or molecule. So only the types of radiation with high enough photon energy can cause ionisation — ultraviolet, X-rays and gamma rays. These types of electromagnetic radiation are called ionising radiation.
6) Some substances (radioactive materials) emit ionising gamma radiation all the time.

Ionisation is Dangerous if it Happens in Your Cells

1) In the cells in your body, there are many important molecules, including DNA molecules. DNA molecules contain all the instructions for the cell, and they're important in cell division.
2) If your cells are exposed to ionising radiation, the damage to DNA molecules can cause mutations, and the cells might start dividing over and over again, without stopping — this is cancer.
3) Very high doses of radiation can kill your cells altogether — this is what happens in 'radiation sickness'.
4) We're all exposed to ultraviolet radiation from the Sun. UV radiation is ionising, and can damage living cells in the skin. This can lead to sunburn or even skin cancer.
5) Increased exposure causes more damage — so the longer you're exposed to the radiation the more damage it causes.

You Need Protection Against Dangerous Radiation

UV radiation — you can easily protect yourself from UV radiation with physical barriers such as clothes or sunscreen or sunblock.

X-rays — when you have an X-ray taken, the radiographer might put lead shields over parts of your body that aren't being investigated. The lead absorbs X-rays, protecting you from unnecessary exposure. Radiographers also wear lead aprons or stand behind concrete to protect themselves.

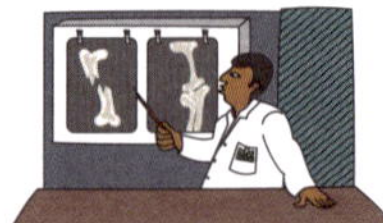

X-rays

Radiographs in hospitals take X-ray pictures of people to see if they have broken bones. X-rays pass easily through flesh but are absorbed by denser materials like bone and metal.
So it's the varying amount of radiation absorbed (or not absorbed really) that makes an X-ray image. X-ray imaging is also used in airports to check the contents of passengers' bags.

Use protection — wear a hat...

There's no point being paranoid about the dangers of radiation. Being exposed to high doses of X-rays doesn't mean you'll definitely get cancer — it increases the risk, but it's well worth having an X-ray to find out if you're seriously injured or ill. Sunbathing for hours with no protection is just stupid, though.

Some Uses of EM Radiation

No phones, no dinner — what would we do without EM radiation?

EM Radiation Can Cause Heating

1) Non-ionising radiation, e.g. light, doesn't have enough energy to change atoms. When it's absorbed by a substance it transfers energy to the atoms or molecules of the substance — and heats them up.
2) The more intense the radiation (see p. 19) and the longer the exposure, the greater the heating effect.
3) This heating effect can damage living cells, e.g. you get burned if you absorb too much infrared radiation.
4) Heating can be pretty useful though — it's how we cook food, after all. 'Normal' ovens do this with infrared radiation and microwave ovens do it with microwaves (surprise):

Microwaves make particles vibrate, heating them up. Some microwaves are strongly absorbed by water molecules and so can heat things containing water. This is handy, because there's water in all food substances.

Light waves aren't strongly absorbed by water molecules so they can't be used to cook food.

Microwave ovens come in different power ratings (e.g. 800 W, 1200 W). More powerful ovens produce higher intensity radiation, so less time is needed to produce the same heating effect — food cooks more quickly.

Microwave radiation would heat up the water in your body's cells if you were exposed to it. Microwave ovens have metal cases and screens over their glass doors which reflect and absorb the microwaves, stopping them getting out.

Some People Say There are Health Risks with Using Microwaves

1) Microwaves are used to send signals between mobile phones and mobile phone masts.
2) When you make a call on your mobile, the phone emits microwave radiation. Some of this radiation is absorbed by your body, and causes heating of your body tissues (which all contain water).
3) There are concerns that heating of tissues like the brain and jaw could increase the risk of some medical conditions, possibly including cancers. There is no conclusive evidence to show this, though.
4) The radiation is quite low intensity, so the heating is probably very minor and nothing to be too worried about. If you only talk for a short time, you'll minimise the heating effect (see above).
5) Mobile phone masts also emit microwave radiation. Some people who live very close to masts are worried about their possible effects. Again, there isn't much evidence — and any health problems might take a long time to emerge, so we might not know either way for many years.

Microwaves — for when you're only slightly sad to say goodbye...

Ovens and mobile phone networks both use microwaves, but with different energies. In an oven, the whole idea is for water molecules to absorb the microwave energy. But that's not ideal with a phone network — if all the energy was absorbed by water molecules, the signals would never get through clouds.

EM Radiation and the Atmosphere

The atmosphere keeps us warm by trapping heat — lovely jubbly.

Some Radiation from the Sun Passes Through the Atmosphere

1) The Earth is surrounded by an atmosphere made up of various gases — the air.
2) The gases in the atmosphere filter out certain types of radiation from the Sun — they absorb or reflect the radiation, so it never reaches the Earth's surface.
3) But some types of radiation (mainly visible light and some radio waves) pass through quite easily.

The Greenhouse Effect Helps Regulate Earth's Temperature

1) The Earth absorbs EM radiation from the Sun. This warms the Earth's surface up. The Earth then emits some EM radiation back out into space — this tends to cools us down.
2) Most of the radiation emitted from Earth is infrared radiation — heat. It's at a lower frequency than most of the radiation emitted by the Sun because the Earth is cooler.

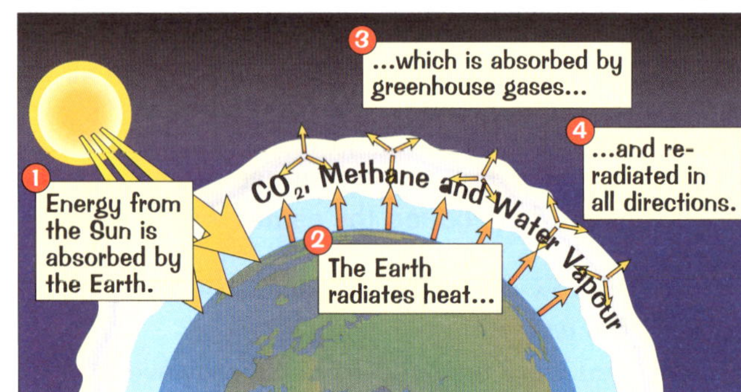

3) A lot of this infrared radiation is absorbed by atmospheric gases, including carbon dioxide, methane and water vapour.
4) These gases then re-radiate heat in all directions, including back towards the Earth.
5) So the atmosphere acts as an insulating layer, stopping the Earth losing all its heat at night.
6) This is known as the 'greenhouse effect'. (In a greenhouse, the sun shines in and the glass helps keep some of the heat in.) Without the greenhouse gases (CO_2, methane, water vapour) in our atmosphere, the Earth would be a lot colder than it is. But too much greenhouse gas could lead to global warming (see p. 24).

The Ozone Layer Protects Us from Too Much UV Radiation

In part of the atmosphere, there's a gas called ozone which absorbs UV radiation.

1) Ozone is a form of oxygen. An ozone molecule is just three oxygen atoms joined together — O_3.
2) Ozone occurs naturally at a certain height in the atmosphere — the 'ozone layer'. It's formed like this:

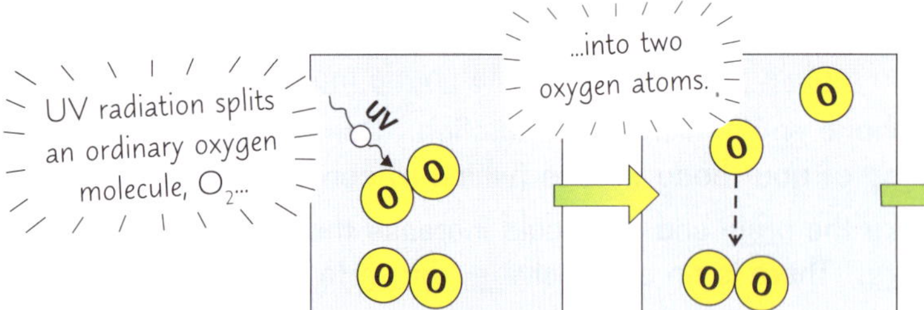

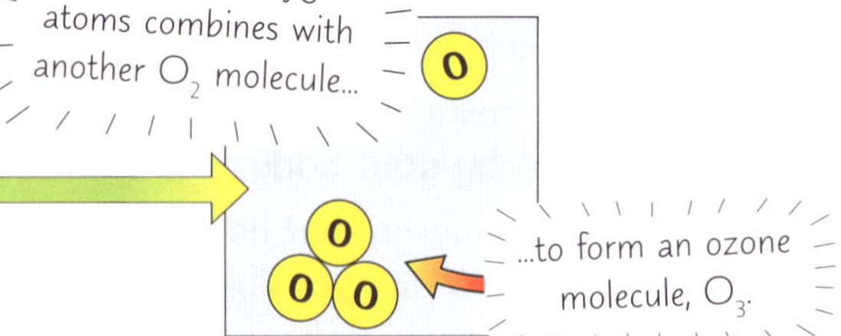

3) When an ozone molecule, O_3, absorbs more UV radiation, it splits into O_2 and O again. So the reaction is reversible (can go forwards and backwards) — causing a chemical change each time.

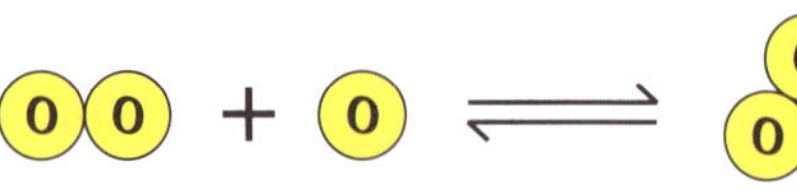

$$O_2 + O \rightleftharpoons O_3$$

4) Most of the time, the amount of ozone is constant. But loss of ozone can cause holes in the ozone layer.

5) Without ozone, a lot more UV radiation (from the Sun) would reach us here on Earth.
6) UV is ionising radiation (see p. 20) so it can be very harmful, especially to complex organisms.
7) So the ozone layer is very important — it protects us from too much UV radiation.

The ozone layer — free sunscreen...

We've been very careless with the ozone layer in the past, and made 'holes' in it. We did this by releasing gases called CFCs into the atmosphere. CFCs are man-made gases which were once used in fridges and aerosols.

The Carbon Cycle

The carbon cycle and carbon dioxide — you can't avoid hearing about them, so read on.

The Carbon Cycle Shows How Carbon is Naturally Recycled

Two of the 'greenhouse gases' which keep the Earth warm are carbon dioxide (CO_2) and methane (CH_4). There's a fairly small amount of CO_2 and just trace amounts (a tiny tiny bit) of methane. Both of these gases contain carbon.

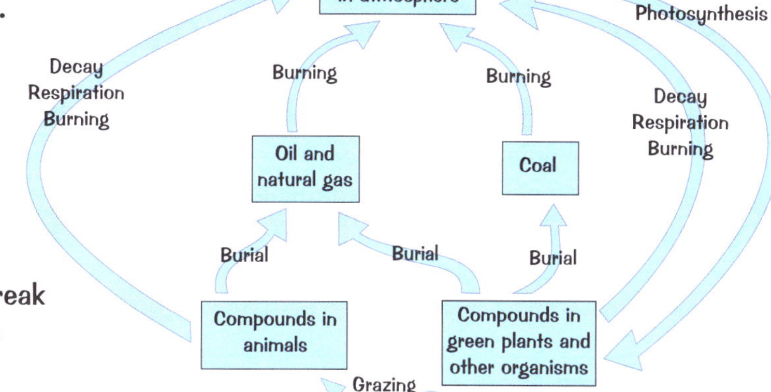

1) All the carbon on Earth moves in a big cycle.
2) Some processes (mainly respiration) return CO_2 to the atmosphere as part of the carbon cycle:
   - Respiration in plants and animals.
   - Respiration in decomposers — all plants and animals contain carbon. When they die, decomposers (bacteria and fungi) break them down. As they do so, they respire and produce CO_2.
   - Burning, e.g. trees or coal, also releases CO_2 into the atmosphere.

3) Photosynthesis in green plants and other organisms removes carbon dioxide from the atmosphere.
4) For thousands of years, these processes have all balanced out — carbon dioxide has been removed from the air and added to the air in approximately equal quantities.
5) So the concentration of CO_2 in the atmosphere has been almost constant for thousands of years. But recently that's been changing...

Humans are Upsetting the Carbon Cycle

Over the last 200 years or so, the concentration of CO_2 in the atmosphere has been increasing. That must be because carbon dioxide is being released into the air faster than it's being removed. There are several reasons for this:

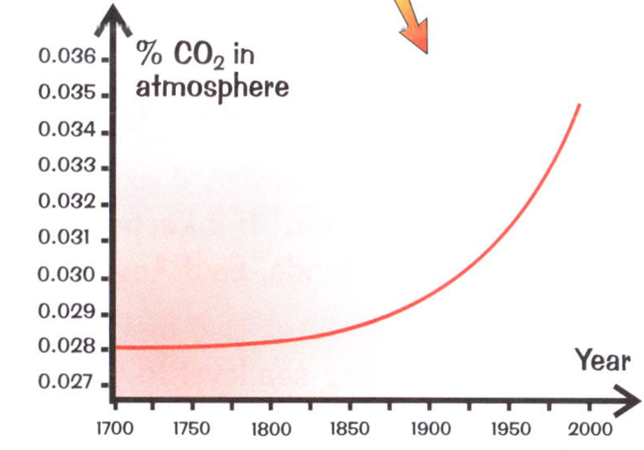

1) People's lifestyles have changed, e.g. we use more electrical gadgets, and travel more in cars and planes. All this needs energy — which we get mainly from burning fossil fuels... which releases more carbon dioxide.
2) The population is rising, so more land is needed to build houses and grow food. This space is often made by chopping down and burning trees. This also adds to the carbon dioxide levels in the atmosphere:
   - Plants are the main things which remove carbon dioxide from the atmosphere (as they photosynthesise) — so fewer trees means less carbon dioxide is taken out of the atmosphere.
   - Burning the trees adds lots of carbon dioxide into the atmosphere.

Eeeek — the carbon cycle's got a puncture...

For each person on a one-way flight from London to New York, a whopping 600 kg of carbon dioxide is added to the air. You can now pay to plant some trees to try and 'soak up' the carbon emissions you're responsible for. This sounds great, but there can be problems, e.g. for people living where the new plantations are planned. It might be better to release less CO_2 from fossil fuels in the first place.

Global Warming and Climate Change

Without any 'greenhouse gases' in the atmosphere, the Earth would be about 30 °C colder than it is now. So we need the greenhouse effect — just not too much of it...

Upsetting the Greenhouse Effect Has Led to Global Warming

1) Since we started burning fossil fuels in a big way, the level of carbon dioxide in the atmosphere has increased (see previous page).
2) The global temperature has also risen during this time (global warming). There's a link between concentration of CO_2 and global temperature.
3) A lot of evidence shows that the rise in CO_2 level is causing global warming by increasing the greenhouse effect (see p. 22).
4) So there's now a scientific consensus (general agreement) that humans are causing global warming.
5) Global warming is a type of climate change, and it also causes other types, e.g. changing weather patterns.

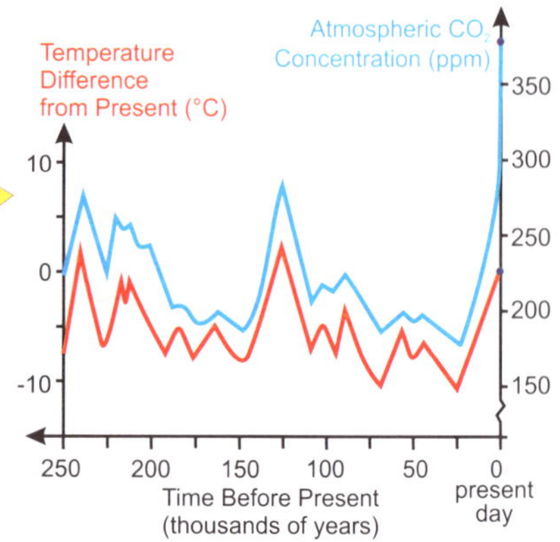

Scientists Use Computer Models to Understand Climate Change

The climate is very complicated — conditions in the atmosphere, oceans and land all affect one another.

1) A climate model is a great big load of equations linking these various parts of the climate system. The idea is to mimic what goes on in the real climate by doing calculations.
2) Once you've programmed a big computer with your equations, you need some data to start the calculations off. E.g. you might put in some data about temperature at the surface of the ocean in various places. The computer uses this data to work out, say, the speed and direction of ocean currents... then uses those results to work out air temperatures around the world. (It's a lot more complicated than this, but you don't have to know any details.)
3) Climate models can also be used to explain why the climate is changing now. We know that the Earth's climate varies naturally — changes in our orbit around the Sun cause ice ages, for instance. Climate modelling over the last few years has shown that natural changes don't explain the current 'global warming' — and that the increase in greenhouse gases due to human activity is the cause.

The Consequences of Global Warming Could be Pretty Serious

1) As the sea gets warmer, it expands, causing sea level to rise. Sea level has risen a little bit over the last 100 years. If it keeps rising it'll be bad news for people living in low-lying places like the Netherlands, East Anglia and the Maldives — they'd be flooded.
2) Higher temperatures also make ice melt. Water that's currently 'trapped' on land as ice runs into the sea, causing sea level to rise even more.
3) Global warming has changed weather patterns in many parts of the world. It's thought that many regions will suffer more extreme weather because of this, e.g. longer, hotter droughts. Hurricanes form over water that's warmer than 27 °C — so with more warm water, you'd expect more hurricanes.
4) The extra heat in the atmosphere will also increase convection (stronger winds) and result in more water vapour (more rain), causing more storms and floods.
5) Changing weather patterns also affect food production — some regions are now too dry to grow food, some too wet. This will get worse as temperature increases and weather patterns change more.

Be a climate model — go on a diet and solve lots of equations...

'Global warming' could mean that some parts of the world cool down. For instance, as ice melts, lots of cold fresh water will enter the sea and this could disrupt the ocean currents. This could be bad news for us in Britain — if the nice warm currents we get at the moment weaken, we'll be a lot colder.

EM Waves and Communication

You use EM waves for all sorts of stuff — your satellite TV (and your terrestrial TV), your radio, your microwave, your pet dog Jimbo... OK maybe not that last bit.

EM Radiation Can Transmit Information

EM radiation has been used to send information for years — e.g. using light to send signals in Morse code. Different frequencies are used for different things:

- Infrared — TV remote controls and 'night vision' cameras.
- Microwave — Mobile phones and satellite communication.
- Radio — TV & radio transmissions and radar.

Radio Waves are Used Mainly for Communications on Earth

1) Radio waves and microwaves are good at transmitting information over long distances.
2) This is because they don't get absorbed by the Earth's atmosphere as much as most waves in the middle of the EM spectrum (like heat), or those at the high-frequency end of the spectrum (e.g. gamma rays or X-rays).
3) The radio waves used for TV and FM radio transmissions have very short wavelengths compared to most radio waves.
4) Microwaves used for mobile phone communications have very long wavelengths compared to most microwaves, but are still titchy compared to radio waves.

You couldn't use high-frequency waves anyway, they'd be too dangerous.

Microwaves are Used for Satellite Communication

1) Communication to and from satellites (including for satellite TV and phones) uses microwaves that can pass easily through the atmosphere.
2) For satellite TV, the signal from a transmitter is transmitted into space...
3) ... where it's absorbed by the satellite receiver dish orbiting thousands of kilometres above the Earth. The satellite transmits the signal back to Earth in a different direction...
4) ... where it's received by a satellite dish on the ground.
5) These dishes are made of metal — metal reflects microwaves well, so the dish can focus the waves onto its receiver, rather than just absorbing them.

Infrared and Light are Used in Optical Fibres

Optical fibres work by bouncing waves off the sides of a thin inner core of glass or plastic. The wave enters one end of the fibre and is reflected repeatedly until it emerges at the other end.

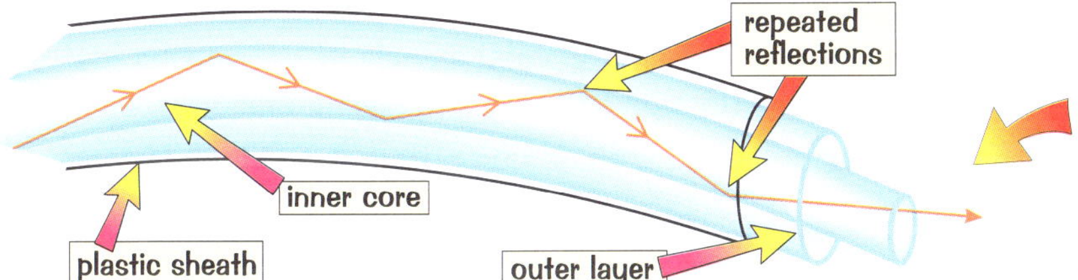

Light and infrared are great for transmitting information along optical fibres — the signal doesn't weaken too much as it travels along, as glass doesn't absorb much of the radiation.

EM waves? Plastic cups and string, that's all we had in my day...

It's pretty logical really that EM waves with different wavelengths have quite different properties and completely different uses. I mean, you wouldn't try and cook your dinner using X-rays, would you...

Analogue and Digital Signals

Sound and images can be sent as analogue or digital signals, but digital technology is gradually taking over.

Information is Converted into Signals

Information is being transmitted everywhere all the time.

1) Whatever kind of information you're sending (text, sound, pictures...) it's converted into electrical signals before it's transmitted.
2) It's then sent long distances down telephone lines or...
3) ...superimposed (mixed) onto 'carrier' EM waves.
4) It's then sent out as either analogue or digital signals.

Analogue Signals Vary but Digital's Either On or Off

1) The amplitude or frequency of an analogue signal varies continuously. An analogue signal can take any value in a particular range.
2) Digital signals can only take one of a small number of discrete values (usually two), e.g. 0 or 1, on or off, true or false.
3) The information is carried by switching the EM carrier wave on or off.
4) This creates pulses — short bursts of waves, e.g. where 0 = off (no pulse) and 1 = on (pulse).
5) A digital receiver will decode these pulses to get a copy of the original signal.

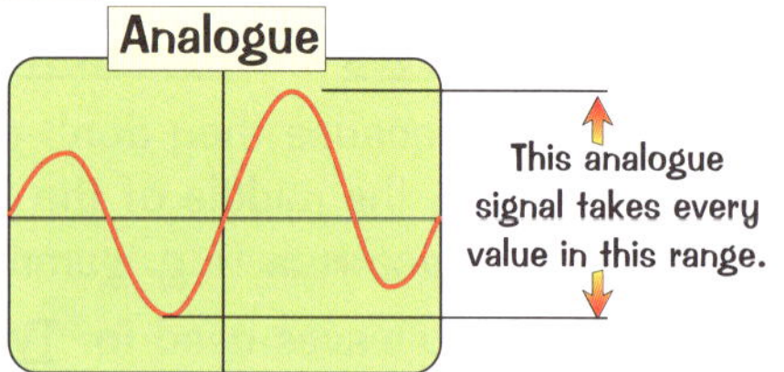

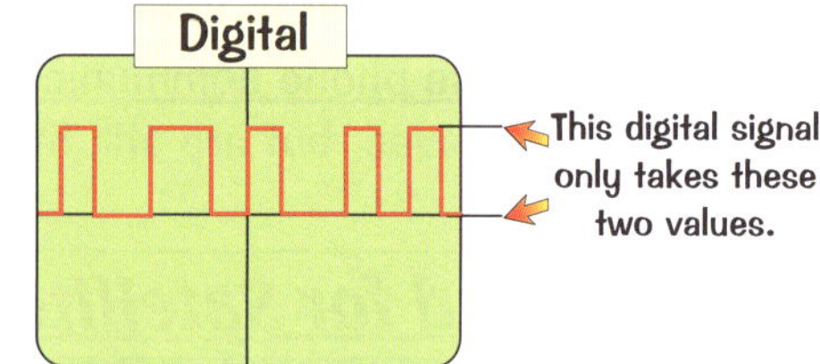

Signals Have to be Amplified

Both digital and analogue signals weaken as they travel, so they may need to be amplified along their route. They also pick up interference or noise from electrical disturbances or other signals.

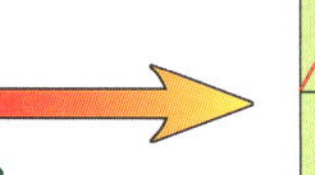

A nice smooth analogue signal

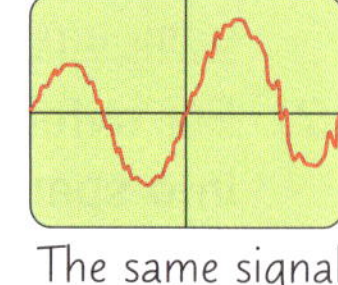

The same signal with noise

Digital Signals are Far Better Quality

1) Noise is less of a problem with digital signals than with analogue. If you receive a 'noisy' digital signal, it's pretty obvious what it's supposed to be. So it's easy to 'clean up' the signal — the noise doesn't get amplified.

This noisy digital signal... ...is obviously supposed to be this.

2) But if you receive a noisy analogue signal, it's difficult to know what the original signal would have looked like. And if you amplify a noisy analogue signal, you amplify the noise as well.

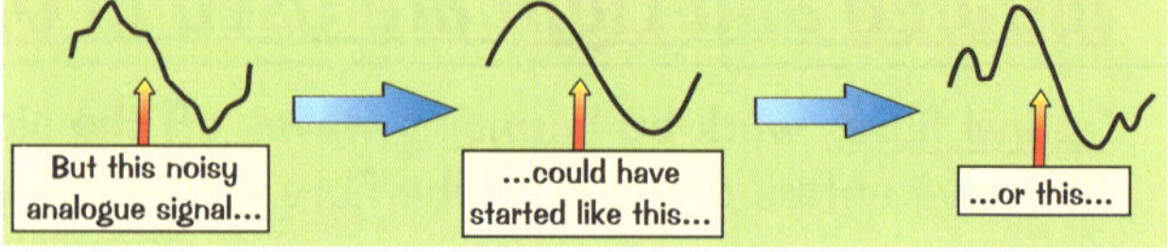

3) This is why digital signals are much higher quality — the information received is the same as the original.
4) Another advantage of digital technology is you can transmit several signals at once using just one cable or EM wave — so you can send more information (in a given time) than using analogue signals.
5) Also, digital signals are easy to process using computers, since computers are digital devices.
6) The amount of information used to store a digital image or sound is measured in bytes. Images and sounds will be of higher quality when the amount of information stored is higher.

I've got loads of digital stuff — watch, radio, fingers...

Digital signals are great — unless you live in a part of the country which currently has poor reception of digital broadcasts, in which case you get no benefit at all. This is because if you don't get spot-on reception of digital signals in your area, you won't get a grainy picture (as with analogue signals) — you'll get nothing at all.

Revision Summary for Module P2

Try these lovely questions. Go on — you know you want to. It'll be nice.

1) Electromagnetic waves don't transfer any matter. What do they transfer?
2) Sketch the EM spectrum, with all the details you've learned. Put the lowest frequency waves first.
3) How is the frequency of EM radiation related to the energy carried by its photons?
4) What does the 'intensity' of a beam of EM radiation mean?
5) Name three types of ionising radiation.
6) Why is ionisation dangerous if it occurs in your cells?
7) How do radiographers protect themselves from X-rays?
8) What sort of radiation is used in conventional cookers?
9) Briefly explain how microwaves cook food.
10) Name three greenhouse gases.
11) How is ozone made in the atmosphere?
12) How is carbon dioxide returned to the atmosphere in the carbon cycle?
13) What has been happening to levels of carbon dioxide in the atmosphere in the last 150 years?
14) What two effects does chopping down and burning trees have on the atmospheric carbon dioxide level?
15) What is global warming?
16) What's causing global warming? How do we know this?
17) Give two possible consequences of global warming.
18) Why are radio waves good at transmitting information over long distances?
19) Describe two uses of microwaves.
20) Draw diagrams illustrating analogue and digital signals.
21) What advantages do digital signals have over analogue signals?

Electrical Energy

I hope you're feeling lively — this whole module is about energy. How we use it, where we get it from, and, importantly, how we can make sure we have enough for the future without messing up the environment. First, a look at electrical energy — the stuff we rely on for light, heat, a nice cuppa, straight hair...

Energy is Transferred from Cells and Other Sources

Anything that supplies electricity is also supplying energy. So cells, batteries, generators etc. all transfer energy to the charge in the wire, which then transfers it to the components or devices in the circuit:

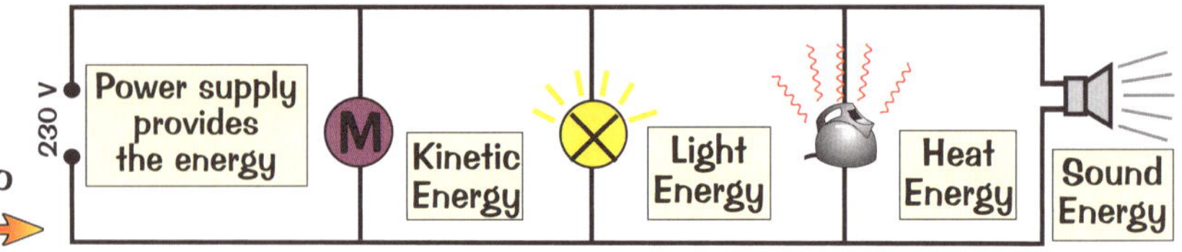

The components can then transfer energy to the environment — in the form of light, sound, heat etc.

Power is the Rate of Energy Transfer

The power of an appliance tells you how fast it transfers energy from the charge passing through it. Power is usually measured in watts, W, or kilowatts, kW. (1 kW = 1000 W)

A light bulb converts electrical energy into light energy and heat energy. A power rating of 100 W means it transfers 100 joules of energy every second.

A kettle converts electrical energy into heat energy. If it has a power rating of 2.5 kW, it transfers 2500 joules every second.

The total energy transferred by an appliance depends on how long the appliance is on and its power rating. The formula:

ENERGY TRANSFERRED (in joules) = POWER (in W) × TIME (in s)

Flick to the inside front cover for more on formula triangles.

EXAMPLE 1: How much energy is transferred by a 2.5 kW kettle left on for 5 minutes?

ANSWER: Energy (in J) = Power (in W) × Time (in s) = 2500 W × 300 s (300 s = 5 minutes)
= 750 000 J

EXAMPLE 2: What is the power of a light bulb that transfers 54 000 J in 15 minutes?

ANSWER: Power = Energy ÷ Time = 54 000 J ÷ 900 s = 60 W

Kilowatt-hours (kWh) are "UNITS" of Energy

Energy is usually measured in joules. The trouble is, one joule is a tiny, tiny amount of electrical energy — so your electricity meter records how much energy you use in units of kilowatt-hours, or kWh.

A KILOWATT-HOUR is the amount of electrical energy converted by a 1 kW appliance left on for 1 HOUR.

Using kilowatt-hours, the energy transfer equation above becomes:

Energy transferred (in KILOWATT-HOURS) = Power (in KILOWATTS) × Time (in HOURS)

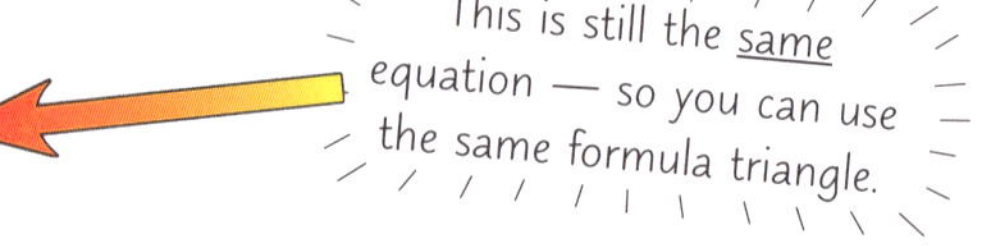

The higher the power rating of an appliance, and the longer you leave it on, the more energy it transfers — and the more it costs...

COST = NUMBER OF kWh × COST PER kWh

EXAMPLE: Find the cost of leaving a 60 W light bulb on for 30 minutes if one kWh costs 10p.

ANSWER: Energy (in kWh) = Power (in kW) × Time (in hours) = 0.06 kW × ½ hr = 0.03 kWh
Cost = number of kWh × cost per kWh = 0.03 × 10p = 0.3p

Kilo-what? Hours — exactly, well almost...

You've got to be careful with your units in this topic — power is in kilowatts, energy is in kilowatt-hours. Kilowatt-hours can also remind you of the equation for electrical energy — power × time.

Electrical Energy

Electrical appliances transfer energy from the charge passing through them (to do whatever they're designed to do), but not all of the energy is used usefully — some always gets wasted.

Power Ratings of Appliances

An appliance with a high power rating transfers a lot of energy in a short time. This energy comes from the current flowing through it. This means that an appliance with a high power rating will draw a large current from the supply.

1) The formula for electrical power is: POWER (in W) = VOLTAGE (in V) × CURRENT (in A) $(P = V \times I)$

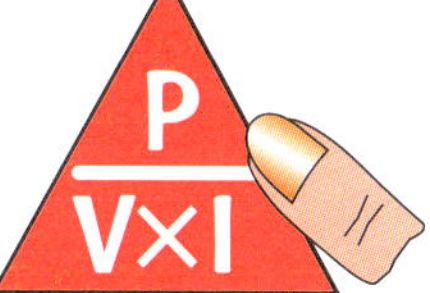

2) So to find the power of a component in a circuit you'd measure the voltage across it and the current flowing through it, then multiply them together. Simple.
3) Most electrical goods show their power rating and voltage rating. To work out the current that the item will normally draw you need to rearrange the equation:

Example: A hairdrier is rated at 230 V, 1 kW. Find the current it draws.
ANSWER: Rearranging, I = P/V = 1000 ÷ 230 = 4.3 A.

More Efficient Machines Waste Less Energy

Efficiency is sometimes considered in terms of power — just replace 'energy' with 'power' in the equation below.

Appliances convert electrical energy taken from the charge passing through them to other forms. Some of these forms will be useful, but some are not wanted so are wasted (often as heat or sound). The efficiency of a machine (or a power station — see page 30) is defined as:

$$\text{Efficiency} = \frac{\text{ENERGY USEFULLY TRANSFERRED}}{\text{TOTAL ENERGY SUPPLIED}} \times 100\%$$

You can also calculate the efficiency as a decimal instead of a percentage — just don't do the '× 100%' bit.

1) To work out the efficiency of a machine, first find out the total energy supplied — the energy input.
2) Then find how much useful energy the machine transfers. The question might tell you this directly, or it might tell you how much energy is wasted as heat/sound.
3) Then just divide the smaller number by the bigger one to get a value for efficiency somewhere between 0 and 1. Easy. If your number is bigger than 1, you've done the division upside down.

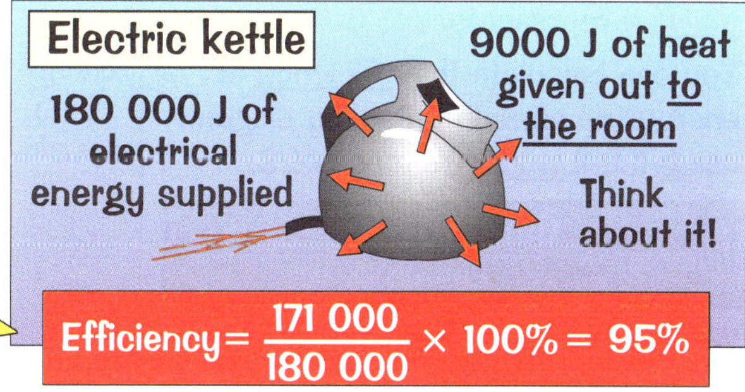

$$\text{Efficiency} = \frac{171\,000}{180\,000} \times 100\% = 95\%$$

4) Then convert the efficiency to a percentage, by multiplying it by 100. E.g. 0.6 = 60%.
5) In the exam you might be told the efficiency and asked to work out the total energy supplied, the energy usefully transferred or the energy wasted. So you need to be able to rearrange the formula.

EXAMPLE: An ordinary light bulb is 5% efficient. If 1000 J of light energy is given out, how much energy is wasted?

ANSWER: $\text{Total Energy Supplied} = \frac{\text{Energy Usefully Transferred}}{\text{Efficiency}} = \frac{1000\text{ J}}{0.05} = 20\,000\text{ J}$

so Energy Wasted = 20 000 – 1000 = 19 000 J.

Shockingly inefficient, those ordinary light bulbs. Low-energy light bulbs are roughly 4 times more efficient, and last about 8 times as long. They're more expensive to buy though.

Efficiency = pages learned ÷ cups of tea made...

Some new appliances (like washing machines and fridges) come with a sticker with a letter from A to H on, to show how energy efficient they are. A really well insulated fridge might have an 'A' rating. But if you put it right next to the oven, or never defrost it, it will run much less efficiently than it should.

Sankey Diagrams

This is another opportunity for a MATHS question. Fantastic.
So best prepare yourself — here's what those Sankey diagrams are all about...

Energy is Always Conserved — even if it's Wasted

1) Whether you're using electricity to power an appliance, or generating electricity in a power station, none of the energy involved is actually 'lost' — it's all conserved but just converted to different forms. Some of this energy is converted to a useful form, and the rest we say is 'wasted energy'.
2) Sankey diagrams are just energy transformation diagrams — they make it easy to see at a glance how much of the input energy is being usefully employed compared with how much is being wasted.
3) The thicker the arrow, the more energy it represents — so you see a big thick arrow going in, then several smaller arrows going off it to show the different energy transformations taking place.
4) You can have either a little sketch (see right) or a properly detailed diagram (see below). With sketches, they're likely to ask you to compare two different devices and say which is more efficient. You generally want to be looking for the one with the thickest useful energy arrow(s).

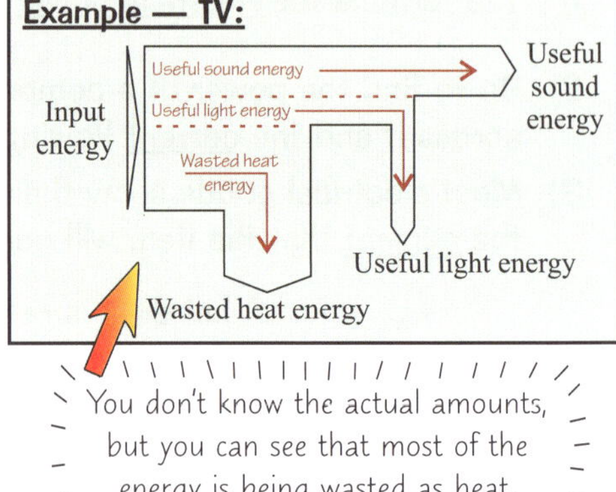

You don't know the actual amounts, but you can see that most of the energy is being wasted as heat.

Supplying Electricity isn't Close to 100% Efficient

1) Power stations generate electricity — but they aren't very efficient. They produce lots of waste energy (heat and noise) as well as useful electricity. Some energy is also lost as heat in the transmission wires as the electricity is distributed from the power station to people's homes. All this can be shown in a Sankey diagram.
2) In a detailed Sankey diagram like the one shown, the width of each arrow is proportional to the number of joules it represents.
3) You can calculate the efficiency of energy transfers in a Sankey diagram using the formula from page 29:

$$\text{Efficiency} = \frac{\text{USEFUL Energy OUTPUT}}{\text{Energy INPUT}}$$

4) When generating electricity, energy is wasted in both generation and distribution, so you can calculate the efficiency of each process:

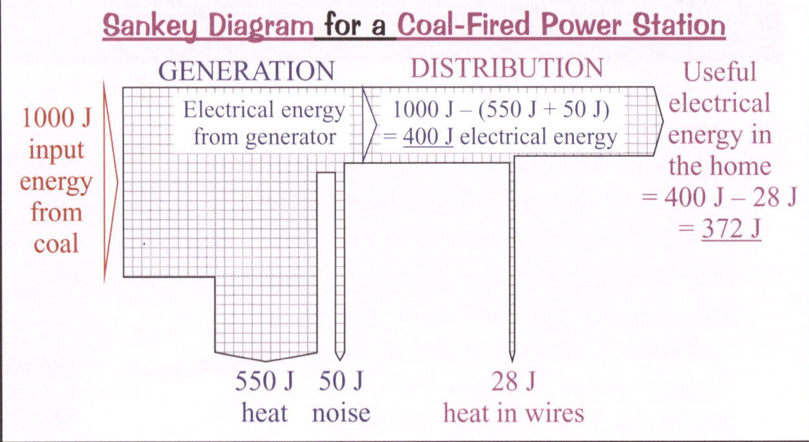

Efficiency of GENERATION: $\text{Efficiency} = \frac{\text{electrical energy from generator}}{\text{energy input from coal}} = \frac{400}{1000} = 0.4$

Efficiency of DISTRIBUTION: $\text{Efficiency} = \frac{\text{useful electrical energy output}}{\text{electrical energy from generator}} = \frac{372}{400} = 0.93$

OVERALL efficiency: $\text{Efficiency} = \frac{\text{useful electrical energy output}}{\text{energy input from coal}} = \frac{372}{1000} = 0.372$

Skankey diagrams — to represent the smelliness of your socks...

If they ask you to draw your own Sankey diagram in the exam, and don't give you the figures, a sketch is all they'll expect. Just give a rough idea of where the energy goes. E.g. a filament lamp turns most of the input energy into heat, and only a tiny proportion goes to useful light energy.

Saving Energy

We can all do our bit to save energy — for example, I typieed this put in thee durk.

Reducing Energy Usage begins At Home

As the world's population continues to grow, more and more energy is needed for fuel and power. The fossil fuels we rely on for most of our energy are pretty bad for the environment and will eventually run out (see page 32). We can all help the situation by reducing the amount of energy we use every day.

Reducing Heat Transfer stops Energy being Wasted

1) A lot of the things you can do to save energy at home involve stopping heat escaping — the less energy you waste, the less you need to use in the first place.
2) Installing cavity wall- and loft-insulation, double glazing and draught-proofing reduces the heat lost through gaps in walls, ceilings, windows and around doors.
3) Cheap and cheerful things such as a buying a fibreglass wool hot water tank jacket and thick curtains can also reduce heat loss, and are often more cost-effective methods (see below).
4) It's not just heat you can save — you can reduce the amount of electricity you use by buying efficient appliances and energy-saving light bulbs, as well as by simply switching things off when you're not using them. Washing clothes at lower temperatures and turning down the heating can also help.

Some Improvements are More Cost-effective than Others

The figures are all rough. It'll vary from house to house.

1) Saving energy at home can save you a few quid too.
2) The methods that save the most money each year are considered the most 'effective' — but 'cost-effectiveness' depends on timescale.
3) You can work out the 'payback time' — how long it takes for the money saved to match the initial cost (divide initial cost by the annual saving). The smaller the payback time, the better.
4) E.g. the energy-saving lightbulb is much more cost-effective than double glazing.

Hot Water Tank Jacket
Initial Cost: £15
Annual Saving: £30
Payback time: 6 mths

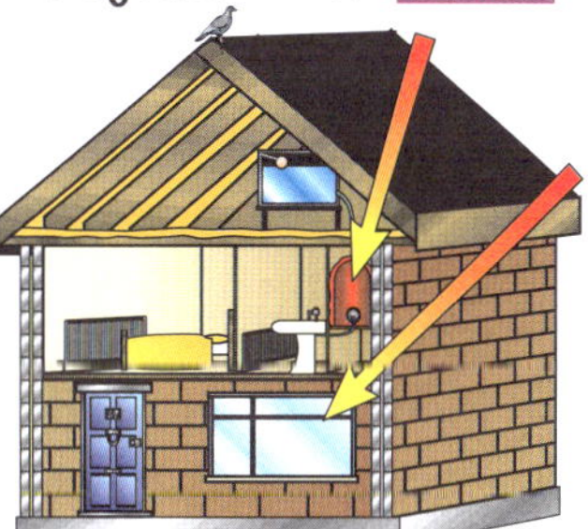

Double Glazing
Initial Cost: £3000
Annual Saving: £60
Payback time: 50 yrs

Energy-saving Bulbs
Initial Cost: £3
Annual Saving: £12
Payback time: 3 mths

Workplaces and The Government have Responsibilities too

1) The methods for saving energy in the home do just as well in the workplace, e.g. lights, computers and appliances should be switched off when not in use.
2) Many businesses also generate lots of paperwork. Energy can be saved by not printing and photocopying things unnecessarily.
3) Some workplaces offer their employees incentives for using energy-efficient ways to travel to work — such as cycling, car-sharing or using public transport.
4) The government can encourage people to save energy too. E.g. by offering grants for better home insulation, running schemes to trade in old boilers for more efficient ones, and by improving public transport.
5) They can help control energy use on a national scale too. E.g. by investing in alternative energy sources, improving recycling services, and making laws to ensure new housing and businesses are energy efficient.

It's payback time...

Makes sense — save energy wherever you can so: a) the world's a nicer place, and b) you'll have more money.

Energy Sources and Power Stations

Electricity doesn't grow on trees you know... We use different energy sources to generate it.

Electricity is a Convenient Way to Supply Energy

1) Electricity is a secondary energy source because it is produced using other energy sources, e.g. coal, nuclear fuel, wind power (known as primary energy sources).
2) Electricity is convenient because it can be easily transmitted over long distances via the National Grid (see page 38), and can be used in many different ways.
3) There are lots of different types of energy sources, which are either renewable or non-renewable:

NON-RENEWABLE SOURCES

1) Fossil Fuels: coal, oil, natural gas.
2) Nuclear fuels (uranium and plutonium)

- They will all 'run out' one day.
- They all do damage to the environment.
- They currently provide most of our energy.

RENEWABLE SOURCES

1) Wind
2) Waves
3) Tides
4) Hydroelectric
5) Biofuels
6) Geothermal
7) Solar (radiation from the Sun)

- They will never run out.
- They do damage the environment, but in less nasty ways than non-renewables.
- They don't provide much energy and can be unreliable if they depend on the weather.

There's more on each type on the next few pages.

Energy Sources Produce Steam to Drive Turbines in Power Stations

Most of the electricity we use is generated by using primary energy sources to heat water in power stations. These are called thermal power stations, and the process is always pretty much the same:

1) Energy is released from the fuel (usually by burning in a boiler) and used to generate steam. →
2) The steam turns a turbine. →
3) A generator converts the movement of the turbine (kinetic energy) into electricity (p. 38).

In many renewable sources (hydroelectric, wind and wave), the energy drives the turbine directly.

Fossil Fuels are Linked to Environmental Problems

1) All three fossil fuels (oil, natural gas and coal) release carbon dioxide (CO_2) into the atmosphere when burnt in power stations.
2) All this CO_2 contributes to global warming and climate change (see p. 24).
3) Burning coal and oil also releases sulfur dioxide, which causes acid rain. Acid rain can harm trees and soils and can have far-reaching effects in ecosystems.
4) Coal mining makes a mess of the landscape, especially "open-cast mining".
5) Oil spillages cause serious environmental problems, affecting mammals and birds that live in and around the sea. We try to avoid them, but they'll always happen.
6) BUT the upside of using fossil fuels is that they produce a lot of energy, relatively cheaply, and do not rely on the weather. We have lots of fossil fuel power stations already, so we don't need to spend money on new technology to carry on using them.

I'm all natural baby!

It all boils down to steam...

Steam engines were invented as long ago as the 17th century, and yet we're still using that idea to produce most of our electricity today, over 300 years later. Surely we could have thought of something better by now...

Nuclear Energy

Nuclear power stations can make lots of energy without releasing lots of CO_2 into the atmosphere. Some people think nuclear power is the best way to reduce CO_2 emissions, but others think it's just too dangerous.

Nuclear Power Stations Release Energy by Splitting Atoms

1) A nuclear power station is mostly the same as the one on page 32, but with nuclear fission producing the heat to make steam to drive turbines, etc. The difference is in the boiler, as shown below:
2) In nuclear fission, atoms in the nuclear fuel (e.g. uranium) are split in two, releasing lots of heat energy.
3) Water is used as a coolant to take away the heat produced by the fission process. This heat is used to produce steam to drive a turbine and generator.
4) You can draw a block diagram of a nuclear power plant:

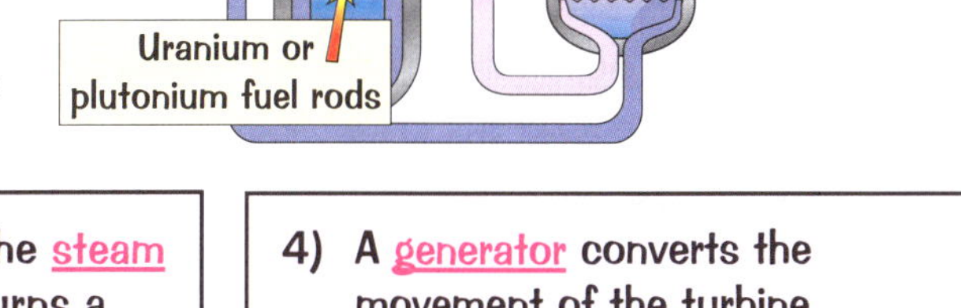

1) Energy is released from the nuclear fuel (e.g. uranium) by nuclear fission.	→	2) The heat energy heats water to make steam.	→	3) The steam turns a turbine.	→	4) A generator converts the movement of the turbine (kinetic energy) into electricity.

Nuclear Power Produces Radioactive Waste

As with any type of energy source, there are advantages and disadvantages to using nuclear energy:

ADVANTAGES

1) Nuclear reactions release a lot more energy than chemical reactions (like burning).
2) A nuclear power station doesn't produce CO_2 when making electricity.
3) Nuclear fuel (e.g. uranium) is relatively cheap.

A gram of uranium releases over 10 000 times more energy than burning a gram of oil.

DISADVANTAGES

1) Nuclear power stations produce radioactive waste — this can be very dangerous and difficult to dispose of as it emits ionising radiation and stays radioactive for a long time:
   - Increased exposure to ionising radiation increases the damage done to cells.
   - High doses of ionising radiation tend to kill cells outright, causing radiation sickness.
   - Lower doses tend to damage cells without killing them, which can cause cancer.
2) Radioactive waste can put people at risk through:
   - IRRADIATION — being exposed to radiation without coming into contact with the source. The damage to your body stops as soon as you leave the area where the radioactive waste is. This means you're only exposed for a short period of time, so will receive a lower dose. Not as bad as...
   - CONTAMINATION — picking up some radioactive waste, e.g. by breathing it in, drinking contaminated water or getting it on your skin. You'll still be exposed to the radiation once you've left the area. Contamination is worse because it leaves people exposed to ionising damage for a long time, leading to more damage.
3) Nuclear power needs extra safety precautions — waste needs disposing of carefully (e.g. it's buried deep underground), the surrounding area needs to be tested for contamination of the soil and water, and workers need to be tested regularly to check they've not been exposed to too much radiation.
4) Nuclear power is supported by some people, but people who live close are often more scared of the risks.
5) Nuclear power stations take the longest time of all the power stations to start up. The overall cost of nuclear power is high due to the cost of the power plant and final decommissioning.

I never thought fishin' was that energetic...

There are arguments for and against nuclear power. Learn these, and the block diagram for a nuclear power plant.

Wind and Solar Energy

Renewable energy sources, like wind, waves and solar energy, will not run out. What's more, they do a lot less damage to the environment. They don't generate as much electricity as non-renewables though — if they did we'd all be using solar-powered toasters by now.

Wind Power — Lots of Little Wind Turbines

1) This involves putting lots of windmills (wind turbines) up in exposed places like on moors or round coasts.
2) Each wind turbine has its own generator inside it so the electricity is generated directly from the wind turning the blades, which turn the generator.
3) There's no pollution (except for a little bit when they're manufactured).
4) But they do spoil the view. You need about 1500 wind turbines to replace one coal-fired power station and 1500 of them cover a lot of ground — which would have a big effect on the scenery.
5) And they can be very noisy, which can be annoying for people living nearby.
6) There's also the problem of no power when the wind stops, and it's impossible to increase supply when there's extra demand.
7) The initial costs are quite high, but there are no fuel costs and minimal running costs.
8) There's no permanent damage to the landscape — if you remove the turbines, you remove the noise and the view returns to normal.

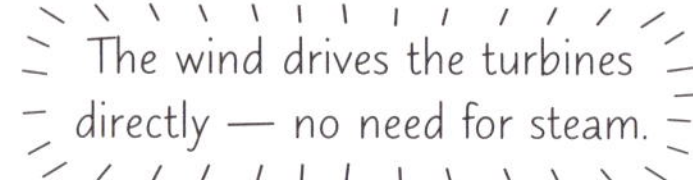
The wind drives the turbines directly — no need for steam.

Solar Cells — Expensive but No Environmental Damage

(well, there may be a bit caused by making the cells)

1) Solar cells generate electric currents directly from sunlight. They're expensive initially. Solar cells are often the best source of energy for calculators and watches which don't use much electricity.

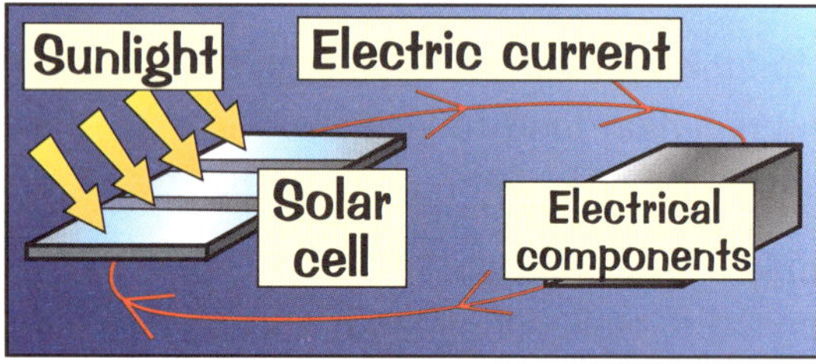

2) Solar power is often used in remote places where there's not much choice (e.g. the Australian outback) and to power electric road signs and satellites.
3) There's no pollution. (Although they do use quite a lot of energy to manufacture in the first place.)
4) In sunny countries solar power is a very reliable source of energy — but only in the daytime. Solar power can still be cost-effective even in cloudy countries like Britain.
5) Initial costs are high but after that the energy is free and running costs almost nil.
6) Solar cells are usually used to generate electricity on a relatively small scale, e.g. powering individual homes.
7) It's often not practical or too expensive to connect them to the National Grid — the cost of connecting them to the National Grid can be enormous compared with the value of the electricity generated.

People love the idea of wind power — just not in their backyard...

Did you know you can now get rucksacks with built-in solar cells to charge up your mobile phone, MP3 player and digital camera while you're wandering around. Pretty cool, huh.

Wave and Tidal Energy

More renewable energy sources — wave power and tidal power. It's easy to get confused between these two because they're both to do with the seaside — but don't. They're completely different.

Wave Power — Lots of Little Wave-Powered Turbines

1) You need lots of small wave-powered turbines located around the coast.
2) As waves come in to the shore they provide an up and down motion that can be used to directly drive a turbine, which then drives a generator.
3) There's no pollution. The main problems are spoiling the view and being a hazard to boats.
4) They are fairly unreliable, since waves tend to die out when the wind drops.
5) Initial costs are high, but there are no fuel costs and minimal running costs. Wave power is never likely to provide energy on a large scale, but it can be very useful on small islands.

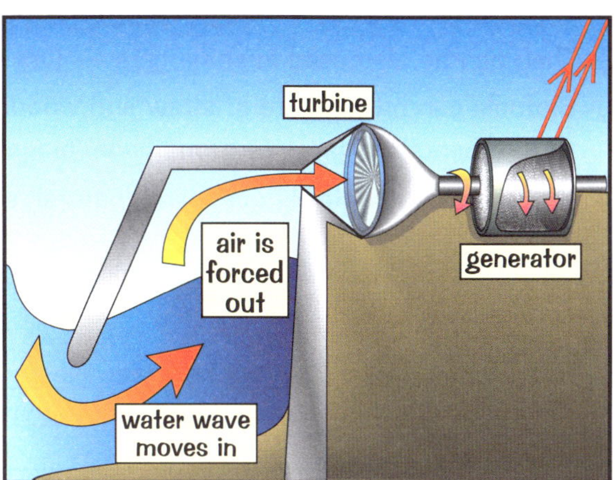

Tidal Barrages — Using the Sun and Moon's Gravity

1) Tidal barrages are big dams built across river estuaries, with turbines in them.
2) As the tide comes in it fills up the estuary to a height of several metres — it also drives the turbines. This water can then be allowed out through the turbines at a controlled speed.
3) The source of the energy is the gravity of the Sun and the Moon.
4) There's no pollution. The main problems are preventing free access by boats, spoiling the view and altering the habitat of the wildlife, e.g. wading birds, sea creatures and beasties who live in the sand.

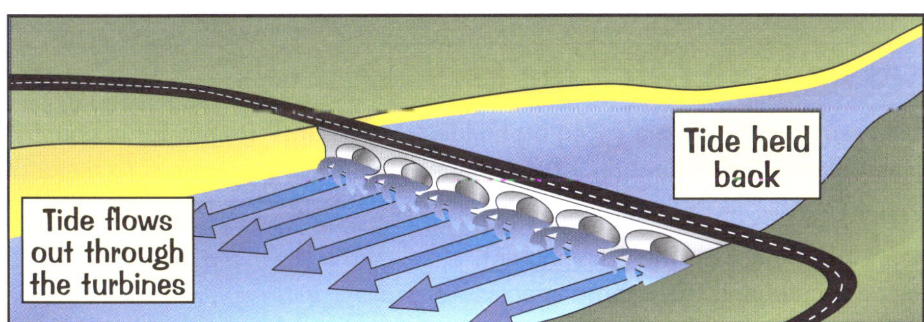

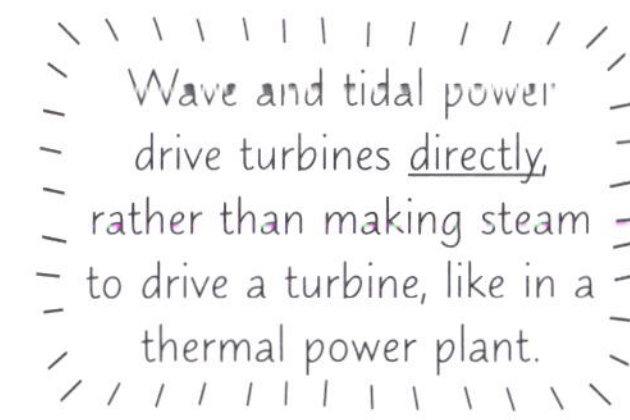

5) Tides are pretty reliable in the sense that they happen twice a day without fail, and always near to the predicted height. The only drawback is that the height of the tide is variable so lower (neap) tides will provide significantly less energy than the bigger 'spring' tides. They also don't work when the water level is the same either side of the barrage — this happens four times a day because of the tides. But tidal barrages are excellent for storing energy ready for periods of peak demand.
6) Initial costs are moderately high, but there are no fuel costs and minimal running costs. Even though it can only be used in some of the most suitable estuaries tidal power has the potential for generating a significant amount of energy.

Learn about Wave Power — and bid your cares goodbye...

I do hope you appreciate the big big differences between tidal power and wave power. They both involve salty seawater, sure — but there the similarities end. Lots of jolly details then, just waiting to be absorbed into your cavernous intracranial void. Smile and enjoy. And learn.

Biofuels, Geothermal and Hydroelectricity

Well, whaddaya know — there's more energy lurking about in piles of rubbish, rocks and rainwater.

Biofuels are Made from Plants and Waste

1) Biofuels are renewable energy resources. They're used to generate electricity in thermal power stations (see p. 32) — they're burnt to heat up water, which makes steam, which drives a turbine...
2) They can be also used in some cars — just like fossil fuels.
3) Biofuels can be solids (e.g. straw and woodchips), liquids (e.g. ethanol) or gases (e.g. methane 'biogas' from sludge digesters).
4) Biofuels are a relatively quick and 'natural' source of energy and are supposedly carbon neutral:

The plants that grew to produce the waste absorbed carbon dioxide from the atmosphere as they were growing. When the waste is burnt, this CO_2 is re-released into the atmosphere. So it has a neutral effect on atmospheric CO_2 levels.

5) But in some regions, forest has been cleared to make room to grow biofuels, resulting in species losing their natural habitats. The decay and burning of this vegetation also increases CO_2 and methane emissions.

Geothermal Energy — Heat from Underground

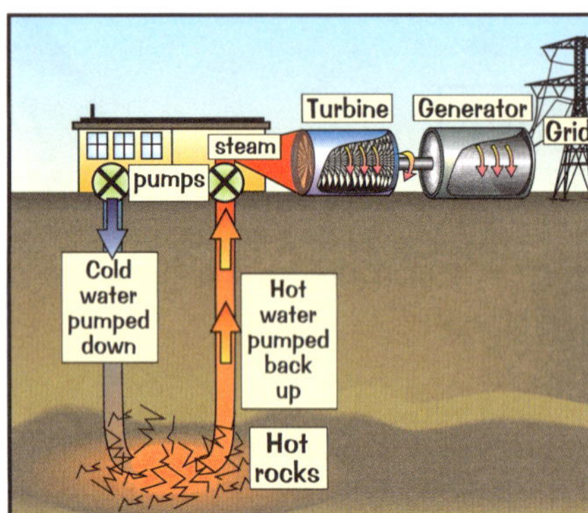

1) This is only possible where hot rocks lie quite near to the surface.
2) Geothermal energy is used to drive generators in thermal power stations (see p. 32). E.g. water is pumped in pipes down to hot rocks and returns as steam to drive a turbine.
3) This is actually brilliant free, renewable energy with no real environmental problems.
4) The main disadvantage is the cost of drilling down several km to the hot rocks.
5) Unfortunately there are very few places where this seems to be an economic option (for now).

Hydroelectricity uses Dams to catch the Rain

1) Hydroelectric power usually requires flooding a valley by building a big dam. Rainwater is caught and allowed out through turbines, driving them directly. The turbines then drive generators to make electricity.
2) There is no pollution (as such)...
3) ...but flooding a valley has a big impact on the environment. Rotting vegetation releases methane and CO_2, some species lose their habitat, and the reservoirs can also look very unsightly when they dry up. Location in remote valleys can reduce the human impact.
4) A big advantage is immediate response to increased demand, and it's fairly reliable except in times of drought.
5) Initial costs are high, but there's no fuel and minimal running costs.
6) The block diagram for the process looks like this:

1) Water stored in reservoir above the turbines using a dam. → 2) Gravity causes the water to rush through the turbines. → 3) A generator converts the movement of the turbines (kinetic energy) into electricity.

Hydroelectric power — pretty dam good...

There's so much to learn on this page — I'll not keep you a minute longer. Get and learn it...

Comparison of Energy Resources

So with all these lovely renewables around, who needs smelly old fossil fuels? If only it were that simple...

We Need a Steady, Reliable Fuel Supply to provide Enough Energy

1) The UK uses a lot of electricity, and demand is increasing.
2) We ideally need a reliable, affordable, large and environmentally-friendly energy source to keep us going.
3) But no single source of energy can provide for all these needs:
   - Renewable sources struggle to produce the same sort of energy output as conventional power stations. E.g. it would take 800 wind turbines to provide the same amount of energy as Drax (the UK's biggest coal-fired power station).
   - All our uranium and over half of the coal we burn is currently imported from other countries. This makes us dependent on other countries and involves transport-related costs and CO_2 emissions.
   - Our supply of fossil fuels will probably run out within 50 years or so, and uranium will run out eventually.
   - Renewable fuel sources are free and won't run out, but some of them are quite variable — it's not always sunny and the wind doesn't blow all the time.
4) So we need to compromise and use a mix of sources to make sure the UK doesn't run out of electricity.

We Need to Consider Environmental Impact as well as Cost

When choosing an energy source there are lots of things to consider:

Economics

Running Costs:
Renewables usually have the lowest running costs, because there's no actual fuel involved.

Setup Costs:
Renewable resources often need bigger power stations than non-renewables for the same output. And as you'd expect, the bigger the power station, the more expensive.

Nuclear reactors, hydroelectric dams and geothermal power stations need lots of engineering which bumps up the cost.

Environmental Impact

If there's a fuel involved, there'll be waste pollution, CO_2 emissions (except nuclear), and you'll be using up resources.

If it relies on the weather, it's often got to be in an exposed place where it sticks out like a sore thumb.

Waste and Air Pollution
Coal, Oil, Gas, Nuclear
(+ others, though less so)

Carbon Dioxide
Coal, Oil, Gas

Visual Pollution
Coal, Oil, Gas, Nuclear, Tidal, Waves, Wind, Hydroelectric, Geothermal

Using Up Resources
Coal, Oil, Gas, Nuclear

Noise Pollution
Coal, Oil, Gas, Nuclear, Wind

Disruption of Habitats
Hydroelectric, Tidal, Biofuels

Disruption of Leisure Activities
(e.g. boats): Waves, Tidal

Other Problems
Nuclear (explosions), Hydroelectric (dams bursting)

No Energy Source is Perfect

You might have to interpret information on different energy sources. This table shows comparison data for some large, modern, UK power stations:

E.g. nuclear power has low CO_2 emissions, so it's fairly environmentally friendly. But it costs a lot per unit of energy and the power station has a relatively short lifetime, so it's not a good long-term solution.

	Coal	Gas	Nuclear	Wind
Efficiency	36%	50%	38%	35%
Energy output per year (millions of units)	8000	5000	7000	150
CO_2 emissions per unit of electricity (g)	920	440	110	none
Lifetime of the site (years)	50	30	25	25
Cost of energy per unit (p)	2.5-4.5	2-3	4-7	3-4

Of course the biggest problem is that we use too much electricity...

It would be lovely if we could get rid of all the nasty polluting power stations and replace them with clean, green fuel... but it's not quite that straightforward. Renewable energy has its own problems too.

Generators and the National Grid

As if by magic, the kinetic energy from the power station turbines goes into a generator and comes out as electricity. Well it's not magic — it's electromagnetic induction...

Moving a Magnet in a Coil of Wire Induces a Voltage

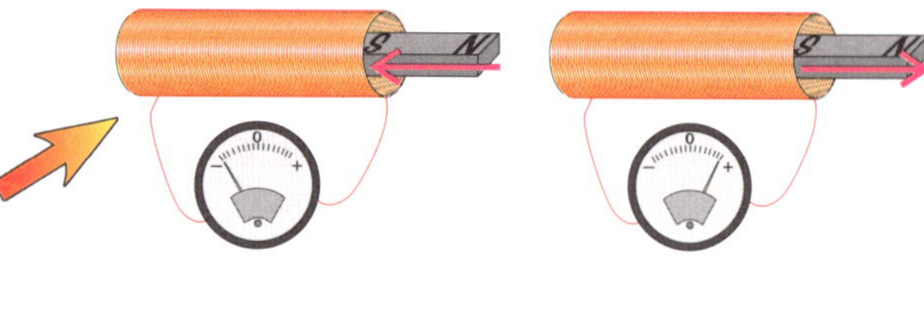

1) You can create a voltage and maybe a current in a conductor by moving a magnet in or near a coil of wire. This is called electromagnetic induction.
2) As you move the magnet, the magnetic field through the coil changes — this change in the magnetic field induces (creates) a voltage, and a current flows in the wire (if it's part of a complete circuit).

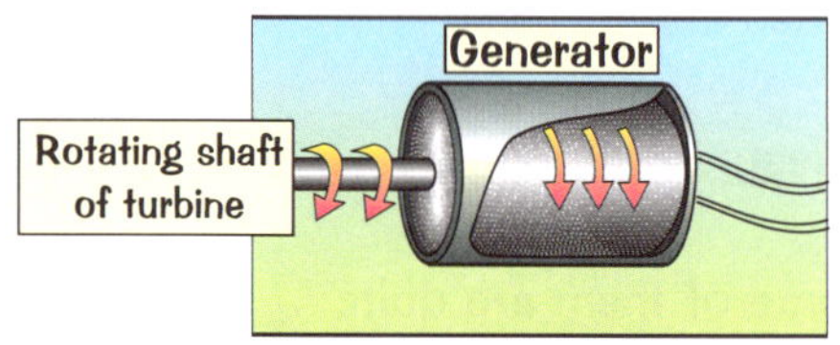

3) Generators use electromagnetic induction to turn kinetic energy from the turbines in power stations into mains electricity.

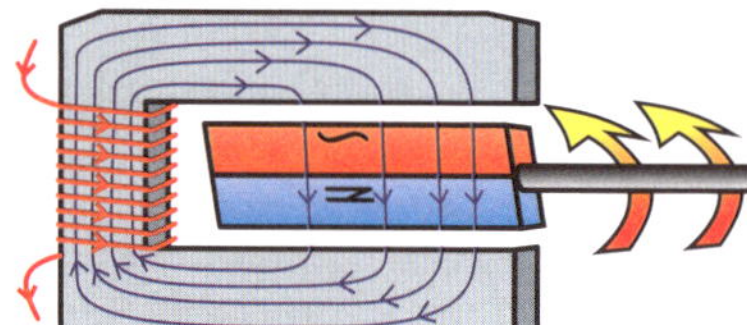

4) In a generator a magnet rotates in a coil of wire. As the magnet turns, the magnetic field through the coil changes — this change in the magnetic field induces a voltage, which makes a current flow in the coil.
5) If you want a bigger voltage and current in the wire, you can turn the magnet faster.
6) To move the magnet faster you need to put more energy in to turn the turbine, which uses up more of the primary energy source (what's being used to power the turbine, e.g. coal).
7) So the bigger the current and voltage, the more fuel we use up every second.

Electricity is Distributed via the National Grid

1) The National Grid is the network of pylons and cables that covers the whole of Britain.
2) It takes electrical energy from power stations to where it's needed in homes and industry.
3) It enables power to be generated anywhere on the grid, and then be supplied anywhere else on the grid.
4) To transmit the huge amount of power needed, you need either a high voltage or a high current.

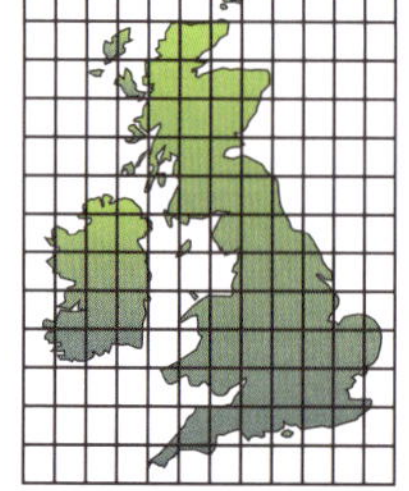
The National Grid.

5) The problem with a high current is that you lose loads of energy through heat in the cables.
6) So it's much cheaper and more efficient to distribute at a really high voltage (400 000 V) — this keeps the current very low and so reduces energy loss.
7) The voltage is reduced before it gets to our homes so it reaches us at 230 V — this is the mains supply voltage.

Talkin' 'bout my generation...

Generators are vital for changing all the energy from power stations into a usable, electrical form. The National Grid is what then gets it from the power stations to wherever it's needed, in a convenient 230 V supply. Magic.

Revision Summary for Module P3

You've finally got to the end of the Module. But do you know all there is to know about electricity? Make sure that it really has sunk in, and that you're ready for anything those examiners can throw at you. Have a go at every single one of these, and if any cause you problems you know what to do — go back and learn it properly.

1) What equation links energy transferred, power and time?
2)* Calculate the cost of using a 5 W energy-saving bulb for 3 hours if one kWh costs 10p.
3)* What is the power rating (in kW) of a pair of straighteners using a voltage of 230 V and a current of 5 A?
4) What two formulas could you use to calculate the efficiency of a hairdrier?
5) Why is a hairdrier not 100% efficient?
6) What does a Sankey diagram show?
7) List one way that energy can be saved: a) at home, b) at work and c) on a national scale.
8) What's the difference between primary and secondary energy sources?
9) Is electricity a primary or secondary energy source?
10) Describe the basic features of a thermal power station.
11) Name two sources of energy that power turbines directly without the use of steam.
12) List four disadvantages of using fossil fuels as an energy source. Why do we still need to use them?
13) Describe the main features of a nuclear power station.
14) List three advantages and three disadvantages of using nuclear power.
15) Explain the difference between irradiation and contamination.
16) Give one advantage and one disadvantage for using the following types of power:
a) wave, b) tidal, c) wind, d) solar, e) biofuels, f) geothermal.
17) Describe the process of generating hydroelectricity. Draw this as a block diagram.
18) Describe two disadvantages of using hydroelectricity.
19) Why can't we carry on using fossil fuels forever?
20) Explain why we can't easily replace fossil fuels with renewable energy sources.
21) List five things that need to be considered when choosing an energy source for a power station.
22) Explain why renewable energy sources aren't necessarily cheap.
23) Explain how kinetic energy is magically transformed to electricity in a generator.
24) What is the National Grid?
25) What voltage is the mains supply voltage to our homes?

* Answers on p.96.

Speed

This whole speed thing's pretty easy really — just make sure you've had lots of practice at calculating speeds, distances and times, and you'll have it sorted.

Speed is Just the Distance Travelled in a Certain Time

1) To find the speed of an object (in metres per second, m/s), you need to know the distance it travels (in metres) and the time it takes (in seconds).
2) You really ought to get pretty slick with this very easy formula:

$$\text{Speed (m/s)} = \frac{\text{Distance travelled (m)}}{\text{Time taken (s)}}$$

You can use a formula triangle to easily rearrange this equation...

1) A formula triangle can help with calculations, especially if you need to find the distance or time rather than the speed...
2) You just cover up the thing you're trying to find, and the triangle magically tells you how to calculate it:

There's a bit about formula triangles on the inside front cover too.

Distance travelled is speed × time taken...

...and time taken is distance travelled ÷ speed.

Now you just need to try and think up some interesting word for remembering the order of the letters in the triangle, s^{d}t. Errm... sedit, perhaps... I'm sure you can think up something better...

EXAMPLE: A cat skulks 20 metres in 40 seconds.
Find: a) its speed, b) how long it will take to skulk 75 m.

ANSWER: Using the formula triangle: a) s = d/t = 20/40 = 0.5 m/s
b) t = d/s = 75/0.5 = 150 s = 2 min 30 s

The Speed of an Object Normally Changes

1) In real life, it's pretty rare for an object to go at exactly the same speed for a long period of time. Cars, for example, have to start off at 0 m/s, then accelerate up to speed. Even if you're on the motorway, you'll have to alter your speed depending on other traffic, etc.
2) So it's usually more useful to know average speed, and that's what the speed formula will normally tell you — the skulking cat averaged 0.5 m/s over its journey.
3) Sometimes though, it's handy to know something's 'instantaneous' speed (or velocity — see next page). Most speed cameras, for instance, use lines painted on the road to measure the distance travelled by a vehicle in a set time.
(So here 'instantaneous' speed is still an average, just over a really short time period...)

Don't speed through this page — learn it properly...

Calculating speed is easy — you know the units are m/s, so it's pretty obviously metres ÷ seconds...

Speed, Distance and Velocity

One way to look at the movement of an object is to draw a lovely old distance-time graph...

Distance-Time Graphs

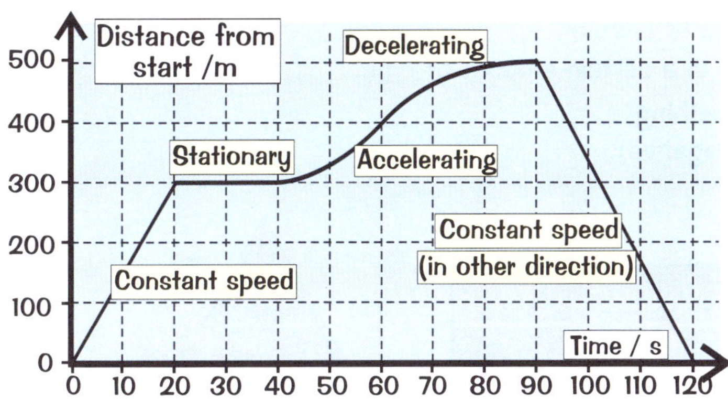

Examiners love to ask you to calculate speed from a distance-time graph. It's pretty easy...
For example, for the first section of the graph:

$$\text{Speed} = \text{gradient} = \frac{\text{vertical}}{\text{horizontal}} = \frac{300}{20} = 15 \text{ m/s}$$

Don't forget that you have to use the scales of the axes to work out the gradient. Don't measure in cm.

Very Important Notes:

1) GRADIENT = SPEED.
2) Flat sections are where it's stationary.
3) The steeper the gradient, the faster it's going.
4) 'Downhill' sections mean it's coming back toward its starting point.
5) Curves represent acceleration or deceleration.
6) A steepening curve means it's speeding up (increasing gradient) — it's accelerating.
7) A levelling-off curve means it's slowing down (decreasing gradient) — it's decelerating.
8) Displacement-time graphs are almost the same idea as distance-time graphs, except the gradient tells you the velocity (see below).

Don't worry too much about curved bits of the graph — you need to know what they mean, but you don't need to calculate anything from them.

Displacement can be Positive or Negative

1) You might see distances referred to as either positive or negative.
2) All this means is that an object can be going in one direction or in the opposite direction.
3) When distance is given with a particular indication of direction, it's called displacement. Or to give it its fancy definition — the displacement of something is its distance in a given direction, from its starting point, at any particular moment in time.
4) For example, imagine that Wayne and Garth are at point A. When they leave, Garth heads towards point B, and Wayne heads in the opposite direction, to point C.
5) So at the end of their journeys, Garth's displacement is 40 m from A and Wayne's is –35 m from point A.

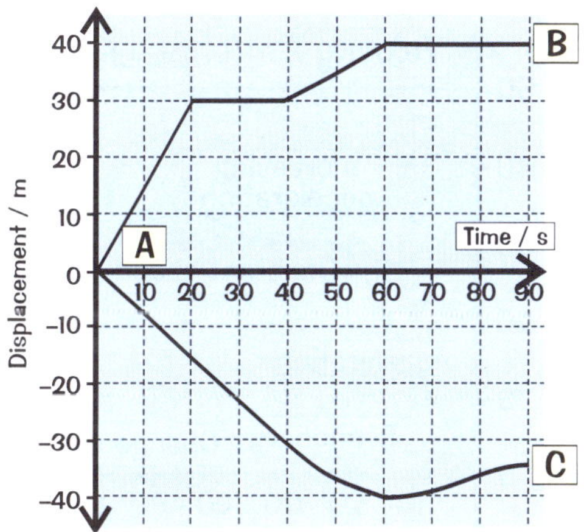

Speed is Just a Number, but Velocity Has Direction Too

1) The speed of an object is just how fast it's going — the direction isn't important. E.g. speed = 30 mph.
2) Velocity is sometimes a more useful measure of motion, because it describes both the speed and direction. E.g. velocity = 30 mph due north.
3) Instantaneous velocity is its speed and direction at a given moment in time.
4) Just like negative displacements, you'll also come across negative velocities. If a car's travelling in a straight line at 20 m/s but then turns around and travels in a straight line in the opposite direction, its speed may still be 20 m/s, but its velocity's changed from 20 m/s to –20 m/s. (Remember, velocity has direction...)
5) Likewise, if two objects are heading in opposite directions, you can say that one has positive velocity and the other has negative velocity.

All speeds = 0.5 m/s
Velocities = completely different

Distance-time graphs — almost as fun as watching dried paint...

These graphs aren't exactly exciting, but you need to be really comfortable with calculating speed from them.

Acceleration and Velocity

Accellll-er-a-tion time, come on — as Kool & The Gang never sang...

Acceleration is How Quickly You're Speeding Up

1) Acceleration is definitely not the same as velocity or speed.
2) Acceleration is the change in velocity (or speed) in a certain amount of time.
3) Deceleration is just negative acceleration (if something slows down then the change in velocity will be negative).

Acceleration — the Formula:

$$\text{Acceleration (m/s}^2) = \frac{\text{Change in Velocity (m/s)}}{\text{Time Taken (s)}}$$

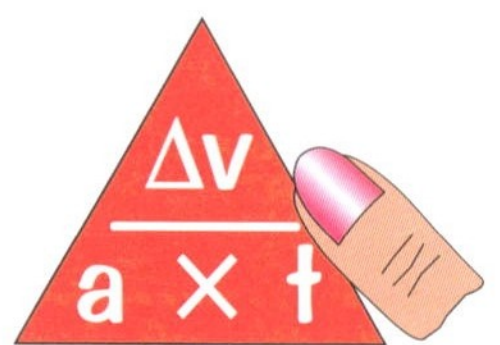

There are two tricky things with this formula. First there's the "Δv", which means working out the "change in velocity", as shown in the example below, rather than just putting a simple value for speed or velocity in. Secondly there's the units of acceleration, which are m/s^2.

EXAMPLE: A skulking cat accelerates steadily from 2 m/s to 6 m/s in 5.6 s. Find its acceleration.

ANSWER: Using the formula triangle: $a = \Delta v \div t = (6 - 2) \div 5.6 = 4 \div 5.6 = \underline{0.71\ m/s^2}$

Velocity-Time Graphs

You might be asked to draw a graph of velocity against time, or to answer questions about a graph you're given.

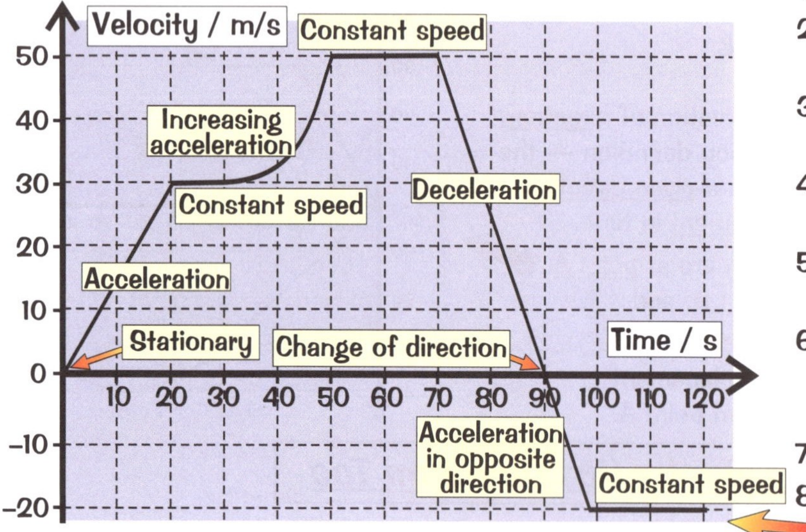

You might be asked to find the acceleration from a velocity-time graph. You do it by finding the gradient. Here's an example:

The acceleration during the first section of the graph is:

$$\text{Acceleration} = \text{gradient} = \frac{\text{vertical}}{\text{horizontal}} = \frac{30}{20} = 1.5\ m/s^2$$

Very Important Notes:

1) Gradient = acceleration.
2) Flat sections represent moving in a straight line at constant speed.
3) The steeper the gradient, the greater the acceleration or deceleration.
4) Uphill sections (/) are acceleration in a straight line.
5) Downhill sections (\) are deceleration in a straight line.
6) The area under any section of the graph (or all of it) is equal to the displacement (distance) travelled in that time interval.
7) A curve means changing acceleration.
8) Negative velocity means that the object is travelling in the opposite direction.
9) Speed-time graphs are similar to velocity-time graphs but ignore direction.
10) You can calculate acceleration from a speed-time graph too, but only if the direction of movement doesn't change. (You can't tell if something's changed direction from a speed-time graph.)

Ch-ch-ch-ch-changes (in velocity)...

Most of the time you can just think of acceleration as how fast the speed of something's changing (such as how quickly a car stops, or how long it takes for a plane to go fast enough to take off). But, because velocity's involved, direction matters. So, a car going around a roundabout at a constant speed is actually accelerating.

Forces and Friction

A force is just a push or a pull, but they never come on their own — there's always at least one force in the opposite direction too. Force is measured in Newtons (N).

Forces Occur When Two Objects Interact

When an object exerts a force on another object, it always experiences a force in return. These two are called 'partner forces' or an 'interaction pair'. Because there are two of them. And they interact...

1) That means if you push against a wall, the wall will push back against you in the opposite direction with exactly the same force. And as soon as you stop pushing, so does the wall.
2) If you think about it, there must be an opposing force when you push (or lean) against a wall — otherwise you (and the wall) would fall over.
3) Although the forces are equal, they can still cause things to move because they act on different objects.
4) Think of a jet engine that uses air to burn fuel, producing exhaust gases. The jet engine exerts a force on the exhaust gases, making them accelerate backwards. The exhaust gases exert an equal but opposite force on the jet, giving it forward momentum (see p. 45) so it moves forwards.
5) A similar thing happens in rockets — the forces on the gas and the rocket are an interaction pair.

An Object Resting on a Surface Experiences a Reaction Force

If you put a book on a table, the book pushes down on the table with a force equal to its weight — and the table exerts an equal and opposite force upwards on the book. This upward force is called a reaction force — because it's the table's 'response' to the force exerted by the book.

Moving Objects Normally Experience Friction

1) When an object is moving relative to another one, both objects experience a force in the direction that opposes the movement — this is called friction.
2) Friction is a reaction force — it happens as a result of an applied force.
3) The frictional force will match the size of the force trying to move an object, up to a maximum point — after this point the friction will be less than the other force and the object will move.
4) There are three types of friction you should know about:

a) FRICTION BETWEEN SOLID SURFACES WHICH ARE GRIPPING

This is the kind of friction that lets you walk around — the friction between your shoes (or feet) and the ground allows you to push against it and move forwards (or backwards if you're doing the Moonwalk*). If there was no friction you'd just slip, look silly and never get anywhere.

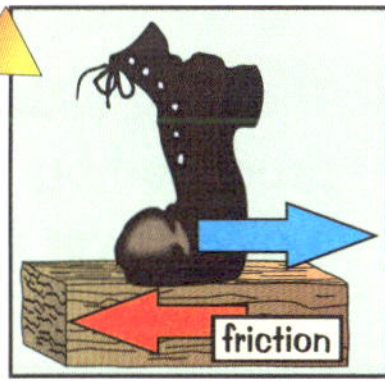

b) FRICTION BETWEEN SOLID SURFACES WHICH ARE SLIDING PAST EACH OTHER

E.g. the moving bits and pieces in a car engine.
You can reduce sliding friction and gripping friction by putting a lubricant like oil or grease between the surfaces.

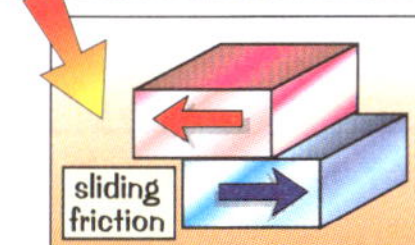

c) RESISTANCE OR "DRAG" FROM FLUIDS (LIQUIDS OR GASES, E.G. AIR)

Drag's basically just the same as other types of friction — an object moving through a fluid has to force its way past all the molecules in that fluid, and that causes friction. Obviously, a big, squarish object like a lorry experiences more drag or air resistance than a streamlined object like a sports car.
Drag only happens if the object is moving through a fluid (i.e. air, water, ketchup).
So there's no drag in space (it's a vacuum, so there's no fluid to move through).

Revision — what a drag...

An obvious joke, I know. But I can't be funny everyday of my life — I'm no Steve Martin** you know.

*ask your parents **ask them again

Forces

It's all very well knowing that there are forces acting all over the place, but you need to be able to show where and when they're acting too...

Arrows Show the Size and Direction of Forces

You might be given a diagram of an object and asked to draw arrows showing the forces acting on it.

1) The length of the arrow shows the size of the force.
2) The direction of the arrow shows the direction of the force (didn't see that one coming, did you...).
3) So if the arrows come in opposite pairs, and they're all the same size, then the forces are balanced...

1) The Reaction of a Surface — Balanced Forces

1) If an object's resting on a surface, it pushes downwards (because of its weight).
2) This causes an equal reaction force from the surface pushing up on the object.
3) The two forces are the same size, so the arrows on the diagram are the same size.

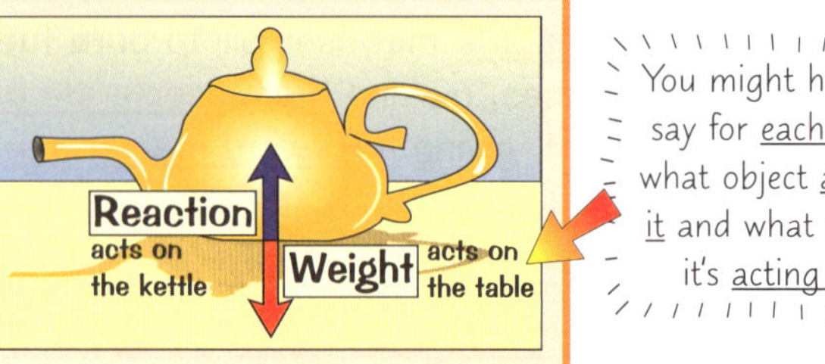

You might have to say for each force what object applies it and what object it's acting on.

2) Steady Speed — Balanced Forces

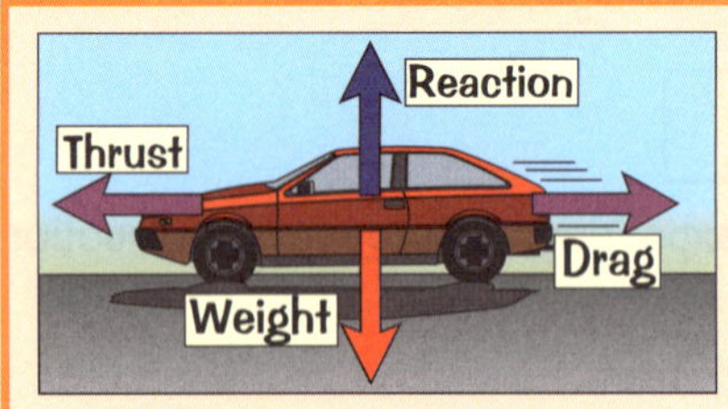

1) If an object is moving with a steady speed the forces must be in balance.
2) Just because something's moving doesn't mean that there's an overall force acting on it — unless it's changing speed or direction, the overall (resultant) force is zero.

You can apply these ideas to lots of other objects...

1) A jet aircraft is moving at a steady speed and at a constant altitude (height).
2) The forces acting on it must therefore be balanced.
3) The drag caused by the air resistance balances the thrust produced by the engines. The lift produced by air moving over the plane's wings balances the weight.

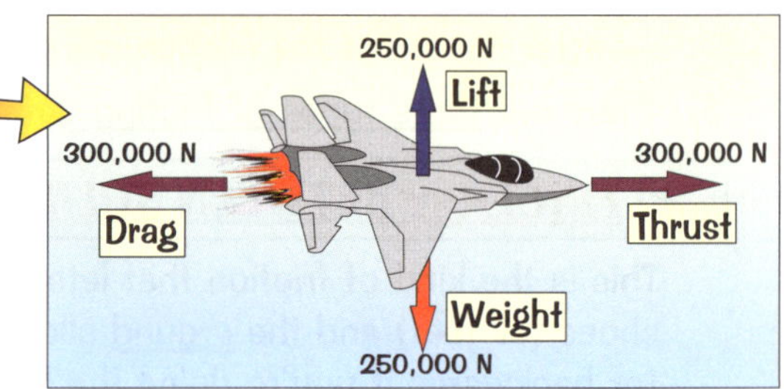

Resultant Force is Really Important

In many real situations, the forces acting on an object are not all the same size — they're unbalanced.

1) The resultant force is the overall force acting on an object — the force you get when you take into account (add up) all the individual forces and their directions.
2) It's this force that decides the motion of the object — whether it will accelerate, decelerate or stay at a steady speed.
3) Remember that 'accelerate' just means change velocity — and since velocity has both speed and direction, accelerating doesn't necessarily mean changing speed — it might just mean changing direction. For example, a car going round a corner is changing velocity (and therefore accelerating), even if it stays at a steady speed.

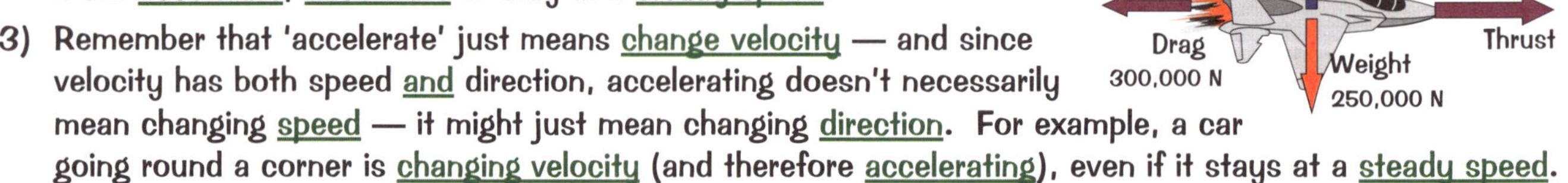

4) So if there's a resultant force acting on an object, its speed or direction (or both) changes.

Resultant force... I'm pretty sure that's a Steven Seagal film...

It's important to understand what object a particular force is acting on. So make sure you revise it well.

Forces and Momentum

"But my forces are unbalanced! What will become of me?!", I hear you scream...
Don't worry my friend, this page has a kangaroo on it. A kangaroo wearing a hat in fact.

Acceleration — Unbalanced Forces

You'll only have to deal with things that are moving in a straight line.

1) If a car's engine exerts a bigger driving force (forwards) than the drag counter force (backwards), the car will accelerate.
2) That's what's happening in this diagram — the thrust (driving force) arrow is bigger than the drag arrow, so there's a resultant force in the forward direction.
3) The bigger this resultant force, the greater the acceleration.
4) If the driving force was less than the drag, the car would slow down.
5) Note that the forces in the other directions (up and down) are still balanced.

acceleration

Thrust

Drag

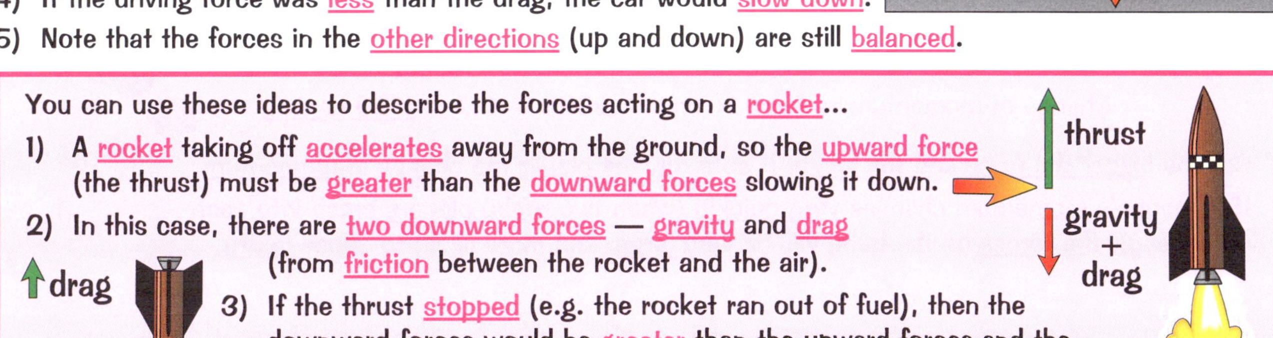

You can use these ideas to describe the forces acting on a rocket...

1) A rocket taking off accelerates away from the ground, so the upward force (the thrust) must be greater than the downward forces slowing it down.
2) In this case, there are two downward forces — gravity and drag (from friction between the rocket and the air).
3) If the thrust stopped (e.g. the rocket ran out of fuel), then the downward forces would be greater than the upward forces and the rocket would slow down until it stopped and then accelerate downward.
4) The same ideas apply to things thrown up in the air (and falling back to Earth). Their motion is all about the relative sizes of the upward and downward forces.

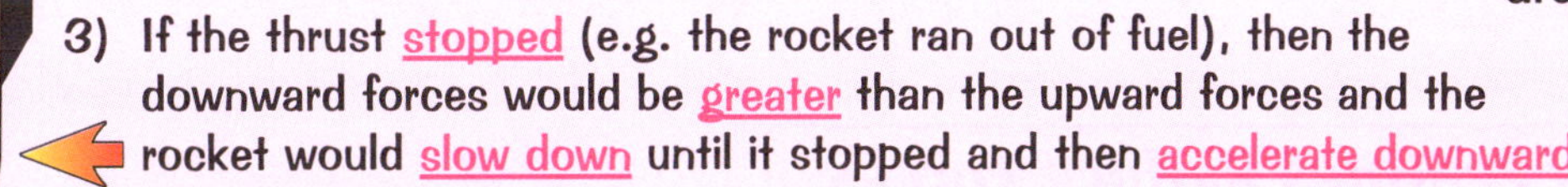

Momentum = Mass × Velocity

Momentum is mainly about how much 'oomph' an object has — how hard it'd be to stop it moving. The heavier an object is, and the faster it's moving, the harder it is to stop.

1) The greater the mass of an object, or the greater its velocity, the more momentum the object has. Here's a nice easy equation:

Momentum (kg m/s) = Mass (kg) × Velocity (m/s)

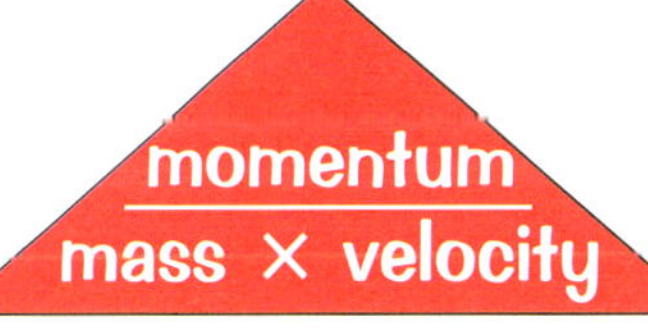

2) Momentum is a vector quantity — it has size and direction (like velocity, but not speed).

EXAMPLE: A 65 kg kangaroo is moving in a straight line at 10 m/s. Calculate its momentum.

ANSWER: Momentum = mass × velocity
= 65 × 10
kg m/s

Easy stuff... You can do that with your eyes closed. As long as you can smell the speed of kangaroos.

3) A resultant force of zero means that a stationary object will stay still. If the object was moving, it stays at a constant velocity (the same speed in the same direction) and constant momentum.
4) If the resultant force on an object is not zero, its momentum changes in the direction of the force.

Accelerate your learning — force yourself to revise...

OK so there's another equation of doom for you to learn, but it's a fairly simple one. In fact, if you remember the units of momentum (kg m/s), then it's pretty obvious that momentum = kg × m/s...

Change in Momentum and Force

Time to get your head around changes in momentum — a faster change = a greater chance of injury.

The Change in Momentum Depends on the Force

1) When a resultant force acts on an object, it causes a change in momentum in the direction of the force.
2) The change of momentum it causes is proportional to the size of the force and the time it acts for:

Change of momentum (kg m/s) = Resultant force (N) × Time for which the force acts (s)

EXAMPLE: A rock with mass 1 kg is travelling through space at 15 m/s. A comet hits the rock, giving it a resultant force of 2500 N for 0.7 seconds. Calculate the rock's initial momentum, and then the change in its momentum resulting from the impact with the comet.

ANSWER: Initial momentum = mass × velocity = 1 × 15 = 15 kg m/s

Change of momentum = force × time = 2500 × 0.7 = 1750 kg m/s

3) So, the bigger the force and the longer it acts for, the bigger the change in momentum.
4) If someone's momentum changes very quickly (when two rugby players crash into each other, say), the forces on the body will be very large, and more likely to cause injury.

Car Safety Features Reduce Forces

1) If you rearrange the equation above, you get force = change in momentum ÷ time. The greater the time for a change in momentum, the smaller the force.
2) So if your momentum changes slowly, like in nice controlled braking in a car, the forces acting on your body are small and you're unlikely to be hurt.
3) In a collision, you can't really affect the change in momentum — whatever you do, the car's mass and its change in velocity stay the same. However, the average force on an object can be lowered by slowing the object down over a longer time.
4) Safety features in a car increase the collision time to reduce the forces on the passengers.

CRUMPLE ZONES crumple on impact, increasing the time taken for the car to stop.

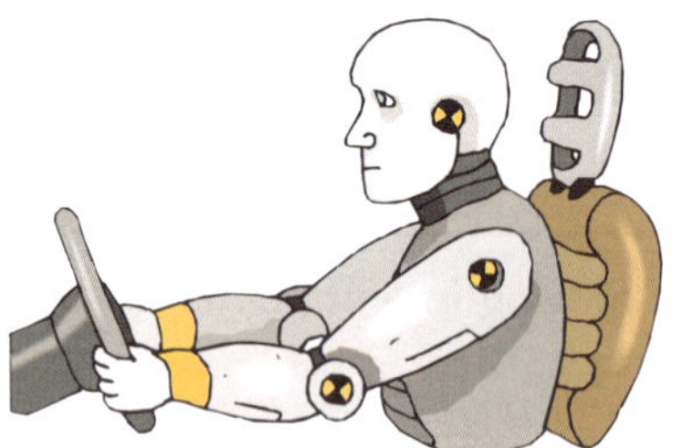

CYCLE AND MOTORCYCLE HELMETS provide padding that increases the time taken for your head to come to a stop if it hits something hard.

AIR BAGS also slow you down more gradually.

SEAT BELTS stretch slightly, increasing the time taken for the wearer to stop. This reduces the forces acting on the chest.

Learn this stuff — it'll only take a moment... um...

Momentum's a pretty fundamental bit of physics — so make sure you learn it properly. There are a few equations to cover in this section, but none of them are too hard, so keep practising different questions and Robert's your mother's brother. And never forget to stick the units on the end of your answers...

Work

In Physics, "work done" means something special — it's got its own formula and everything.

"Work Done" is Just "Energy Transferred"

When a force moves an object it does work and energy is transferred to the object.

That statement sounds far more complicated than it needs to. Try this:

1) Whenever something moves, something else is providing some sort of "effort" to move it.
2) The thing putting the effort in needs a supply of energy (like fuel or food or electricity etc.).
3) It then does "work" by moving the object — and one way or another it transfers the energy it receives (as fuel) into other forms.
4) Whether this energy is transferred usefully (e.g. by lifting a load) or is wasted (e.g. lost as heat), you can still say that work is done. Just like Batman and Bruce Wayne, work done and energy transferred are indeed one and the same. (And they're both in joules.)

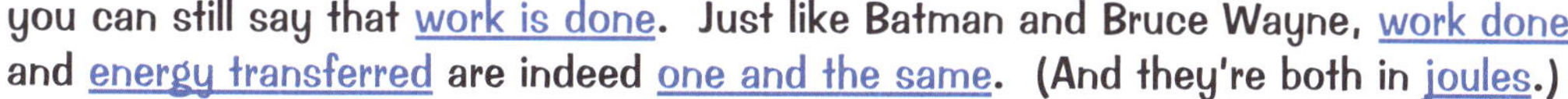

Amount of energy transferred (J) = Work done (J)

5) If energy is transferred then the object doing the work loses energy.
6) In the picture above, the guy doing the sweeping is doing work on the rubbish, so he loses energy — if he does 500 J of work, then he loses 500 J of energy. The rubbish is having work done on it, so it gains energy (though not the full 500 J — some will be lost as noise and heat).

And Another Formula to Learn...

Work done by a force (J) = Force (N) × Distance moved in direction of force (m)

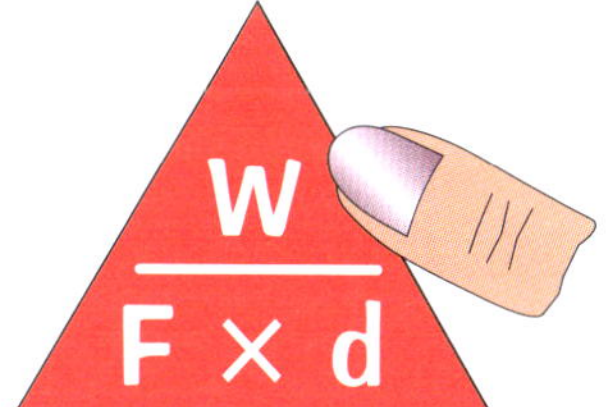

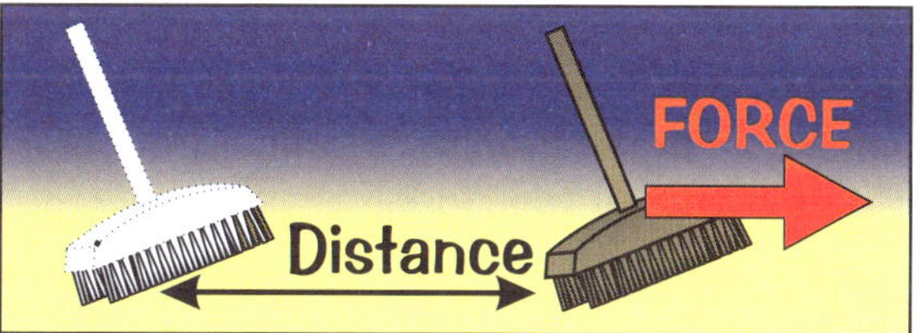

This formula only works if the force is in exactly the same direction as the movement.

To find how much work has been done (in joules), you just multiply the force in newtons by the distance moved in metres. Easy as that. I'll show you...

> EXAMPLE: Some hooligan kids drag an old tractor tyre 5 m over flat ground. They pull with a total force of 340 N. Find the work done.
>
> ANSWER: $W = F \times d = 340 \times 5 = 1700$ J.

Revise work done — what else...

So, work is just energy transferred. Learn the formula, then have a go at this question:
A gorilla finds himself with nothing to do on a Sunday evening, so he does 1050 J of work pushing a log 3 m across the forest floor. What is the average force he exerts on the log?*

*Answers on page 96.

Kinetic Energy

Work done always involves movement. That's where this whole kinetic energy business comes in...

Kinetic Energy is Energy of Movement

1) Anything that's moving has kinetic energy (K.E.).
2) The kinetic energy of something depends both on its mass and speed. The greater its mass and the faster it's going, the bigger its kinetic energy.
3) There's a slightly tricky formula for it, so you have to concentrate a little bit harder for this one:

Kinetic Energy (J) = ½ × mass (kg) × velocity² ([m/s]²)

K.E. / ½×m×v²

EXAMPLE: A car of mass 1450 kg is travelling at 28 m/s. Calculate its kinetic energy.

ANSWER: It's pretty easy. You just plug the numbers into the formula — but watch the "v^2".
K.E. = $\frac{1}{2}mv^2 = \frac{1}{2} \times 1450 \times 28^2 =$ 568 400 J (joules because it's energy)

4) To increase something's kinetic energy, you need to increase its velocity, and the only way to increase something's velocity is to apply a force to it...
5) ...and if you're applying a force to something, you're doing work on it. It doesn't matter what kind of work this is — it could be a person pushing a trolley, a jet engine providing thrust to an aeroplane, a golf club hitting a golf ball. If object A is causing object B's velocity to increase by exerting a force on it, then it's doing work and increasing object B's kinetic energy.
6) On the other hand, kinetic energy is just movement energy, so if you do work on an object but it doesn't accelerate, then you haven't increased its kinetic energy.

Increase in K.E. = Work Done, Just About...

1) OK, so if work is done on an object, then energy is transferred to that object, which is probably going to make it start moving or move faster.

2) Now then, a really important concept in physics is the idea that energy is always conserved. What that means is that you can't create or destroy energy — it just gets transformed from one kind of energy to another. E.g. a light bulb transforms electrical energy into light and heat energy.
3) So if energy is conserved, then you'd expect the increase in an object's kinetic energy to be equal to the amount of work that's been done on it.
4) The problem is, some of the energy that's transferred gets 'wasted' as heat because of friction and air resistance. If you do 30 J of work hitting a stationary ball, the ball's kinetic energy will be a bit less than 30 J because air resistance creates heat (OK, so the ball won't get hot, but it'll be a tiny bit hotter than it would be if there was no air resistance). So...

The increase in an object's K.E. is normally a bit less than the amount of work done on it, because some energy is wasted as heat.

5) BUT if there's no friction or air resistance acting on an object (e.g. a rocket in space), OR you're told to ignore it, then the increase in an object's kinetic energy is equal to the amount of work done on it.

After doing all this work you should be bouncing around...

The kinetic energy equation's the hardest one in this module — make sure you've got it nailed.

Gravitational Potential Energy

It's the last page of this module to learn... and it's got roller coasters on it. Life is good.

G.P.E. is 'Height Energy'

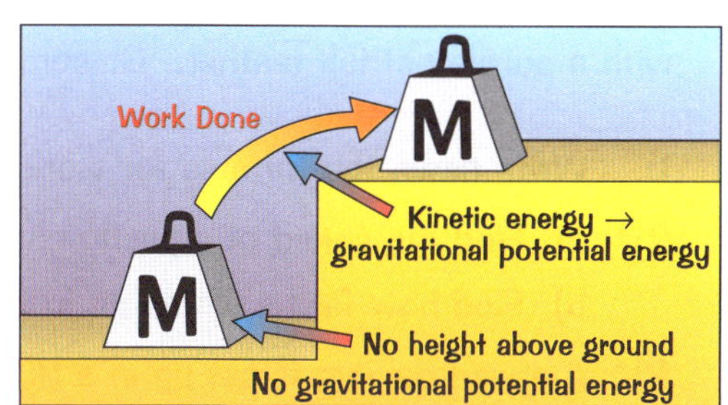

1) Gravitational potential energy (G.P.E.) is the energy stored in an object when you raise it to a height against the force of gravity.
2) If you lift an object, its G.P.E increases as it's raised.
3) As an object falls, its G.P.E. decreases.
4) You increase G.P.E. by doing work.
5) The increase in the G.P.E. is equal to the work done by the lifting force in order to raise its height.

Change in G.P.E. (J) = Weight (N) × Vertical height difference (m)

EXAMPLE: A 4000 N cow walks onto a geyser, and is propelled 10 m upwards. Calculate its change in G.P.E.

ANSWER: Change in G.P.E. = weight × vertical height difference
= 4000 × 10 = 40 000 J (or 40 kJ)

Falling Objects Convert G.P.E. into K.E.

1) When something falls, its gravitational potential energy is converted into kinetic energy (K.E.). So the further it falls, the faster it goes.
2) In practice, some of the G.P.E. will be dissipated as heat due to air resistance, but in exam questions they'll likely say you can ignore air resistance, in which case you'll just need to remember this simple and really quite obvious formula:

K.E. gained = G.P.E. lost

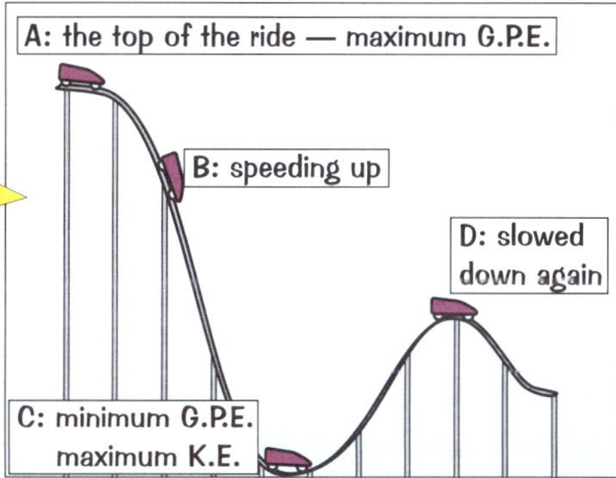

3) For example, the roller coaster to the right will lose G.P.E. and gain K.E. as it falls between points A and C.
4) If you ignore friction (between the tracks and the wheels) and air resistance, the amount of K.E. it gains will be the same as the amount of G.P.E. it loses.
5) Between C and D, it's gaining height, so some of that K.E. is converted back to G.P.E. again.

EXAMPLE: The carriage in the diagram has a weight of 5000 N (mass about 500 kg), and the vertical height difference between A and C is 20 m.

a) Ignoring friction and air resistance, how much K.E. is gained by the carriage in moving from A to C?

b) The roller coaster was stationary at A. Calculate its speed at C.

Weight is the force due to an object's mass and gravity. Weight = mass × acceleration due to gravity (about 10 m/s²).

ANSWER: a) K.E. gained = G.P.E. lost = weight × vertical height difference = 5000 × 20 = 100 000 J

b) At C it has 100 000 J of K.E. You know that K.E. = $\frac{1}{2}mv^2$ (see previous page), so...

$\frac{1}{2}mv^2 = 100\,000$

$v^2 = 100\,000 \div \frac{1}{2}m = 100\,000 \div (\frac{1}{2} \times 500) = 400$

$v = \sqrt{400} = 20$ m/s

If you know how much K.E. something's gained you can calculate it's speed. Handy.

Revise roller coasters — don't let your thoughts wander off into oblivion...

Roller coasters are constantly transferring between potential and kinetic energy. In reality, energy will be lost due to friction, air resistance and even as sound. But in exams you can usually ignore these.

Revision Summary for Module P4

Yay — revision summary. I know these are your favourite bits of the book, all those jolly questions. There are lots of equations and picky little details to learn in this module. So, practise these questions till you can do them all standing on one leg with your arms behind your back while being tickled on the nose with a purple ostrich feather. Or something.

1) Write down the formula for working out speed.
2)* a) Find the speed of a partly chewed mouse which hobbles 3.2 metres in 35 seconds.
b) Find how far he would go in 25 minutes.
3)* A speed camera is set up in a 30 mph (13.3 m/s) zone. It takes two photographs 0.5 s apart. A car travels 6.3 m between the two photographs. Was the car breaking the speed limit?
4) What does the gradient of a distance-time graph tell you?
5) What's the difference between speed and velocity?
6) Sketch a typical velocity-time graph and point out all the important points.
7) Explain how to find acceleration from a velocity-time graph.
8) What is an interaction pair?
9) A man leans on a wall with a force of 50 N. What can you say about the force exerted by the wall?
10) Explain what the 'reaction' of a surface is.
11) Define friction.
12) Give two scenarios where forces are balanced. Draw diagrams.
13) What is meant by resultant force?
14) If an object has zero resultant force on it, can it be moving? Can it be accelerating?
15)* Write down the formula for momentum. Find the momentum of a 78 kg sheep moving at 5 m/s.
16) Write down a formula for change of momentum.
17) Explain how air bags, seat belts and crumple zones reduce the risk of serious injury in a car crash.
18)* A crazy dog dragged a big branch 12 m over the next-door neighbour's front lawn, pulling with a force of 535 N. How much work was done on the branch?
19) What is the formula for kinetic energy (K.E.)?
20)* Calculate the increase in gravitational potential energy (G.P.E.) when a box of weight 120 N is raised vertically through 4.5 m.
21)* At the top of a roller coaster ride when it is stationary, a carriage has 150 kJ of gravitational potential energy. Ignoring friction and air resistance, how much kinetic energy must the carriage have at the bottom (when G.P.E. = 0)?
22)* A 600 kg (6000 N) roller coaster carriage is travelling at 40 m/s. What is the maximum vertical height it could climb to if all its kinetic energy is transferred to gravitational potential energy?
23)* A trolley is stationary at the top of a hill. The trolley weighs 200 N (mass 20 kg), and the hill is 50 m high. Assuming all of its G.P.E. is converted into K.E., how fast will the trolley be going when it reaches the bottom of the hill?

* Answers on page 96.

Static Electricity

Static electricity's all about charges which are not free to move. This causes them to build up in one place, and lead to sparks or shocks when they finally do move — crackling when you take a jumper off, say.

Build-up of Static is Caused by Friction

1) When two insulating materials are rubbed together, electrons are scraped off one and dumped on the other.
2) Electrons are negatively charged.
3) So this leaves a positive static charge on one (electrons scrapped off) and a negative static charge on the other (gained electrons).
4) Which way the electrons are transferred depends on the two materials involved.
5) The classic examples are polythene and acetate rods being rubbed with a cloth duster, as shown in the diagrams.

With the polythene rod, electrons move from the duster to the rod.

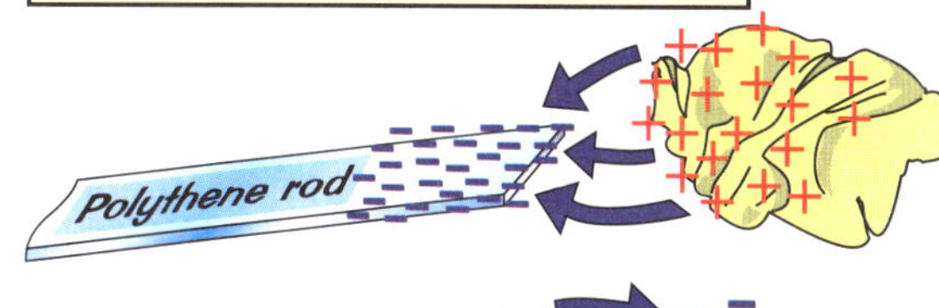

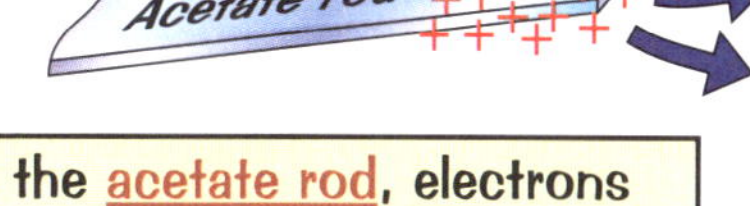

With the acetate rod, electrons move from the rod to the duster.

Only Electrons Move — Never the Positive Charges

When electrons are removed from particles the particles are left positively charged — these charged particles are called ions.

Both +ve and –ve electrostatic charges are only ever produced by the movement of electrons — the negatively charged particles. The positive charges definitely do not move. A positive static charge is always caused by electrons moving away elsewhere, as shown above. Don't forget!

Like Charges Repel, Opposite Charges Attract

Two things with opposite electric charges are attracted to each other.
Two things with the same electric charge will repel each other.

When you rub two insulating materials together a whole load of electrons get dumped together on one of the insulators, which becomes negatively charged. They try to repel each other, but can't move apart because their positions are fixed. The patch of charge that results is called static electricity because it can't move.

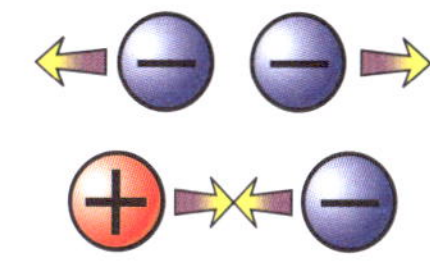

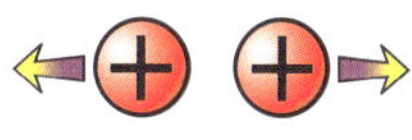

Static Electricity can be a Little Joker

Static electricity is responsible for some of life's little annoyances...

1) Attracting Dust

Dust particles are really tiny and lightweight and are easily attracted to anything that's charged. Unfortunately, many objects around the house are made of insulating materials (e.g. glass, wood, plastic) that get easily charged and attract the dust particles — this makes cleaning a nightmare. (Have a look at how dusty your TV screen is.)

2) Clinging Clothes and Crackles

When synthetic clothes are dragged over each other (like in a tumble drier) or over your head, electrons get scraped off, leaving static charges on both parts, and that leads to the inevitable — attraction (they stick together and cling to you) and little sparks or shocks as the charges rearrange themselves.

3) Bad Hair Days

Static builds up on your hair, giving each strand the same charge — so they repel each other.

Static caravans — where electrons go on holiday...

Static electricity's great fun. You must have tried it — rubbing a balloon against your jumper and trying to get it to stick to the ceiling. It really works... well, sometimes, and if at first you don't succeed, try, try again...

Electric Current

Static electricity's all well and good, but things get much more interesting when the charge can move. Moving charge is called current — you can use it to power all sorts of toys and gadgets. It's great stuff.

Electric Current is a Flow of Charge Round a Circuit

1) Electric current is a flow of charge.
2) In an electrical circuit the metal conductors (components and wires) are full of charges (electrons) that are free to move.
3) So electric charge flows in metal conductors because the electrons are free to move around.
4) Current can't flow in an insulator (like plastic) because there are few charges free to move.
5) The circuit shown is complete — the loop between one side of the battery and the other is continuous.

-ve
+ve
Voltage supply provides the 'push'
Current flows
R
RESISTANCE - opposes the flow

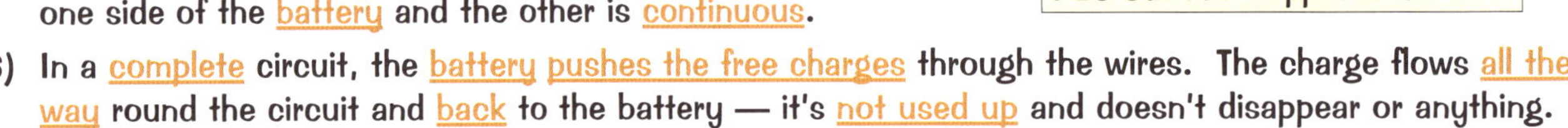

6) In a complete circuit, the battery pushes the free charges through the wires. The charge flows all the way round the circuit and back to the battery — it's not used up and doesn't disappear or anything.

Current Depends on Voltage and Resistance

1) Current (I) will only flow through a component if there's a voltage across that component. Its units are amperes (amps), A.
2) Voltage (V) is the driving force that pushes the current round. Its units are volts, V.
3) Resistance (R) is caused by things in the circuit (such as components, e.g. lamps) that resist the flow of charge (slows the charge down). Its units are ohms, Ω.
4) There's a balance: the voltage is trying to push the current round the circuit, and the resistance is opposing it — the relative sizes of the voltage and resistance decide how big the current will be:

> If you increase the voltage — then more current will flow.
> If you increase the resistance — then less current will flow.

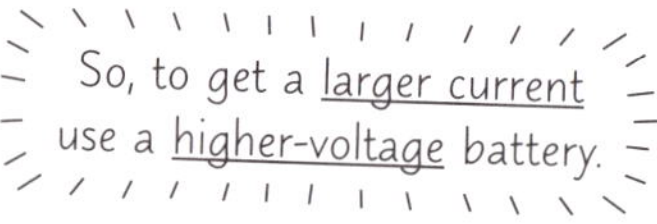

Power is the Rate of Energy Transfer

1) Anything that supplies electricity is also supplying energy.
2) So power supplies (cells, batteries, etc.) all transfer energy to the charge, which then transfers it to the components (and sometimes their surroundings).
3) Work is also done because energy is transferred (p. 47).
4) Power is the rate at which an electrical power supply transfers energy to an appliance.
5) Power is usually measured in watts, W, or kilowatts, kW (1 kW = 1000 W).

Power Ratings of Appliances

An appliance with a high power rating transfers a lot of energy in a short time. This energy comes from the current flowing through it. This means that an appliance with a high power rating will use a large current.

1) The formula for electrical power is: **POWER (W) = VOLTAGE (V) × CURRENT (A)** or $P = V \times I$
2) Most electrical goods show their power rating and voltage rating. To work out the current that the item will normally draw, you need to rearrange the equation:

EXAMPLE: A hairdrier is rated at 230 V, 1 kW. Find the current it draws.
ANSWER: Rearranging, $I = P \div V = 1000 \div 230 = 4.3$ A.

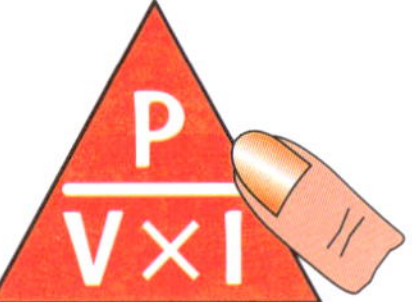

Electric current — always taking a circuitous route...

Electric current can only flow if electric charge (usually electrons) is free to move and the circuit is complete.

Electric Circuits

We use symbols when we're drawing circuit diagrams as it makes it simpler (even if it doesn't look it at first)...

Circuit Symbols You Should Know:

Circuit diagrams can look a little scary at first — all those squiggly pictures. You'll come across these symbols over the next few pages. If you learn what they mean it'll make a whole lot more sense later on...

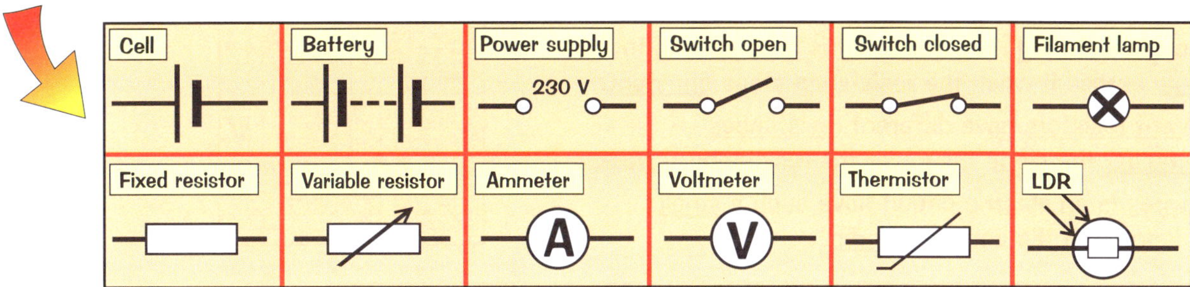

The Standard Test Circuit

This is without doubt the most totally bog-standard circuit the world has ever known. So know it.

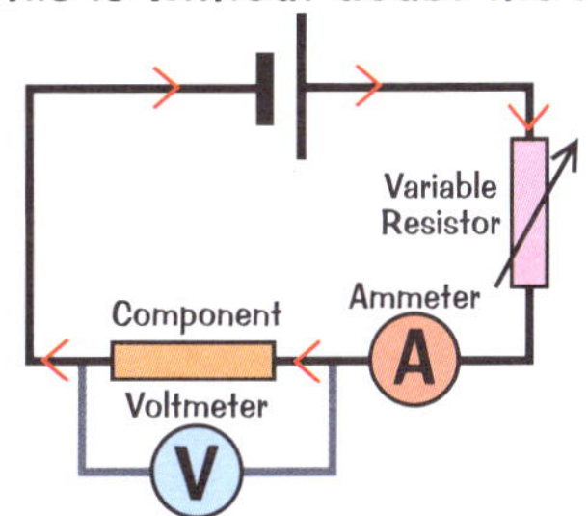

1) This very basic circuit is used for testing components.
2) The component, the ammeter and the variable resistor are all in series (p. 55) which means they can be put in any order in the main circuit.
3) The ammeter needs to be placed in series with the component to measure the flow of current through it.
4) The voltmeter can only be placed in parallel (p. 56) around the component under test, as shown. Anywhere else is a definite no-no.
5) Varying the variable resistor alters the current flowing through the circuit.

A Voltmeter Measures Potential Difference Between Two Points

1) Potential difference (the proper name for voltage) tells us how much energy is transferred to or from each unit of charge as it moves between two points.
2) The battery transfers energy to the charge as it passes — that's the "push" that moves the charge round the circuit.
3) Components transfer energy away from the charge as it passes — e.g. to use as light in a lamp or sound in a buzzer.
4) When energy is transferred, work is done. So potential difference is also a measure of the work done on or by a charge as it passes between two points.
5) The voltage of a battery shows how much work the battery will do to charge that passes through it (how big a "push" it gives it).
6) A voltmeter is used to measure the potential difference between two points.
7) A voltmeter must be placed in parallel (see p. 56) with a component so it can compare the energy the charge has before and after passing through the component (as in the diagram).

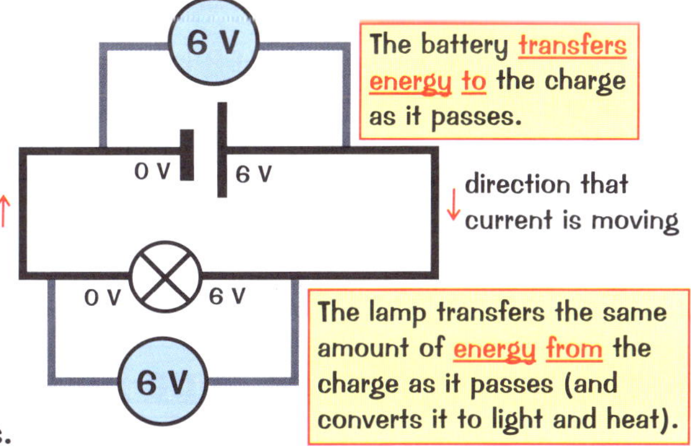

Measure gymnastics — use a vaultmeter...

An interesting fact — voltage is named after Count Alessandro Volta, an Italian physicist. I heard once that potential difference was named after his cousin — Baron Potentialo Differenché. I'm not so sure if it's true... What is true and very important is that voltage and potential difference are the same thing.

Resistance

Resistance resists the flow of current — simple. Resistors come in all shapes and sizes — and some have fixed resistance while others can change their resistance.

The Slope of a Voltage-Current Graph Shows Resistance

Voltage-current (V-I) graphs show how the current in a circuit varies as you change the voltage.

1) The current through a component is proportional to the voltage across it when the resistance stays constant.
2) Different resistors have different resistances — the steeper the slope the lower the resistance.
3) The wires in an electric circuit have such a small resistance that it's usually ignored.

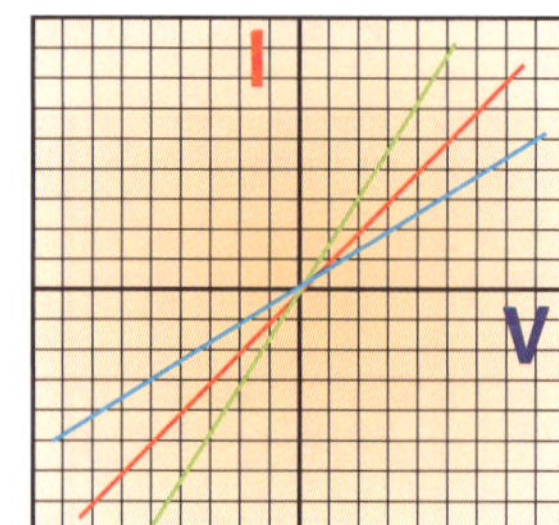

Calculating Resistance: R = V/I (or R = 1/gradient)

At a constant temperature the resistance of a component is steady and is equal to the inverse of the gradient of the line, or "1/gradient". In other words, the steeper the graph the lower the resistance. Alternatively, you can take any pair of values (V, I) and stick them in the formula R = V/I.

$$\text{Resistance } (\Omega) = \frac{\text{Voltage (V)}}{\text{Current (A)}}$$

Resistors Get Hot When Current Passes Through Them

When electrons move through a resistor, they collide with positive ions in the resistor. These collisions make the ions vibrate more, which causes an increase in temperature. A filament lamp contains a piece of wire with a really high resistance. When current passes through it, its temperature increases so much that it glows — which is the light you see.

Light-Dependent Resistor or "LDR" to You

A light-dependent resistor or LDR is a special type of resistor that changes its resistance depending on how much light there is:

1) In bright light, the resistance falls.
2) In darkness, the resistance is highest.

This makes it a useful device for various electronic circuits, e.g. automatic night lights.

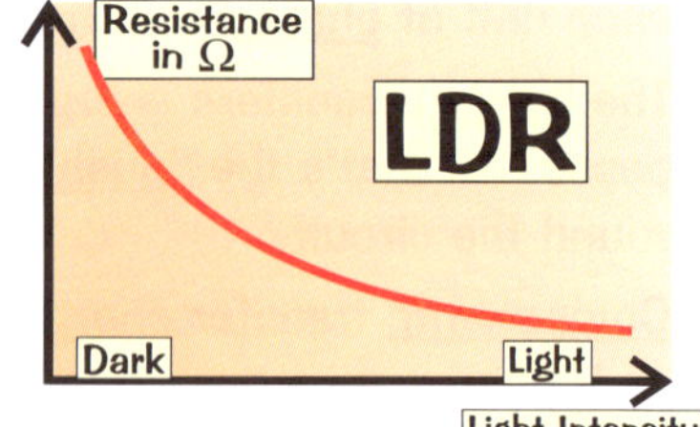

Thermistor (Temperature-Dependent Resistor)

A thermistor is like an LDR — but its resistance depends on temperature.

1) In hot conditions, the resistance drops.
2) In cool conditions, the resistance goes up.

Thermistors make useful temperature detectors, e.g. electronic thermostats.

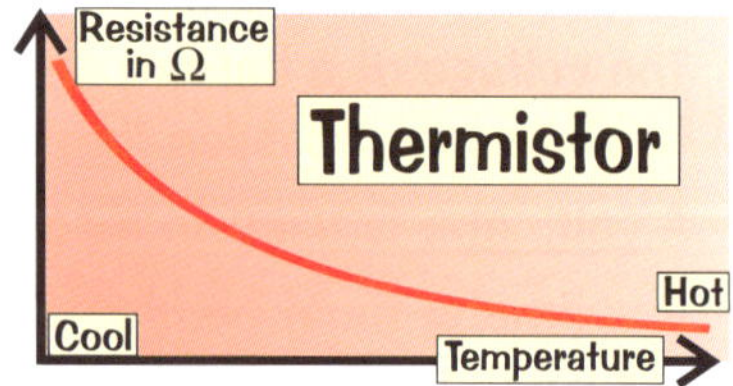

In the end you'll have to learn this — resistance is futile...

This page is packed full of useful stuff. You have to be able to interpret those voltage-current graphs. Remember — the steeper the slope, the lower the resistance. That equation's important too — make sure you learn it. You'll need to be able to rearrange it too — I didn't put that formula triangle in for fun.

Series Circuits

You need to be able to tell the difference between series and parallel circuits just by looking at them.

Series Circuits — Everything in a Line

In series circuits, the different components are connected in a line, end to end, between the +ve and –ve of the power supply (except for voltmeters, which are always connected in parallel, but they don't count).

Potential Difference is Shared:

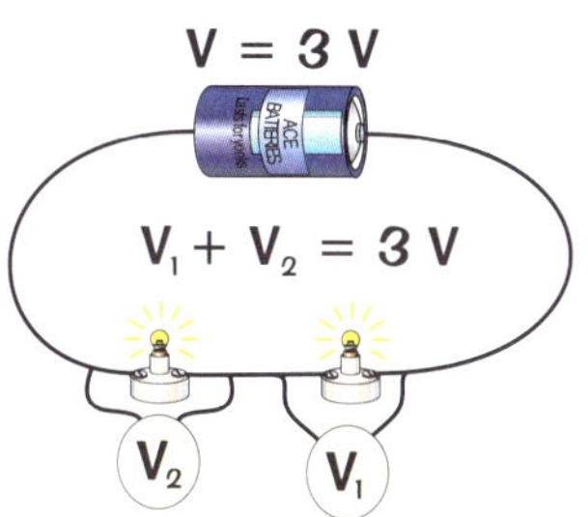

1) In series circuits, the total potential difference (P.D.) of the supply is shared between the various components. So the P.D.s round a series circuit always add up to equal the P.D. across the battery: $V = V_1 + V_2$
2) This is because the total work done on the charge by the battery must equal the total work done by the charge on the components.

Current is the Same Everywhere:

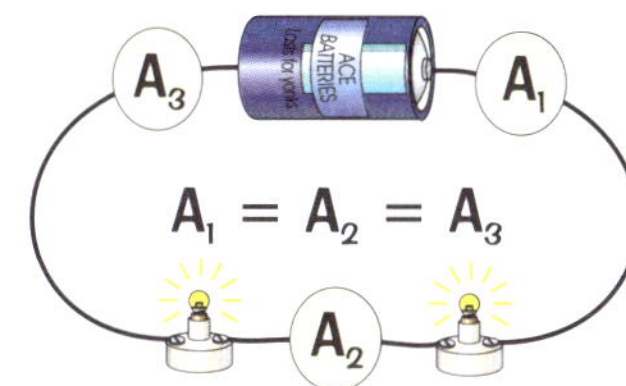

1) In series circuits the same current flows through all parts of the circuit: $A_1 = A_2 = A_3$
2) The size of the current is determined by the total P.D. of the cells and the total resistance of the circuit: i.e. I = V/R. This means all the components get the same current.

Resistance Adds Up:

1) In series circuits, the total resistance is just the sum of the individual resistances: $R = R_1 + R_2 + R_3$
2) The resistance of two (or more) resistors in series is bigger than the resistance of just one of the resistors on its own because the battery has to push charge through all of them.
3) The bigger the resistance of a component, the bigger its share of the total P.D. because more work is done by the charge when moving through a large resistance, than through a small one.

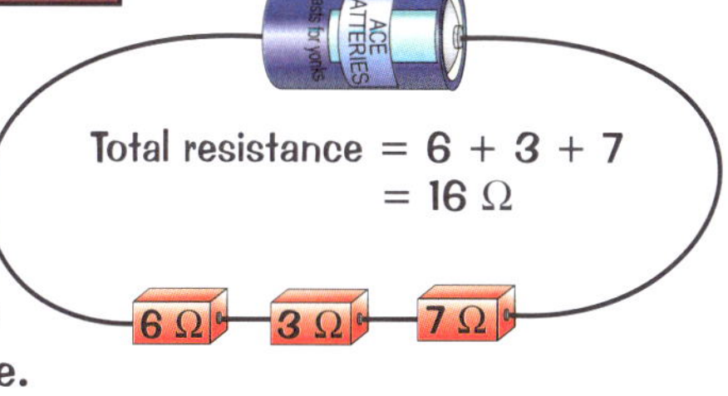

4) If the resistance of one component changes (e.g. if it's a variable resistor, light-dependent resistor or thermistor) then the potential difference across all the components will change too.

Cell Voltages Add Up:

1) If you connect several cells in series, all the same way (+ to –) you get a bigger total voltage — because each charge in the circuit passes though all the cells and gets a 'push' from each cell in turn.
2) So two 1.5 V cells in series would supply 3 V in total.
3) Cell voltages don't add up like that for cells connected in parallel. Each charge only goes through one cell.

+ 12 V
- 12 V
Total = 24 V

+ 12 V + 12 V
Total = 12 V

Cell Current Doesn't Add Up:

1) Adding cells in series doesn't increase the current in a circuit. The maximum current in the circuit will just be the same as if you had one cell in the circuit.
2) Cells connected in parallel increase the total current in the circuit. However, the current through each cell is less than in the rest of the circuit because they join together to make the total current.

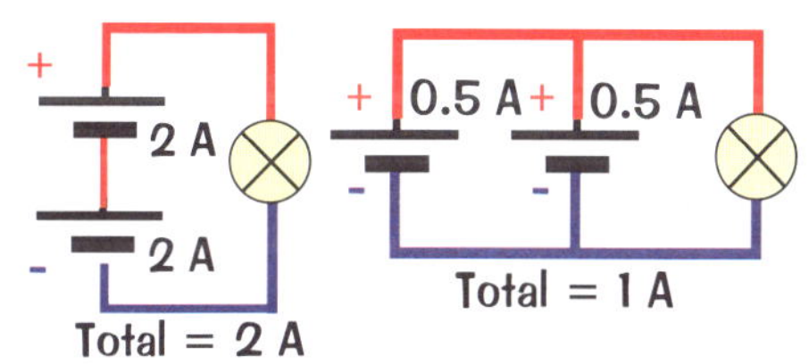

Series circuits — they're no laughing matter...

If you connect some lamps in series and one of them breaks then all of them stop working. This is unhelpful.

Parallel Circuits

Parallel circuits are much more sensible than series circuits so they're much more common in real life.

Parallel Circuits — Independence and Isolation

1) In parallel circuits, each component is separately connected to the +ve and –ve of the supply.
2) If you remove or disconnect one of them, it will often hardly affect the others at all.
3) This is obviously how most things must be connected, for example in cars and in household electrics. You have to be able to switch everything on and off separately.

P.D. is the Same Across All Components:

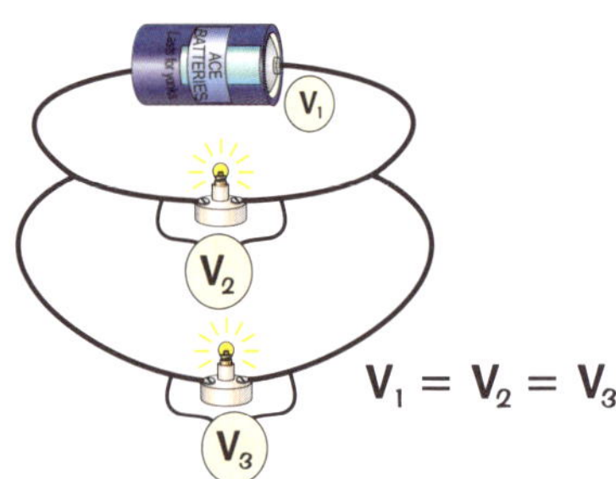

1) In parallel circuits the P.D. across each component is equal to the P.D. of the battery, so the P.D. is the same across all components:

$$V_1 = V_2 = V_3$$

2) This means that identical bulbs connected in parallel will all be at the same brightness.

Total Current is Shared Between Branches:

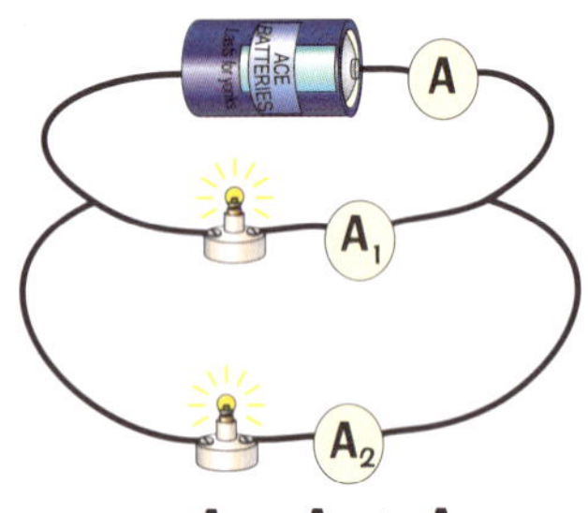

$A = A_1 + A_2$

1) In all circuits, the current flowing from the battery is the same as the current flowing back to it — there's nowhere else for the charge to go.
2) In parallel circuits, the current flowing from the battery is shared between the branches. So the total current leaving the battery is equal to the total of the currents in the separate branches.

$$A = A_1 + A_2$$

3) In a parallel circuit, there are junctions where the current splits or rejoins. The total current going into a junction equals the total current leaving.

Resistance Is Tricky:

R_1

R_2

Total $R < R_1$
and
Total $R < R_2$

1) The total resistance of a parallel circuit is tricky to work out, but it's always less than that of the branch with the smallest resistance.
2) The resistance is lower because the charge has more than one branch to take — only some of the charge will flow along each branch.
3) A circuit with two resistors in parallel will have a lower resistance than a circuit with either of the resistors by themselves — which means the parallel circuit will have a higher current.

The Current Through a Component Depends on its Resistance

1) Each component in a parallel circuit is separately connected to the battery. This means the current through each component is the same as if that component was the only one in the circuit.
2) The resistance of a component controls how much current the voltage is able to push through it.
3) The component with the least resistance has the largest current.
4) This is because in a parallel circuit all the components have the same P.D. across them — the same P.D. causes a larger current to flow through a smaller resistance than through a bigger one.

A current shared — is a current halved...*

Parallel circuits might look a bit scarier than series ones, but they're much more useful. Remember that each component has the same P.D. across it, the current is shared between branches, the total resistance is lower than that of the least resistant branch, and components work as if they were on their own. Phew.

* Conditions may apply. CGP takes no responsibility for the accuracy of this proverb.

Mains Electricity

It's difficult to imagine a world without electricity — it would be hard to bake cakes at night, for a start.

Mains Supply is AC, Battery Supply is DC

You might remember bits of this from P3, but now you need to know it in more detail.

1) The UK mains domestic electricity supply is 230 volts.
2) It's produced by generators using a process called electromagnetic induction (see below).
3) Mains electricity is an AC supply (alternating current) — the current is constantly changing direction.
4) Batteries supply direct current (DC). This just means the current always flows in the same direction.
5) AC is used for mains electricity because it's easier to generate than DC and is easier and simpler to distribute over long distances.

Moving a Magnet into a Coil of Wire Induces a Voltage

1) You can create a voltage, and maybe a current, in a conductor by moving a magnet in or near a coil of wire. This is called electromagnetic induction.
2) As you move the magnet, the magnetic field through the coil changes — this change in the magnetic field induces (creates) a voltage across the ends of the coil.
3) If the ends of the wire are connected to make a closed circuit then a current will flow in the wire.
4) The direction of the voltage depends on which way you move the magnet:

If you move the magnet into the coil the voltage is induced in the opposite direction from when you move it out of the coil.

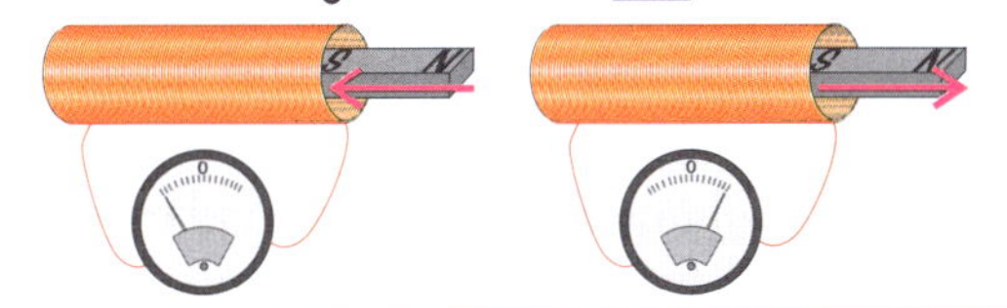

If you reverse the magnet's North-South polarity — so that the opposite pole points into the coil, the voltage is induced in the opposite direction.

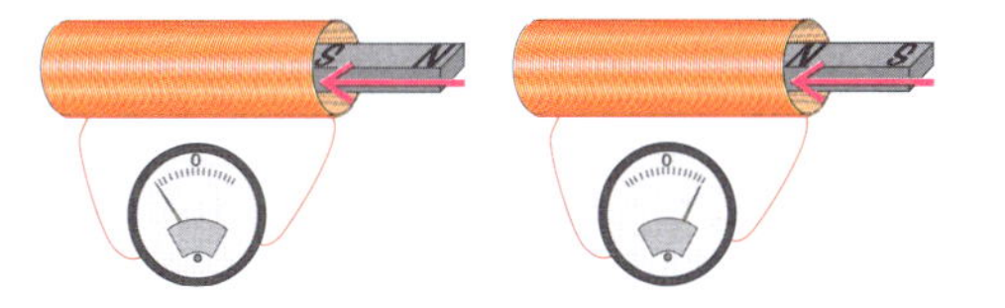

AC Generators — Just Turn the Magnet and There's a Current

1) In a generator, a magnet (or an electromagnet) rotates in a coil of wire. As the magnet turns, the magnetic field through the coil changes — this change in the magnetic field induces a voltage, which makes a current flow in the coil.
2) When the magnet is turned through half a turn, the direction of the magnetic field through the coil reverses. When this happens, the voltage reverses, so the current flows in the opposite direction around the coil of wire.
3) If the magnet keeps turning in the same direction — clockwise, say — then the voltage keeps on reversing every half turn and you get an AC current.

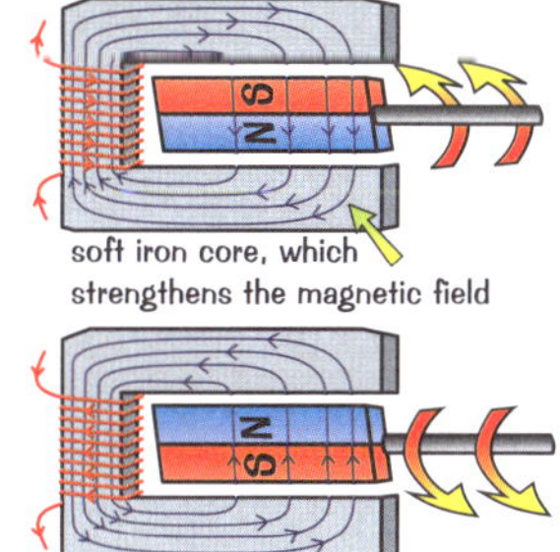

Four Factors Affect the Size of the Induced Voltage

1) If you want a bigger peak voltage (and current) you could do one or more of these four things.
2) To reduce the voltage, you would reduce one of the factors or take the iron core out.

1) Add an IRON CORE inside the coil
2) Increase the STRENGTH of the MAGNETIC FIELD
3) Increase the SPEED of ROTATION
4) Increase the number of TURNS on the COIL

So THAT's how they make electricity — I always wondered...

Generators are mostly powered by burning things to make steam, to turn a turbine, to rotate the magnet. You can get portable generators too, to use in places without mains electricity — like at music festivals.

Transformers

So you've generated your electricity, but it's not at the right voltage — what do you need? A transformer.

Transformers Change the Voltage — but Only AC Voltages

Transformers are used to change the size of the voltage — they use electromagnetic induction to 'step up' or 'step down' the voltage. They have two coils of wire, the primary and the secondary coils, wound around an iron core.

The alternating current in the primary coil causes changes in the iron core's magnetic field, which induces a changing voltage in the secondary coil (see below).

STEP-UP TRANSFORMERS step the voltage up (increase it). They have more turns on the secondary coil than the primary coil.

STEP-DOWN TRANSFORMERS step the voltage down (decrease it). They have more turns on the primary coil than the secondary.

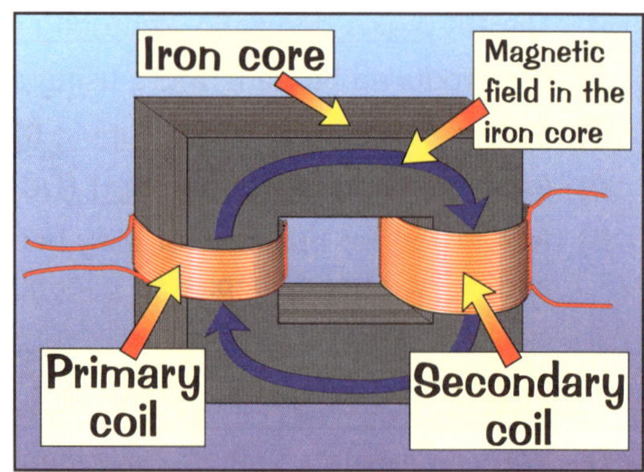

Transformers Work by Electromagnetic Induction

1) The primary coil produces a magnetic field which stays within the iron core.
2) Because there's an alternating current (AC) in the primary coil, the magnetic field in the iron core constantly changes direction (100 times a second if it's at 50 Hz) — i.e. it's a changing magnetic field.
3) This changing magnetic field induces an alternating voltage in the secondary coil (with the same frequency as the alternating current in the primary) — electromagnetic induction of a voltage in fact.
4) The relative number of turns on the two coils determines whether the voltage induced in the secondary coil is greater or less than the voltage in the primary coil (see equation below).
5) If you supplied direct current (DC) to the primary coil, you'd get nothing out of the secondary coil at all. Sure, there'd still be a magnetic field in the iron core, but it wouldn't be constantly changing, so there'd be no induction in the secondary coil — because you need a changing field to induce a voltage. So don't forget it — transformers only work with AC. They won't work with DC at all.

The Transformer Equation — Use It Either Way Up

You can calculate the output voltage from a transformer if you know the input voltage and the number of turns on each coil.

$$\frac{\text{Voltage across primary coil}}{\text{Voltage across secondary coil}} = \frac{\text{Number of turns in primary coil}}{\text{Number of turns in secondary coil}}$$

Well, it's just another formula. You stick in the numbers you've got and work out the one that's left. And you can write the formula either way up — you should always put the thing you're trying to find on the top.

$$\frac{V_P}{V_S} = \frac{N_P}{N_S}$$

or

$$\frac{V_S}{V_P} = \frac{N_S}{N_P}$$

EXAMPLE: A transformer has 40 turns on the primary coil and 800 on the secondary coil. If the input voltage is 1000 V, find the output voltage.

ANSWER: The question asks you to find V_S, so put it on the top: $\frac{V_S}{V_P} = \frac{N_S}{N_P}$

Substitute the values: $\frac{V_S}{1000} = \frac{800}{40}$, $V_S = 1000 \times \frac{800}{40} = 20\ 000\ V$

Which transformer do you need to enslave the Universe — Megatron...

You'll need to practise with those tricky equations. They're unusual because they can't be put into formula triangles, but other than that, the method is the same — stick in the numbers. Just practise.

Magnetic Fields

Loads of electrical appliances use magnetic fields generated by electric currents.

A MAGNETIC FIELD is a region where MAGNETIC MATERIALS (like iron and steel) and also WIRES CARRYING CURRENTS experience a FORCE acting on them.

Magnetic fields can be shown on field diagrams.
The arrows on the field lines point from the North pole of the magnet to the South pole.

A Current-Carrying Wire Creates a Magnetic Field

1) There is a magnetic field around a straight, current-carrying wire.
2) The field is made up of concentric circles with the wire in the centre.

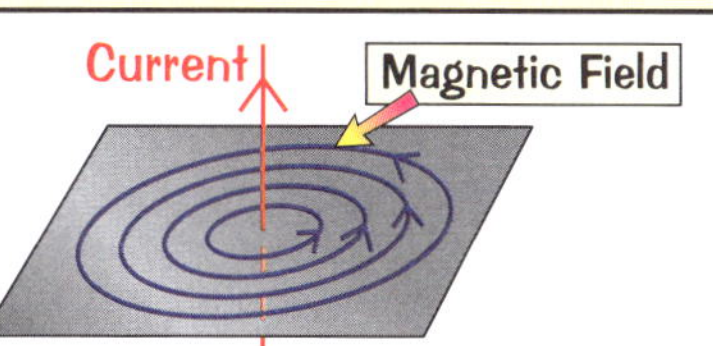

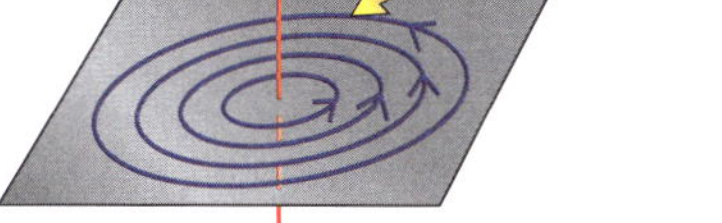

A Rectangular Coil Reinforces the Magnetic Field

1) If you bend the current-carrying wire round into a coil, the magnetic field looks like this.
2) The circular magnetic fields around the sides of the loop reinforce each other at the centre.
3) If the coil has lots of turns, the magnetic fields from all the individual loops reinforce each other even more.

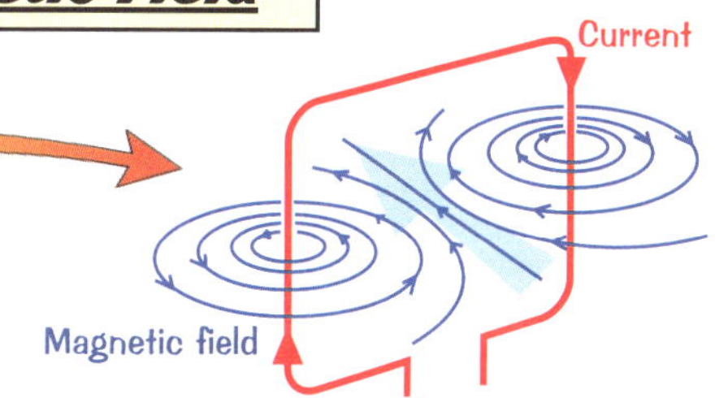

A Current in a Magnetic Field Experiences a Force

1) Because of its magnetic field, a current-carrying wire or coil can exert a force on another current-carrying wire or coil, or on a permanent magnet.
2) When a current-carrying wire is put in a different magnetic field, the two magnetic fields affect one another. The result is a force on the wire.

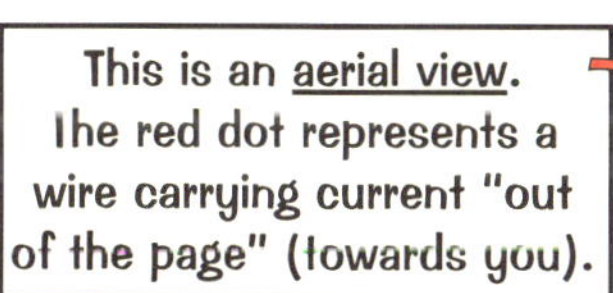

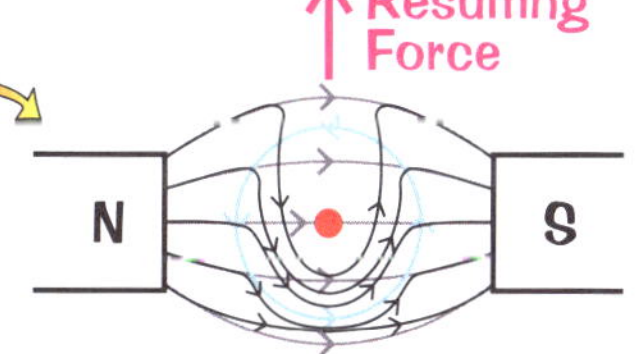

Normal magnetic field of wire
Normal magnetic field of magnets
Deviated magnetic field of magnets

3) To feel the full force, the wire has to be at right-angles (90°) to the lines of force of the magnetic field it's placed in. (As it is in the diagram above.)
4) If the wire runs parallel to the lines of force of the magnetic field, it won't experience any force at all. And at angles in between 0° and 90° it'll feel some force.
5) When the wire is at right-angles to the magnetic field, the force always acts at right-angles to both the lines of force of the magnetic field and the direction of the current.

Fleming's Left-Hand Rule Tells You Which Way the Force Acts

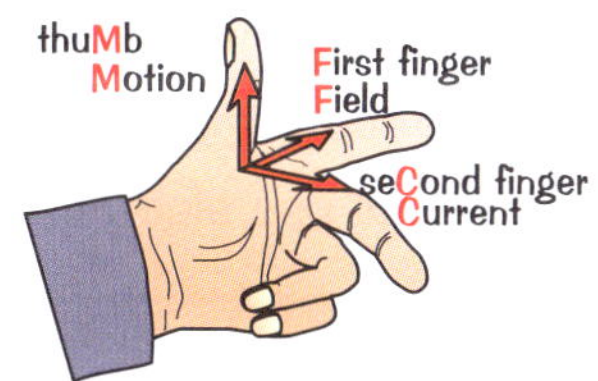

1) Using your left hand, point your First finger in the direction of the Field and your seCond finger in the direction of the Current.
2) Your thuMb will then point in the direction of the force (Motion).

(Give it a try with the diagram of the wire and the magnet field above.)

Use the force — at right-angles to the magnetic field...

When I'm parallel to my bed I don't feel any force pulling me out of it. Just like wires and magnets... Sort of.

The Motor Effect

The motor effect — that's how electric motors work. Should be easy to remember that.

Magnetic Fields Make Current-Carrying Coils Turn

If a rectangular coil of wire carrying a current is placed in a uniform magnetic field, the force will cause it to turn. This is called the motor effect. You can use Fleming's left-hand rule (LHR), from the previous page, to work out which way the coil will turn:

A uniform magnetic field has the same strength everywhere in the field.

EXAMPLE: Is the coil turning clockwise or anticlockwise?

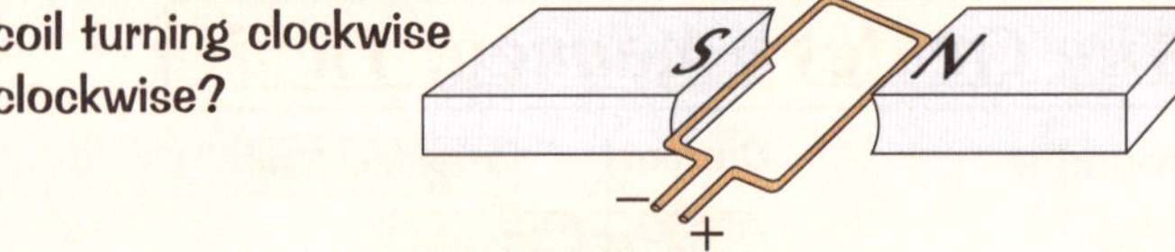

ANSWER:

1) Draw in current arrows (+ve to –ve) and magnetic field lines, which always run from North to South.

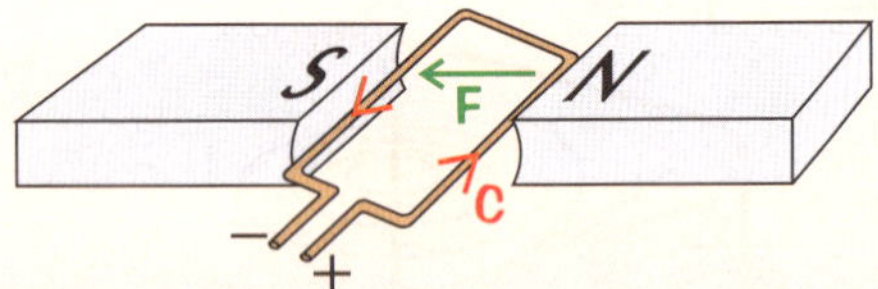

2) Use LHR on one side of the coil (I've used the right-hand side).

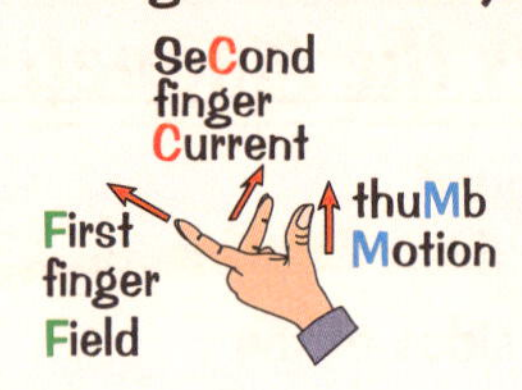

3) Draw in direction of motion (force).

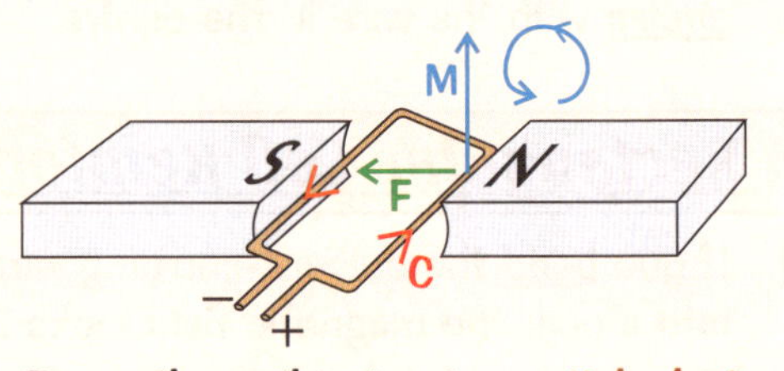

So — the coil is turning anticlockwise.

The Simple Electric Motor

1) The diagram shows the forces acting on the two side arms of a coil.
2) These forces are just the usual forces which act on any current-carrying wire in a magnetic field.
3) Because the coil is on a spindle and the forces act one up and one down, it rotates.
4) The split-ring commutator is a clever way of swapping the contacts every half turn.
5) This reverses the direction of the current every half-turn to keep the coil rotating continuously in the same direction.
6) Otherwise, the direction of the force would reverse every half turn and the coil would change direction every half turn instead of fully rotating.

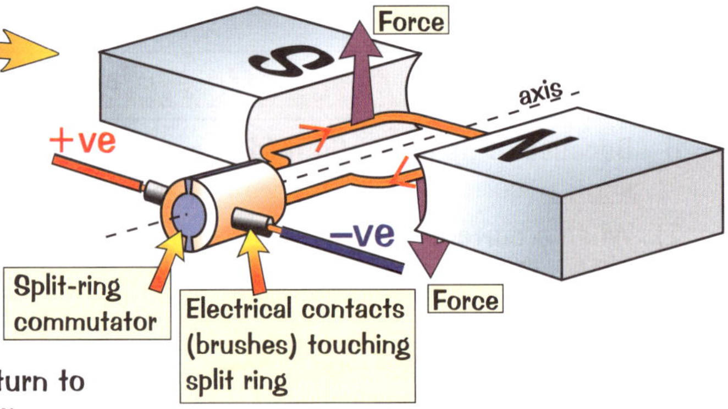

Force
S
axis
N
+ve
–ve
Split-ring commutator
Electrical contacts (brushes) touching split ring
Force

Anything That Uses Rotation can be Powered by an Electric Motor

Lots of devices use rotation. They all work by using an electric motor in a similar way.

1) Link the coil to an axle, and the axle spins round.
2) In the diagram there's a fan attached to the axle, but you can stick almost anything on a motor axle and make it spin round.
3) For example:

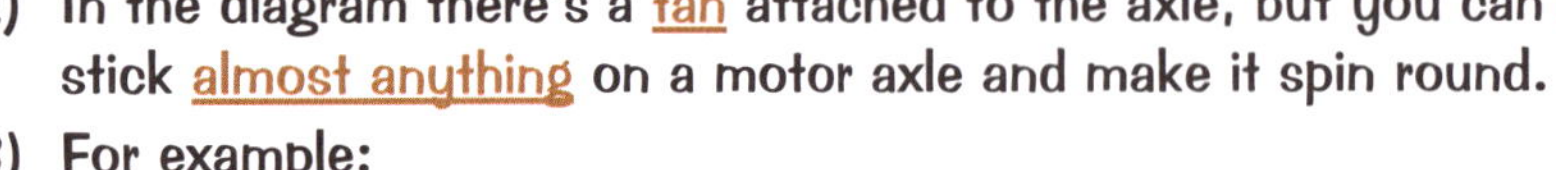

- In a DVD player, the axle's attached to the bit the DVD sits on to make it spin.
- Electric cars and trains have their wheels attached to axles.
- Electric motors spin the platters (the bits where information is stored) of a computer hard disc drive.
- Domestic appliances, such as washing machines, fridges and vacuum cleaners all use electric motors.

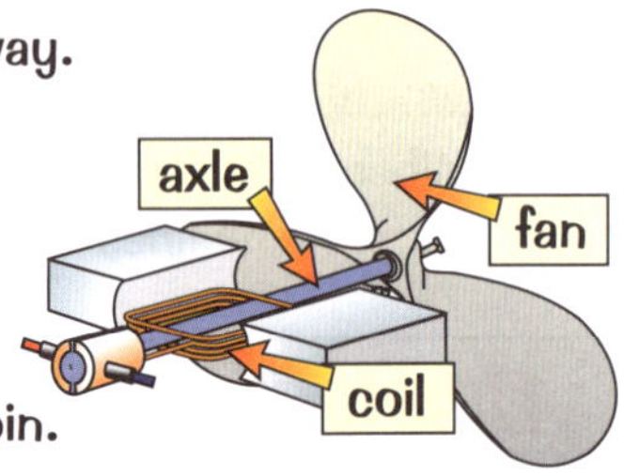

axle
fan
coil

Hello Motor...

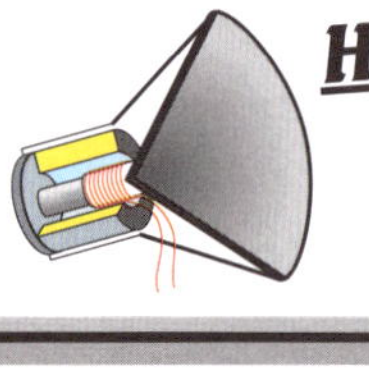

Loudspeakers demonstrate the motor effect. AC electrical signals from the amplifier are fed to the speaker coil (shown red). These make the coil move back and forth over the poles of the magnet. These movements make the cardboard cone vibrate and this creates sounds.

Revision Summary for Module P5

There's some pretty heavy physics in this section. But just take it one page at a time and it's not so bad. When you think you know it all, try these questions and see how you're getting on. If there are any you can't do, look back at the right bit of the section, learn it, then come back here and try again.

1) What causes the build-up of static electricity? Which particles move when static builds up?
2) Describe the forces between objects with: a) like charges, b) opposite charges.
3) Explain how static electricity can make synthetic clothes crackle when you take them off.
4) Explain why metals are good conductors of electricity.
5) Explain what current, voltage and resistance are in an electric circuit.
6) What happens to the amount of current in a circuit if the voltage of the battery is increased?
7) What does the power of an appliance measure?
8) Write down the formula linking voltage, current and power.
9) Sketch a diagram of a circuit containing a cell, filament lamp, switch and fixed resistor.
10) Add an ammeter and voltmeter to your circuit, connected sensibly.
11) What is another name for voltage? What is it a measure of?
12) Sketch a typical voltage-current graph for a resistor at a constant temperature.
13)* Calculate the resistance of a wire if the voltage across it is 12 V and the current through it is 2.5 A.
14) Describe how the resistance of an LDR varies with light intensity. Give an application of an LDR.
15)* Find each unknown voltage, current or resistance in the circuit shown.

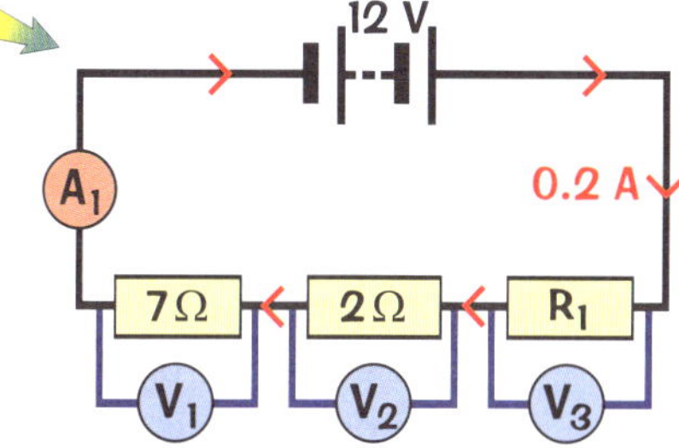

16) Explain, in terms of energy, why P.D. is shared out in a series circuit.
17) What happens to the voltage when cells are added to a series circuit?
18) Two circuits each contain a 2 Ω and a 4 Ω resistor — in one circuit they're in series, in the other they're in parallel. Which circuit will have the higher total resistance? Why?
19)* A current of 0.4 A flows through the filament lamp in this circuit. What current will flow through this lamp if another, identical lamp is connected in parallel to it?

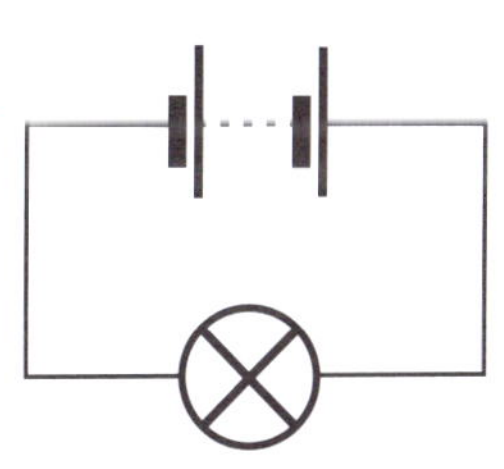

20) What voltage is UK mains electricity supplied at? Why is AC used?
21) Define electromagnetic induction.
22) Explain how a generator works — use a sketch if it helps.
23) What are the four factors that affect the size of the induced voltage produced by a generator?
24) Write down the transformer equation.
25)* A transformer has 500 turns on the primary coil and 20 on the secondary coil. If the output voltage is 9 V, find the input voltage.
26) A current-carrying wire runs parallel to the lines of force of a magnetic field. Does the wire feel a force?
27) Draw a field diagram to show the resulting force on a current-carrying wire placed at right-angles to the lines of force of a magnetic field.
28) What part of an electric motor reverses the direction of the current? Why is this important?
29) Briefly describe three uses of electric motors.

* Answers on page 96.

Radioactivity

Radioactivity — nothing to do with how much you use your radio. It's much more interesting than that.

Atoms Consist of a Nucleus Plus Orbiting Electrons

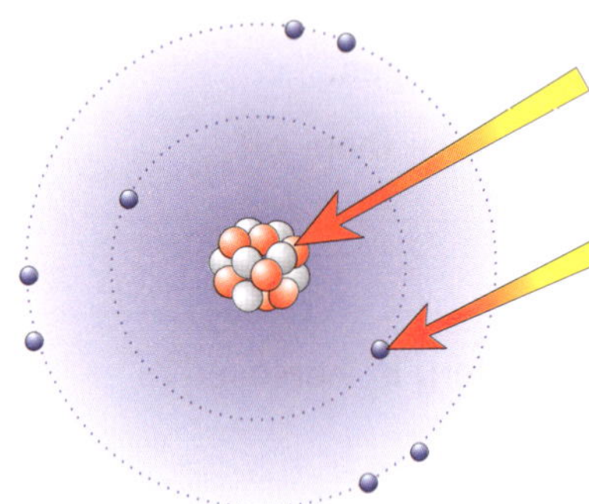

The nucleus of an atom contains protons and neutrons. It makes up most of the mass of the atom, but takes up virtually no space — it's tiny.

The electrons are really really small. They whizz around the outside of the atom. Their paths take up a lot of space, giving the atom its overall size (though it's mostly empty space).

The Number of Neutrons in an Element isn't Fixed

1) Every atom of a particular element has the same number of protons in its nucleus, e.g. every carbon atom has 6 protons in its nucleus, every nitrogen atom has 7 protons in its nucleus, etc.
2) The number of neutrons isn't fixed, though. Many elements have a few different isotopes — atoms with the same number of protons but different numbers of neutrons.
3) E.g. there are two common isotopes of carbon — carbon-14 has two more neutrons than 'normal' carbon (carbon-12).
4) Usually each element only has one or two stable isotopes — like carbon-12.
5) The other isotopes tend to be radioactive — the nucleus is unstable, so it decays (breaks down) and emits radiation. Carbon-14 is an unstable isotope of carbon.

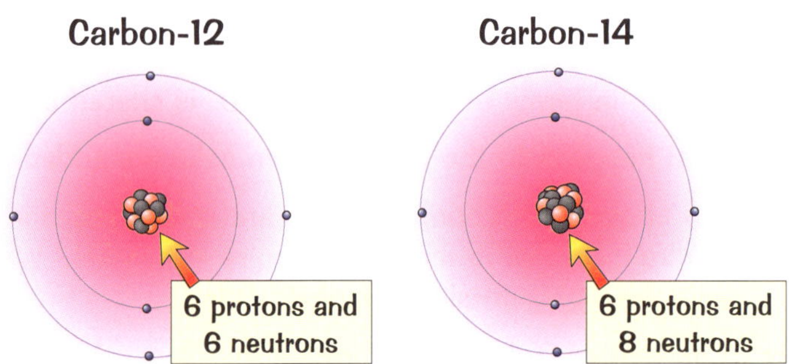

Radioactive Elements Emit Ionising Radiation

1) Some elements emit ionising radiation all the time — these elements are radioactive.
2) Radioactive atoms are unstable — they break up (decay) to make themselves more stable.
3) Unstable atoms decay at random and you can't predict when it will happen — it's completely unaffected by physical conditions (like temperature) or chemical processes (e.g bonding).
4) When an atom does decay, it spits out one or more of three types of ionising radiation — alpha, beta and gamma (see next page).
5) In the process, the atom often changes into a new element.
6) Ionising radiation can transfer enough energy to break an atom or molecule into bits called ions — this is called ionisation.
7) These ions can then go on to take part in other chemical reactions.

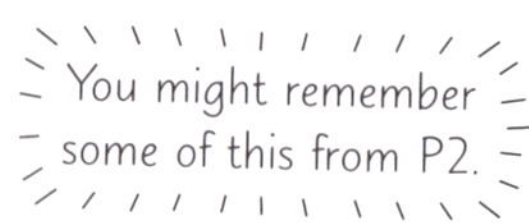

Unstable isotopes — put them in a field...

So, it's the number of protons that decides what element something is. Then the number of neutrons decides what isotope of that element it is. Some isotopes of an element are stable, but others are unstable — it's the unstable ones that undergo radioactive decay and emit ionising radiation.

Radiation

The three types of ionising radiation (alpha, beta and gamma) are all emitted by radioactive materials. You need to remember how an element changes after emitting radiation.

Alpha Radiation is Slow and Heavy

big unstable nucleus — alpha particle

1) Alpha particles (α) are relatively big and heavy and fairly slow-moving.
2) So they don't penetrate far into materials — they're stopped quickly.
3) Alpha particles are released by very heavy nuclei, e.g. uranium.
4) An alpha particle is a helium nucleus (He) — made up of 2 protons and 2 neutrons.
5) Alpha particles have a mass of 4 and a charge of +2.
6) Alpha decay always changes the element of the atom that's decaying, since it loses protons.

A typical alpha emission:

$$^{226}_{88}Ra \rightarrow {}^{222}_{86}Rn + {}^{4}_{2}\alpha$$

$$226 \rightarrow 222 + 4$$

$$88 \rightarrow 86 + 2$$

You might be asked to write decays as nuclear equations. The top (mass number) and bottom (proton number) numbers have to balance on both sides. Make sure you learn the numbers for alpha and beta particles. You can use a periodic table to find out numbers for the elements.

Beta Radiation is Lighter and More Penetrating

1) Beta particles (β) move quite fast and they are quite small.
2) They penetrate moderately into materials before they're stopped.
3) Beta particles are released by nuclei that have too many neutrons.
4) During beta decay, a neutron in the nucleus turns into a proton, so the element changes, and a beta particle is emitted.
5) A beta particle is identical to an electron, with virtually no mass and a charge of –1.

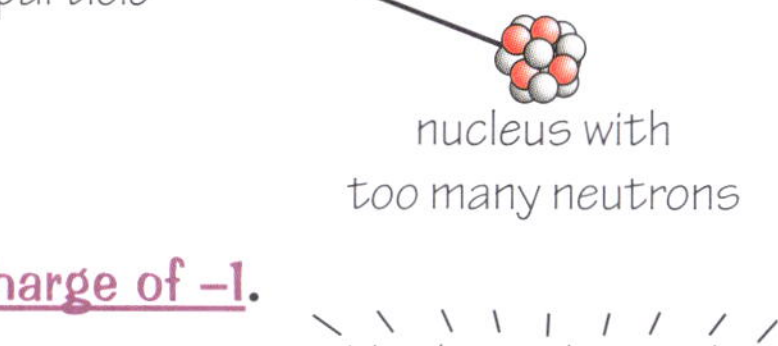

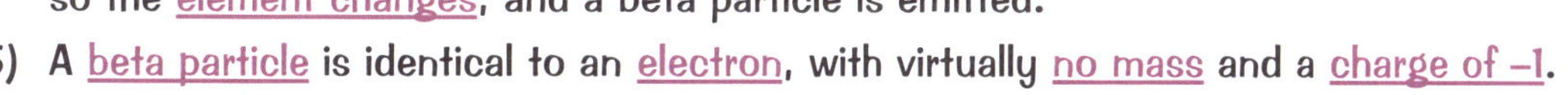

A typical beta emission:

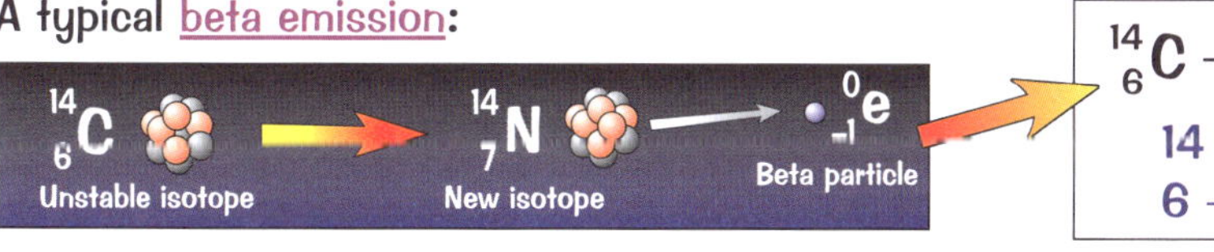

$$^{14}_{6}C \rightarrow {}^{14}_{7}N + {}^{0}_{-1}\beta$$

$$14 \rightarrow 14 + 0$$

$$6 \rightarrow 7 + (-1)$$

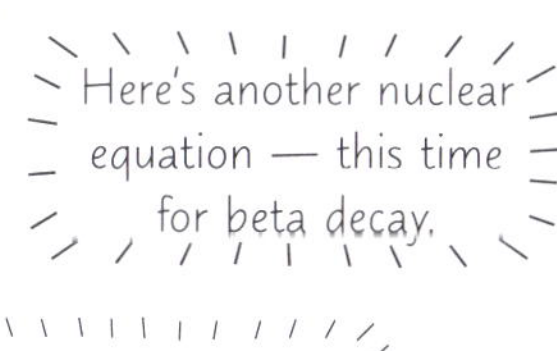

Beta particles can be written as $^{0}_{-1}e$ too.

Gamma Radiation is an Electromagnetic Wave

1) After spitting out an alpha or beta particle, the nucleus might need to get rid of some extra energy.
2) It does this by emitting a gamma ray (γ) — a type of electromagnetic wave. They have no mass.
3) They can penetrate a long way into materials without being stopped.
4) Since a gamma ray is just energy, it doesn't change the element of the nucleus that emits it.

Remember What Blocks the Three Types of Radiation...

Alpha particles are blocked by paper.

Beta particles are blocked by thin aluminium.

Gamma rays are blocked by thick lead.

Similar things will also block them, e.g. skin will stop alpha, a thin sheet of any metal will stop beta, and very thick concrete will stop gamma.

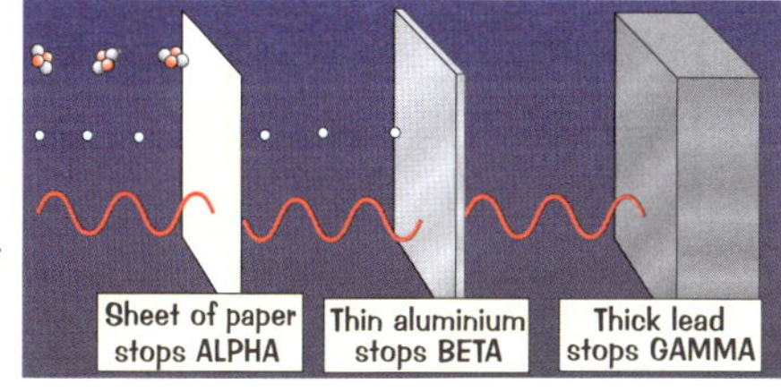

I once beta particle — it cried for ages...

Make sure you know how to complete nuclear equations for both alpha and beta decay. They're really important.

Half-Life

Radioactivity is measured in becquerels (Bq) or counts per minute (cpm). 1 Bq is one decay per second.

The Radioactivity of a Sample Always Decreases Over Time

1) Each time an unstable nucleus decays and emits radiation, that means one more radioactive nucleus isn't there to decay later.
2) As more unstable nuclei decay, the radioactivity of the source as a whole decreases — so the older a radioactive source is, the less radiation it emits.
3) How quickly the activity decreases varies a lot. For some isotopes it takes just a few seconds before nearly all the unstable nuclei have decayed. For others it can take millions of years.
4) The problem with trying to measure this is that the activity never reaches zero, which is why we have to use the idea of half-life to measure how quickly the activity decreases.
5) Learn this important definition of half-life:

HALF-LIFE is the TIME TAKEN for HALF of the radioactive nuclei now present to DECAY.

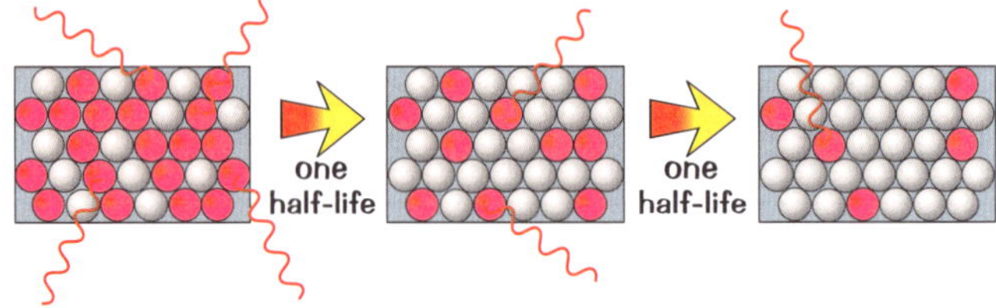

6) A short half-life means the activity falls quickly, because lots of the nuclei decay in a short time.
7) A long half-life means the activity falls more slowly because most of the nuclei don't decay for a long time — they just sit there, basically unstable, but kind of biding their time.

Do Half-Life Questions Step by Step

Half-life can be confusing, but exam calculations are straightforward so long as you do them STEP BY STEP:

A VERY SIMPLE EXAMPLE:

The activity of a radioactive sample is 640 Bq. Two hours later it has fallen to 40 Bq. Find its half-life.

ANSWER: Go through it in short simple steps like this:

INITIAL count:	(÷2) →	after ONE half-life:	(÷2) →	after TWO half-lives:	(÷2) →	after THREE half-lives:	(÷2) →	after FOUR half-lives:
640		320		160		80		40

This careful step-by-step method shows that it takes four half-lives for the activity to fall from 640 to 40. So two hours represents four half-lives — so the half-life is 2 hours ÷ 4 = 30 MINUTES.

You also need to be able to find the half-life of a sample from a graph. Relax, this is (almost) fun.

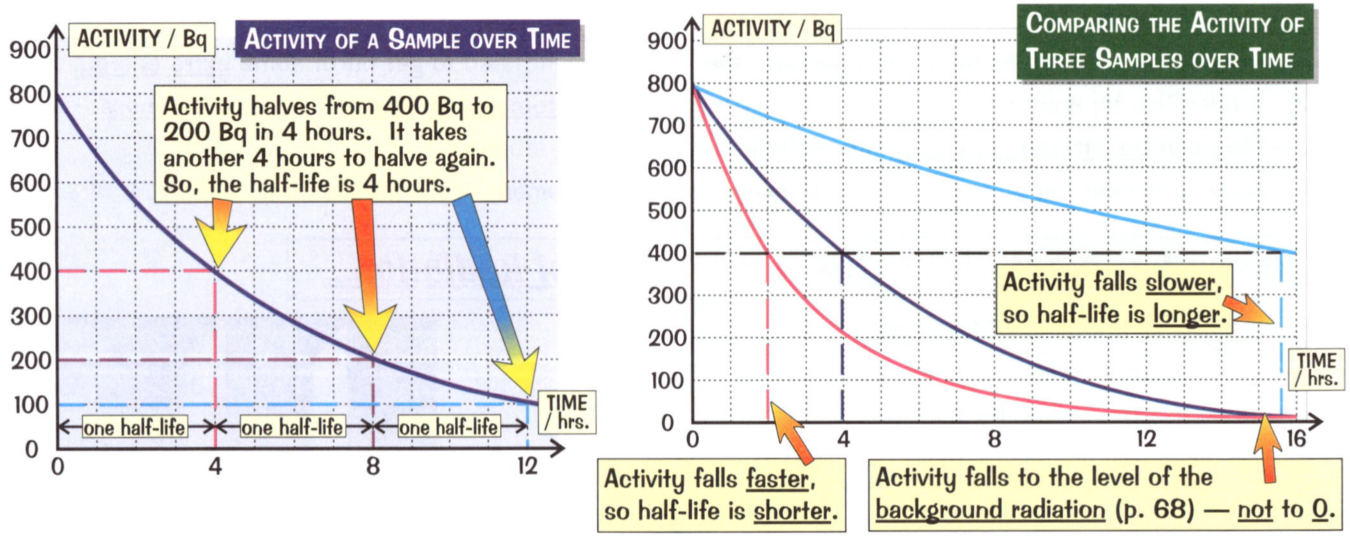

Half-life of a box of chocolates — about five minutes...

To measure half-life, you time how long it takes for the number of decays per second to halve. Simples.

The Atom and Nuclear Fusion

Back in 1904, a guy called J. J. Thomson suggested that atoms were a bit like a plum pudding (a positively charged 'pudding' with negatively charged 'plums' in it). He was wrong.

Rutherford's Scattering Showed that Atoms Have a Positive Nucleus

1) In 1909, Ernest Rutherford and his merry men, Hans Geiger and Ernest Marsden tried firing alpha particles — which are positively charged — at thin gold foil.
2) Most of the alpha particles just went straight through, but the odd one came straight back at them.
3) Being a pretty clued-up guy, Rutherford realised this meant:

Most of the mass of a gold atom was concentrated at the centre in a tiny nucleus. The rest of the atom must be mainly empty space — as most of the alpha particles went straight through the foil.

The nucleus had to have a positive charge — otherwise the positively charged alpha particles wouldn't be repelled by the nucleus and wouldn't scatter.

The Nucleus is Held Together by the Strong Force

1) The nucleus contains positively charged proton particles, which repel each other.
2) The nucleus doesn't fly apart because it's held together by an attractive force much greater than the repulsive electrostatic force between the protons. This force is called the strong force.
3) The strong force only has a very short range — it can only hold protons and neutrons together when they're separated by tiny distances (about 0.000000000000001 m).
4) At larger separations, the strong force is so weak that it effectively disappears.

Nuclei Have to be Brought Close Together to Fuse

1) Two nuclei can combine (fuse) to create a larger nucleus, releasing energy when they do — this is called nuclear fusion.
2) For example, hydrogen nuclei fuse together to make helium nuclei.
3) Nuclei can only fuse if they overcome the repulsive electrostatic force and get close enough for the strong force (see above) to hold them together.
4) For that you need lots of energy — which means a high temperature.

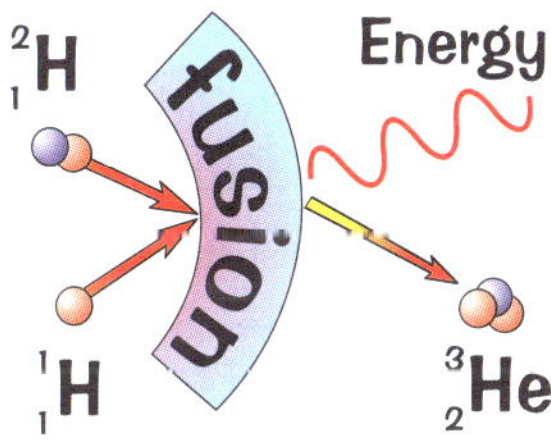

Nuclear Fusion Converts Mass into Energy

1) Albert Einstein reckoned that mass is a form of energy.
2) So, mass can be converted into other forms of energy.
3) This idea is summed up by his famous equation:

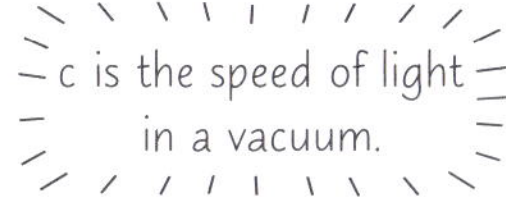

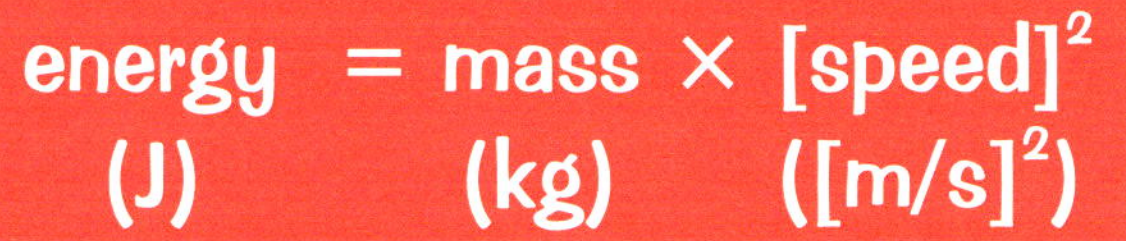

$$E = mc^2$$

4) When nuclei undergo nuclear fusion or fission (see next page) they lose mass and energy is released.
5) You can calculate how much energy is released during fusion or fission using $E = mc^2$.

I've lost a lot of time fusing this knowledge with my brain...

Scientist facts: J. J. Thomson discovered electrons (but called them 'corpuscles'). Ernest Rutherford was the first New Zealander to win a Nobel prize. Hans Geiger invented the 'Geiger counter', to measure radioactivity. Nothing interesting ever happened to Ernest Marsden (apart from Rutherford's scattering experiment).

Nuclear Fission and Nuclear Power

Nuclear fission is the opposite of nuclear fusion — it's where atoms are split apart.
This releases energy which we can use to power stuff...

Nuclear Power Stations Release Energy by Splitting Atoms

1) A nuclear fuel, e.g. uranium or plutonium, releases large amounts of energy when its nuclei split apart.
2) This process is called nuclear fission and starts when neutrons are fired at the fuel, causing some of its large, unstable nuclei to split into two smaller nuclei of roughly equal size.
3) Each split nucleus also releases 2 or 3 more neutrons and lots of energy.

Bits of this may seem familiar from P3, but you need to know more about it now.

Nuclear Fission Releases a Lot of Energy...

1) Nuclear reactions release a lot more energy than chemical reactions (like burning).
2) Splitting a gram of uranium releases over 10 000 times more energy than burning a gram of oil.
3) You can calculate just how much energy is released using $E=mc^2$ (see previous page).

...So It Needs to be Carefully Controlled

1) In nuclear reactors, a chain reaction is set up.
2) A neutron splits a nucleus, releasing more neutrons. These can then go on to split more nuclei and release more neutrons, and so on...
3) The uranium (or plutonium) fuel used in nuclear reactors is contained in fuel rods.
4) These fuel rods capture the neutrons, and emit neutrons when nuclei in the rod split.
5) The chain reaction in the reactor has to be controlled, or the reactor would overheat.

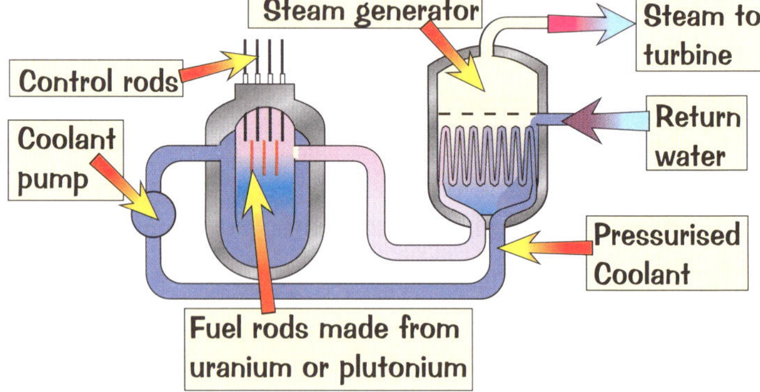

6) Control rods absorb some of the neutrons and slow down the reaction. They can be moved further into and out of the reactor to absorb more or less neutrons.
7) Coolant, e.g. water, is used to take away the heat produced by the fission process.
8) This heat is used to produce steam to drive a turbine and generator... and we get electricity. Ta da.

The Waste from Nuclear Power Stations is Hard to Deal With

The main problem with nuclear power is that it produces radioactive waste.

1) Most waste from power stations (or medical use, see p. 68) is 'low level' (slightly radioactive). E.g. things like paper and gloves, etc. This waste can be disposed of by burying it in secure landfill sites.
2) Intermediate level waste includes things like the metal cases of used fuel rods and some waste from hospitals. It's usually quite radioactive — and some of it will stay that way for tens of thousands of years. It's often sealed into concrete blocks then put in steel canisters for storage.
3) High level waste from nuclear power stations is so radioactive that it generates a lot of heat. This waste is sealed in glass and steel, then cooled for about 50 years before it's moved to more permanent storage.
4) The canisters of intermediate and high level wastes could then be buried deep underground. However, it's difficult to find suitable places. The site has to be geologically stable (e.g. not suffer earthquakes), since big movements in the rock could break the canisters and radioactive material could leak out.
5) Even when geologists do find suitable sites, people who live nearby often object.
6) So, at the moment, most intermediate and high level waste is kept 'on-site' at nuclear power stations.

I'm split over fissi drinks — loads of energy, but bad for your teeth...

There's enough uranium and plutonium around to provide us with energy for years, but it's difficult to deal with the waste we've already got. You need to know all about the three 'levels' of waste and how they're disposed of.

Danger from Radiation

Radioactive materials can be really useful, but they're also dangerous — they need careful handling.

Ionising Radiation can Damage Living Cells

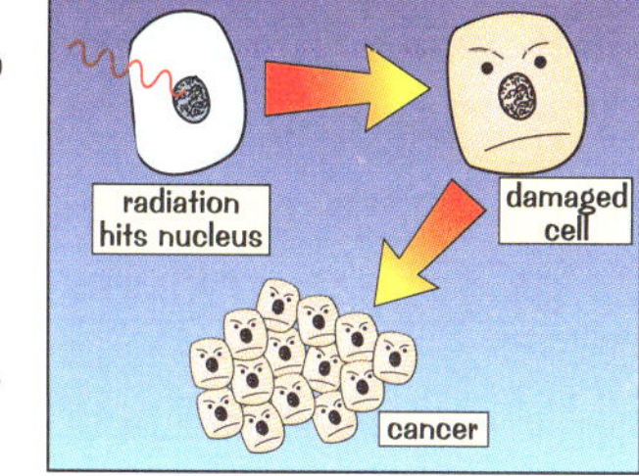

1) Alpha, beta and gamma radiation are all ionising radiation — they can break up molecules into smaller bits called ions. Ions can be very chemically reactive, so they go off and react with things and generally make nuisances of themselves.
2) In humans, ionisation can cause serious damage to the cells in the body.
3) A high dose of radiation tends to kill cells outright, causing radiation sickness. Lower doses tend to damage cells without killing them, which can cause cancer.
4) Radioactive materials put people at risk through either:
   - IRRADIATION — being exposed to radiation without coming into contact with the source. The damage to your body stops as soon as you leave the radioactive area.
   - CONTAMINATION — picking up some radioactive material, e.g. by breathing it in, drinking contaminated water or getting it on your skin. You'll still be exposed to the radiation once you've left the radioactive area.

Sieverts Show Possible Harm from Ionising Radiation

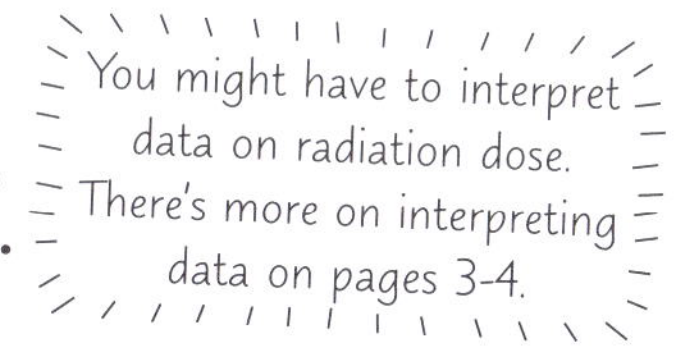

1) How likely you are to suffer damage to your body if you're exposed to radiation depends on the radiation dose.
2) Radiation dose is measured in sieverts (Sv) or more usually millisieverts (mSv). It takes into account the type and amount of radiation you've been exposed to.
3) The following data shows some radiation doses and their effects on the body:

2 mSv/year	Typical background radiation (see p. 68) experienced by everyone.
9 mSv/year	Exposure to airline crew flying the New York to Tokyo polar route.
20 mSv/year	Current limit (averaged) for nuclear industry employees and uranium miners.
100 mSv/year	Lowest level at which an increase in cancer is clearly evident. Above this, the probability of cancer occurrence (rather than the severity) increases with dose.
1000 mSv/dose	Causes (temporary) radiation sickness such as nausea and decreased white blood cell count, but not usually death. Above this, severity of illness increases with dose.
5000 mSv/dose	Would kill about half of those receiving it within a month.
10 000 mSv/dose	Fatal within a few weeks.

Data from the World Nuclear Association

4) Categories of people who are at higher risk of radiation exposure include:
   - uranium miners and processors
   - workers in nuclear power plants
   - airline staff (the radiation comes from cosmic rays)
   - miners (many rocks are naturally radioactive)
   - some medical staff (e.g. radiographers)
   - nuclear researchers

In Britain, people at a higher risk have to have their radiation doses carefully monitored and have regular check-ups to make sure they're not getting sick because of the radiation they're exposed to at work.

Revision sickness — never mind, it'll all be worth it...

Everyone is exposed to some radiation (see next page), but don't worry, the average dose is 10 times less than the limit for people who work with radiation, and even that seems to be pretty safe (as far as we know).

Using Ionising Radiation

We're constantly exposed to very low levels of radiation without us noticing — sneaky.

Background Radiation is Everywhere All the Time

There's low-level background radiation all around us that is constantly irradiating and contaminating us. It comes from radioactive materials:

1) NATURAL RADIOACTIVE ELEMENTS in the air, in soil, in living things, in the rocks under our feet...
2) SPACE (cosmic rays) — these come mostly from the Sun.
3) HUMAN ACTIVITY — e.g. from nuclear explosions or waste from nuclear power plants.

Radioactive sources are considered to be "safe" when the radiation they are emitting is at about the same level as the background radiation. The half-life of the source gives an idea of how long it will take for this to happen. E.g. strontium-90 has a half-life of 29 years so a sample emitting 1000 cpm will take four half-lives, 116 years, to reach roughly the background count of 60 cpm. (1000 cpm → 500 cpm → 250 cpm → 125 cpm → 62.5 cpm.)

Ionising Radiation Can be Very Useful For...

...Treating Cancer

1) Since high doses of gamma rays will kill all living cells, they can be used to treat cancers.
2) The gamma rays have to be directed carefully and at just the right dosage so as to kill the cancer cells, without damaging too many normal cells.
3) However, a fair bit of damage is inevitably done to normal cells, which makes the patient feel very ill.
4) But if the cancer is successfully killed off in the end, then it's worth it.

...Sterilising Medical Equipment

1) Gamma rays are used to sterilise medical instruments by killing all the microbes.
2) This is better than trying to boil plastic instruments, which might be damaged by high temperatures.
3) You need to use a strongly radioactive source that has a long half-life, so that it doesn't need replacing too often.

...Sterilising Food

1) Food can be sterilised in the same way as medical instruments — again killing all the microbes.
2) This keeps the food fresh for longer, without having to freeze it or cook it or preserve it some other way.
3) The food is not radioactive afterwards, so it's safe to eat.

...Detecting Diseases Using Tracers

1) Tracers are radioactive molecules that can be injected into people. Their progress around the body is followed using an external detector. They can detect cancer or whether an organ is working properly.
2) Isotopes used as tracers must be gamma or beta emitters so the radiation passes out of the body.
3) They should have a short half-life so that the radioactivity inside the patient quickly disappears.

Gamma radiation — just what the doctor ordered...

Background radiation was discovered accidentally. Scientists couldn't understand why their detector showed radioactivity when there was no material being tested. They were picking up background radiation.

Revision Summary for Module P6

Phew... what a relief — you made it to the end of yet another section. But don't run off to put the kettle on just yet — make sure that you really know your stuff with these revision questions.

1) What are the three particles found in an atom? Which two are found in the nucleus?
2) What do we mean by an 'unstable' atom?
3) Oxygen contains 8 protons. What is the difference between the oxygen-16 and oxygen-18 isotopes?
4) Is the rate of radioactive decay affected by chemical processes?
5) Describe the nature and properties of the three types of ionising radiation: alpha, beta and gamma.
6) What substances could be used to block: a) alpha radiation, b) beta radiation, c) gamma radiation?
7)* Complete the following nuclear equations by working out the missing numbers shown by the dotted lines:
   a) ${}^{131}_{53}\text{I} \rightarrow {}^{\cdots}_{\cdots}\text{Xe} + {}^{0}_{-1}\beta$ b) ${}^{\cdots}_{\cdots}\text{Gd} \rightarrow {}^{144}_{62}\text{Sm} + {}^{4}_{2}\alpha$
8) Define half-life.
9)* The activity of a radioactive sample is 840 Bq. Four hours later it has fallen to 105 Bq. Find the half-life of the sample.
10) What did the Rutherford-Geiger-Marsden experiment reveal about the nucleus?
11) Why don't positively charged particles in the nucleus fly apart from each other?
12) What idea is summed up in Einstein's equation '$E = mc^2$'?
13) What type of particle keeps a fission chain reaction going?
14) Describe how nuclear power stations generate electricity using uranium or plutonium fuel rods.
15) Briefly describe how the three 'levels' of nuclear waste are disposed of.
16) Describe what kind of damage ionising radiation causes to body cells. What are the effects of high doses? What are the effects of lower doses?
17) What units are doses of radiation measured in? What two things does 'dose' take into account?
18) Give four categories of people who are at a higher than normal risk of exposure to radiation.
19) Give three sources of background radiation.
20) Describe in detail how radioactive sources are used in each of the following:
   a) treating cancer, b) sterilising medical equipment, c) sterilising food, d) medical tracers.

* Answers on page 96.

Observing the Sky

It's easy to see why people thought we were at the centre of the Universe for ages.
The Sun, Moon and stars all seem to orbit around us — but really it's all down to the Earth's spin.

A Sidereal Day is the Time Taken for the Earth to Spin Once

1) If you looked at the night sky for long enough, you'd see distant stars appear to cross the sky from east to west.
2) Astronomers have known for years that it's not the stars that move, but the Earth that spins on its axis.
3) For a star to get to the same position in the sky, the Earth needs to spin 360°. The time taken for this to happen is called a sidereal day.

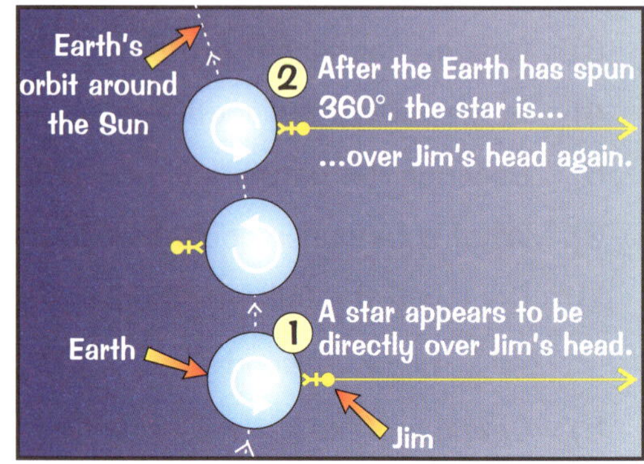

A sidereal day is the time taken for a star to return to the same position in the sky. It's about 23 hours and 56 minutes.

The Sun and Moon Appear to Cross the Sky at Different Speeds

1) It's not just the stars — the Sun and Moon also appear to cross the sky from east to west.
2) The Sun seems to move more slowly across the sky than distant stars — it takes 24 hours to get to the same position in the sky, a whole 4 minutes longer. This is called a solar day.

A solar day is the time taken for the Sun to appear at the same position in the sky. It's 24 hours.

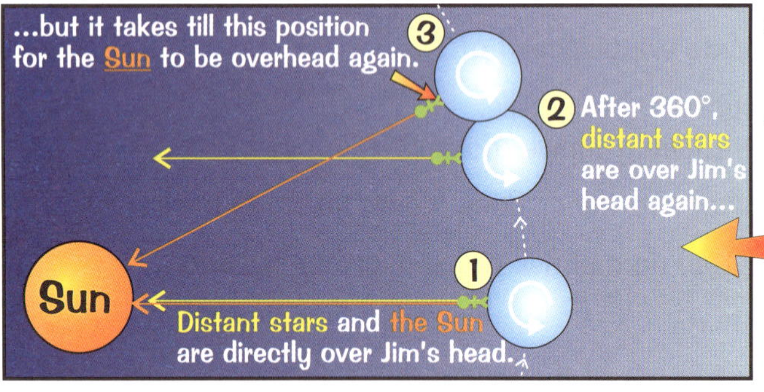

3) Solar and sidereal days are different because the Earth orbits the Sun as well as spinning on its axis.
4) The Earth orbits the Sun in the same direction as it spins — so the Earth needs to spin slightly more than 360° before the Sun appears at the same position in the sky.

5) The Moon seems to go more slowly than the Sun, taking about 25 hours to appear at the same position in the sky.
6) This is because the Moon orbits the Earth in the same direction as the Earth is rotating.

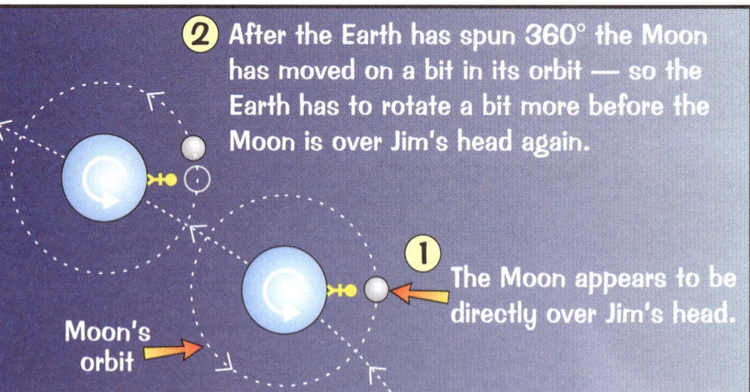

The Stars You Can See in the Sky Change During the Year

1) As the Earth moves around the Sun, the direction we face changes slightly each day.
2) This means we can see a slightly different patch of sky each night — we see different stars.
3) An Earth year is the time it takes the Earth to orbit the Sun once, so on the same day each year you should be able to see the same stars in the night sky.

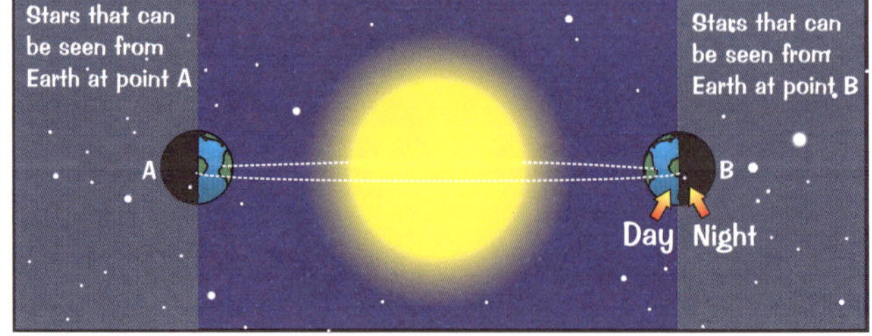

All this spinning is making me dizzy...

The ancient Greeks thought the Sun was a god called Helios riding a golden chariot across the sky. Bit fancier than your average car I suppose. Don't try putting that in your exam though... you won't get any marks.

Eclipses and the Moon

Some more spinning and orbiting, but this time it's the Moon's turn...

The Phases of the Moon

1) The Moon doesn't glow itself — it only reflects light from the Sun. Only the half facing the Sun is lit up, leaving the other half in shadow.
2) As the Moon orbits the Earth, we see different amounts of the Moon's dark and lit-up surfaces.
3) You see a 'full moon' when the whole of the lit-up surface is facing the Earth, and a 'new moon' when the dark half faces us.
4) The rest of the phases are in between these two extremes.

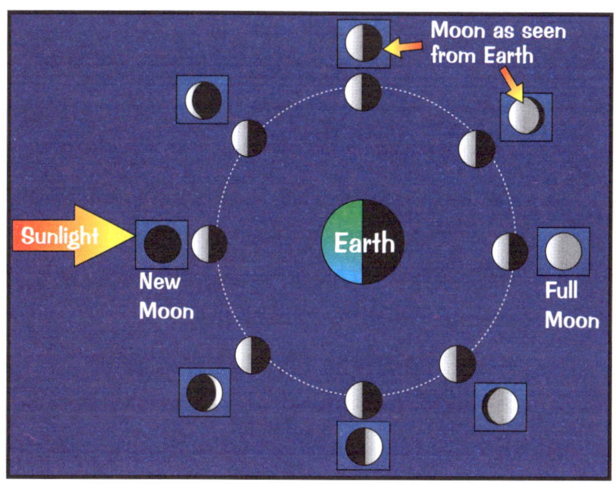

Eclipses Happen When Light from the Sun is Blocked

There are two main types of eclipse: lunar and solar.

LUNAR ECLIPSE

As it orbits, the Moon sometimes passes into the Earth's shadow. The Earth blocks sunlight from the Moon, so almost no light is reflected from the Moon and it just seems to disappear. A total lunar eclipse is where no direct sunlight can reach the Moon. More often, the Moon isn't fully in the Earth's shadow so only part of it appears dark — a partial lunar eclipse.

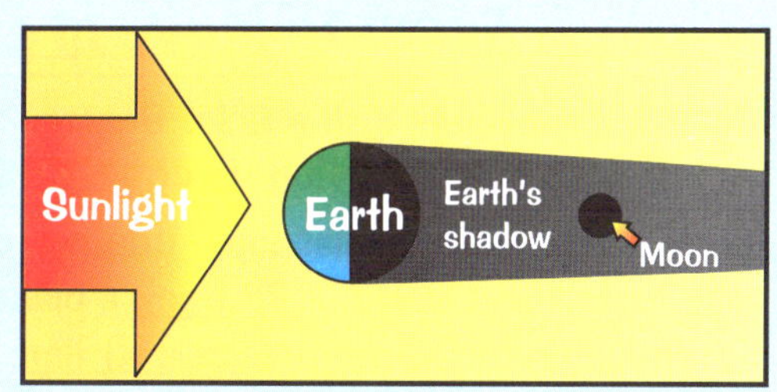

SOLAR ECLIPSE

The Moon is (purely by chance) just the right size and distance away that when it passes between the Sun and the Earth, it can block out the Sun. This is called a solar eclipse. From some parts of the Earth the Sun is completely blocked — a total solar eclipse. From many places on Earth only part of the Sun will be blocked — a partial solar eclipse. From most places on Earth the Sun won't be blocked at all.

Eclipses Don't Happen Very Often

1) It's not every day you see the Sun being blotted out of the sky by the Moon.
2) The Moon orbits the Earth at an angle to Earth's orbit around the Sun. So most of the time the Sun, Moon and Earth don't line up to cause eclipses.
3) Partial eclipses happen a bit more often as they don't have to line up perfectly for this.
4) Even when there is a solar eclipse, there's only a very small region on Earth from which it can be seen. There might be a total solar eclipse in China but we'd hardly notice anything in the UK.

Aaaargh — the Sun's been eaten by a giant sky monster...

If you ever get the chance to see a total solar eclipse, it's amazing (but don't look directly at the Sun). If you want to see it in the UK though, don't buy your popcorn just yet — you'll have to wait 'til 2090...

Coordinates in Astronomy

This page is a bit tricky, but stick with it...

The Positions of Stars are Measured by Angles Seen from Earth

1) The positions of stars are measured by angles seen from Earth. It's just like latitude and longitude on Earth — only for the sky.
2) The sky appears to turn as the Earth spins — so astronomers picked two fixed positions to measure from:

   THE POLE STAR is a star that doesn't seem to move because it's almost directly above the North Pole (and the spin axis) of Earth.

   THE CELESTIAL EQUATOR is an imaginary plane running across the sky, extending out from the Earth's equator.
3) The two angles used to measure positions in the sky are:

   Declination — Celestial latitude, measured in degrees.

   Right Ascension — Celestial longitude (the 'how much across' angle), measured in degrees or time.

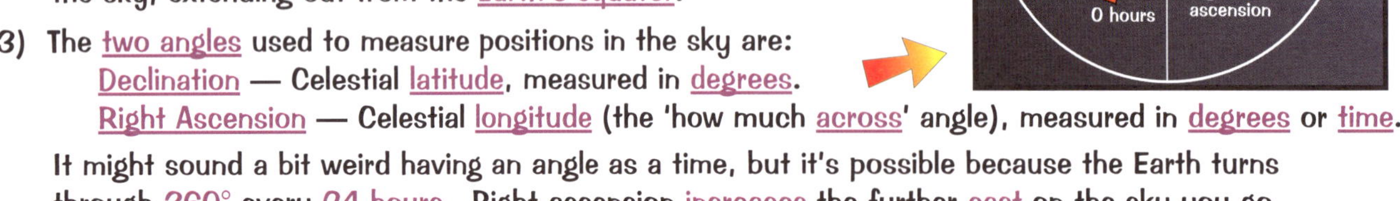

It might sound a bit weird having an angle as a time, but it's possible because the Earth turns through 360° every 24 hours. Right ascension increases the further east on the sky you go.

Planets Seem to Move in Complicated Patterns

1) All the planets in the Solar System orbit the Sun in the same direction but at different speeds. The closer to the Sun, the quicker the planet.
2) Even without a telescope, you can often see the 'naked eye' planets — Mercury, Venus, Mars, Jupiter and Saturn. To track a planet as it goes across the sky, set your alarm clock and note down its position at the same (sidereal) time each night. (That way you rule out the Earth's spin making it cross the sky.) You'll find that the planets seem to gradually travel from west to east.
3) Every so often, though, a planet seems to change direction and go the other way for a bit (in relation to the fixed stars), making a loop or squiggle in its track before carrying on as normal. This is called retrograde motion. It only happens with the outer planets — Mars to Neptune.
4) It happens because both the planet and Earth are moving around the Sun — so we're seeing the motion of the planet relative to Earth.
5) Mars appears to change direction once every two or so years. Slower-moving planets further out 'change direction' less frequently.

Fixed stars are distant background stars that stay in the same position year after year.

From Earth, Mars appears to move to the left (west to east) compared to fixed stars.

About three months later, Earth 'overtakes' Mars, and so Mars appears to change direction (travelling from east to west).

After another few months, Earth moves 'vertically down' while Mars is still moving 'horizontally', so Mars once again appears to move to the left (west to east).

Date	Right Ascension		Declination (degrees)
	hours	minutes	
June 5th 2003	21	51	-16.3
July 31st 2003	22	55	-14.6
Sept 10th 2003	22	45	-16.5
Oct 20th 2003	22	25	-13.2
Dec 1st 2003	23	29	-4.3

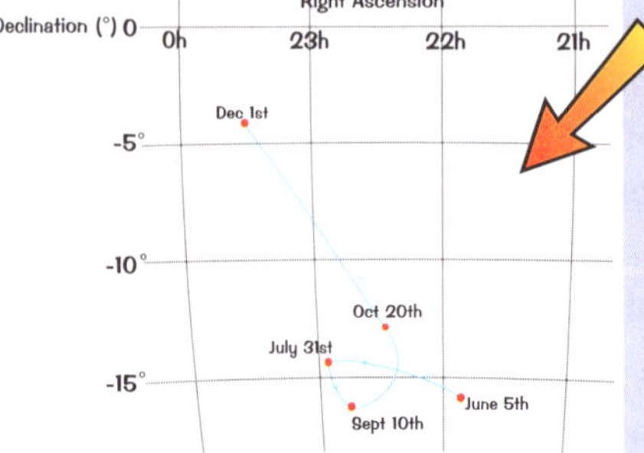

The diagram shows the loop Mars made in 2003. You can tell just from the table of data that Mars has changed direction. Mars travels east (right ascension increases) — then changes direction and moves west (right ascension decreases) before moving east again (right ascension increases).

It's all just loops and squiggles...

Time is an angle? Hmm. And the planets are a bit like athletes running at different speeds on a race track and lapping each other — make sure you can explain how this causes those loops and squiggles.

Refraction

A lot of what we know about stars is based on the light coming from them. This light can bend by refraction.

Refraction — Waves Change Speed and Direction

1) The speed of a wave is affected by the density of the substance or medium it's travelling in. For example, light waves travel more slowly in denser medium (usually).
2) So when a wave crosses a boundary between two substances (from glass to air, say) it changes speed.
3) Since wave speed = frequency × wavelength (you did this in P1), and the frequency is fixed for each type of wave, then if the speed changes, the wavelength must also change. E.g. if speed decreases, the wavelength must decrease.
4) The change in speed and wavelength can cause the wave to change direction too — this is called refraction:

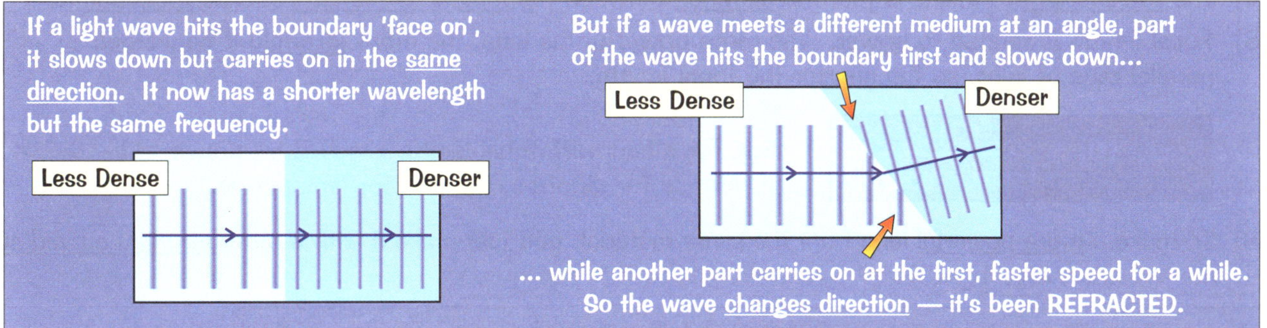

5) Converging or convex lenses (see next page) use refraction to focus light waves to form an image of an object.
6) As a light ray hits the surface of the lens and passes from air to glass, it slows down. This causes the light ray to bend towards the 'normal' (the line at right angles to the boundary at the point where the ray enters or leaves).

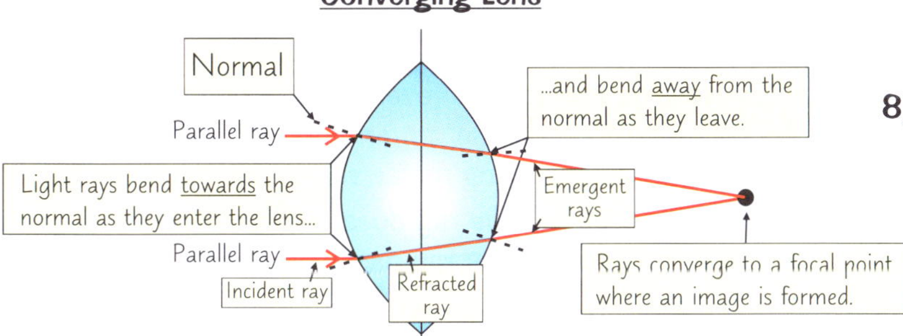

7) When it hits the 'glass to air' boundary on the other side it speeds up and bends away from the normal.
8) The curvature of the lens means all the parallel rays hitting different parts of the lens are bent towards the same focal point, where an image is formed of whatever the light is coming from.

A Triangular Prism Can Refract Light to Form a Spectrum

1) Different wavelengths of light refract by different amounts. So white light (a mixture of lots of wavelengths of coloured light) disperses (spreads out) into its different colours as it enters a prism.
2) A rectangular prism has parallel boundaries, so the rays bend one way as they enter, and then bend back again by the same amount as they leave — the light leaving the glass is parallel to the light entering it, so white light emerges.

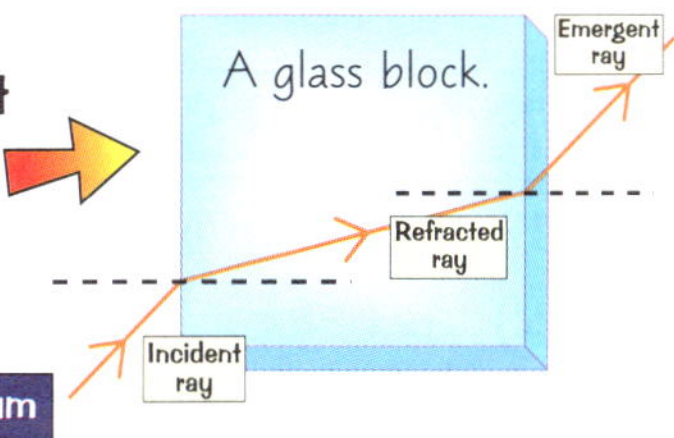

3) But with a triangular prism, the boundaries aren't parallel, which means the different wavelengths don't recombine, and you get a nice rainbow effect — a spectrum.

Prism
White light
A spectrum
Violet is bent the most

My mate Ray got caught speeding — went straight to prism...

You need to get your head around refraction to understand lenses — and there's plenty more on lenses on the next couple of pages. For now, amuse yourself by considering why there are so many songs about rainbows...

Converging Lenses

Lenses are used in telescopes. No, really... They change the direction of light rays by refraction.

Converging Lenses Bring Light Rays Together

1) A converging lens is convex — it gets fatter towards the middle. It causes rays of light to converge (come together) to a focus.
2) All lenses have a principal axis, a line which passes straight through the middle of the lens.
3) The focal point of a lens is where rays initially parallel to the principal axis meet. (All lenses have two focal points, one in front of the lens, and one behind the lens.)

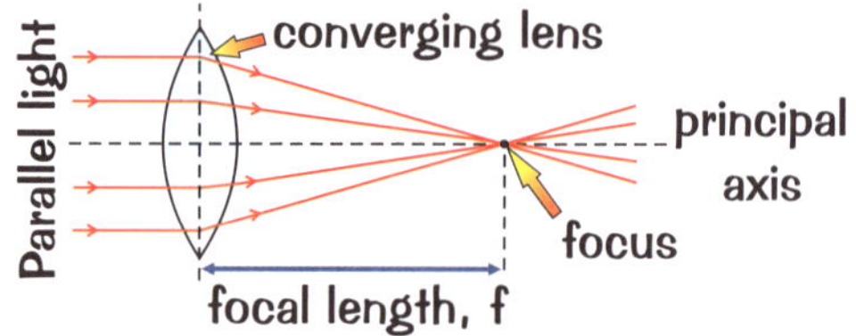

4) The focal length of a lens is just the distance between the middle of the lens and its focal point.
5) Focal length is related to power. The more powerful the lens, the more strongly it converges parallel rays of light, so the shorter the focal length.

$$\text{Power (D)} = \frac{1}{\text{Focal length (m)}}$$

E.g. for a lens with focal length f = 0.2 m, power = 1 ÷ 0.2 = 5 D. (D stands for dioptres, the unit for lens power.)

6) To make a more powerful lens from the same material, you just make it with a more strongly curved surface.

Drawing Ray Diagrams for Light from Objects in Space

A lot of objects like stars are so far away that you can think of them as just dots of light (point sources). Light rays from them are effectively parallel by the time they reach Earth. This makes it nice and easy to draw ray diagrams of the light being focused with a converging lens — here's how:

Point Source

1) parallel light from point source — focal length, f — focal point, F — principal axis

2)

3) image of star

1) Mark the focal point on the principal axis. Draw 3 parallel rays from the star (or whatever it is) — one to the centre of the lens, one towards the top and one towards the bottom. Only draw the rays going as far as the middle of the lens.
2) The middle ray doesn't get refracted, so just extend this ray past the focal point of the lens.
3) Draw in the rest of the top and bottom rays, making them meet the middle ray above or below the focal point. The image is formed at this point — and it's a real image, as all the rays actually meet there.

It's almost exactly the same for light from extended sources (anything that you can't just pretend is a dot, such as a planet or moon in our solar system, or a galaxy etc.)

Extended Source

1) Treat two opposite edges of the object as point sources.
2) As before, the parallel rays for each edge will meet in line with (or at) the focal point of the lens.
3) A real image is formed between the two points where the rays meet.

parallel light from edge 2 — parallel light from edge 1 — F — image of galaxy

Convex lenses — keepin' it real...

A real image — instead of a fake image? Well, kind of. Sometimes virtual images are formed — where light rays appear to have come from. This is really useful in the refracting telescope (see next page).

Telescopes

Telescopes use convex lenses or curved mirrors to magnify light from space. Here's how.

A Simple Refracting Telescope Uses Two Converging Lenses

1) A simple refracting optical telescope is made up of two convex lenses with different powers — an objective lens and a more powerful eye lens (or eyepiece). The objective lens collects the light from the object being observed and forms an image of it, and the eyepiece magnifies this image so we can view it.
2) The lenses are aligned to have the same principal axis and are placed so that their focal points are in the same place.
3) Many objects in space are so far away that by the time their light arrives on Earth, the light rays are effectively parallel.

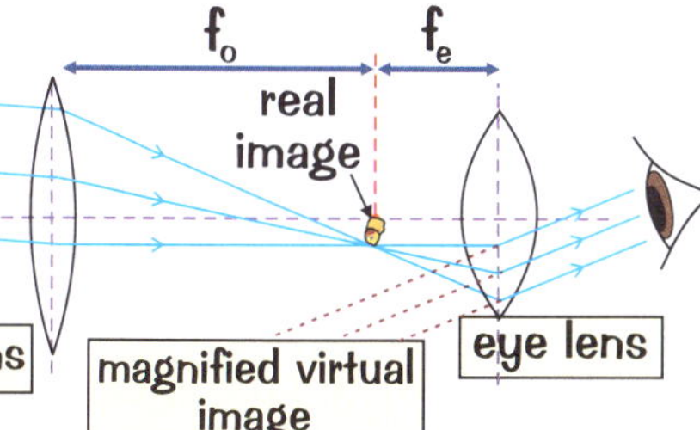

4) The objective lens converges these parallel rays to form a real image between the two lenses.
5) The eyepiece lens is much more powerful than the objective lens (it's much more curved). It acts as a magnifying glass on the real image and makes a virtual image — where the light entering the eye lens appears to have come from.
6) The angular magnification, M, of the telescope can be calculated from the focal lengths of the objective lens, f_o, and the eye lens, f_e.

$$\text{Magnification} = \frac{\text{Focal length of objective lens } (F_o)}{\text{Focal length of eye lens } (F_e)}$$

EXAMPLE 1: An astronomer uses a refracting telescope to look at a distant star. If f_o = 4.5 m and f_e = 0.1 m, find the angular magnification of the telescope.

ANSWER: Angular magnification = $f_o \div f_e = 4.5 \div 0.1 = 45$

EXAMPLE 2: Geoff makes a telescope which has a 0.2 D objective lens and an 8 D eye lens. What is the magnification of Geoff's telescope?

ANSWER: $P = 1 \div f$, so $f = 1 \div P$. So $f_o = 1 \div 0.2 = 5$ m, $f_e = 1 \div 8 = 0.125$ m.
Angular magnification = $f_o \div f_e = 5 \div 0.125 = 40$

See right at the bottom of the page for a shortcut for doing this one.

Most Astronomical Telescopes Use a Concave Mirror

1) Most astronomical telescopes use a concave mirror instead of a convex objective lens.
2) Concave mirrors are shiny on the inside of the curve. Parallel rays of light shining on a concave mirror reflect and converge.
3) Concave mirrors are like a portion of a sphere. The centre of the sphere is the centre of curvature, C.
4) The centre of the mirror's surface is called the vertex.
5) Halfway between the centre of curvature and the vertex is the focal point, F. These points all lie on the axis.
6) Rays parallel to the mirror's axis, e.g. those from a distant star, reflect and meet at the focal point (as with lenses).
7) By putting a lens near the focal point of the mirror to act as an eyepiece, you can form a magnified image — just as in the simple refracting telescope above.

concave mirror
focal point (F)
axis
centre of curvature (C)
vertex

Important stuff this — come on, focus, focus...

There's an alternative magnification formula you can use if you're given the powers rather than focal lengths. It'll save faffing about: Magnification = $\text{Power}_{eye} \div \text{Power}_{objective}$. (It's just upside down.)

Diffraction and Telescopes

With telescopes, it's all about size — especially when you need to deal with diffraction.

Diffraction — Waves Spreading Out

1) All waves spread out ('diffract') at the edges when they pass through a gap or past an object.
2) The amount of diffraction depends on the size of the gap relative to the wavelength of the wave. The narrower the gap, or the longer the wavelength, the more the wave spreads out.
3) A narrow gap is one about the same size as the wavelength of the wave.
4) So whether a gap counts as narrow or not depends on the wave in question.
5) Light has a very small wavelength (about 0.0005 mm) — it can be diffracted but it's only when you have a really small gap that you notice any effects.

Gap much wider than wavelength

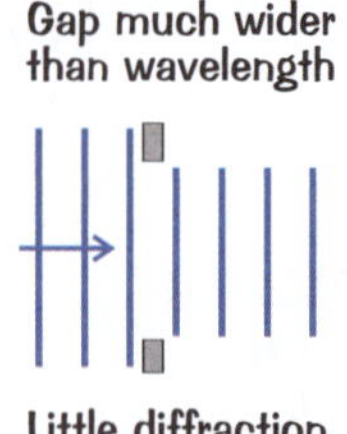

Little diffraction

Gap a bit wider than wavelength

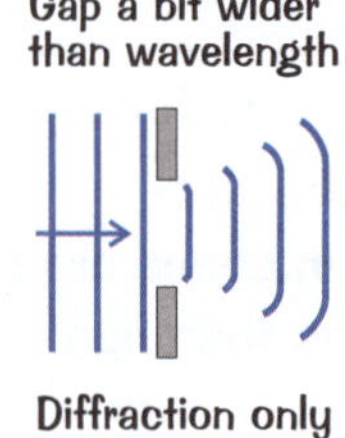

Diffraction only at edges

Gap the same as wavelength

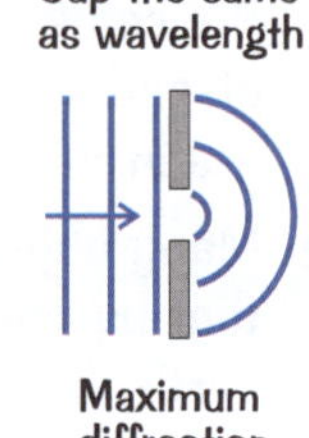

Maximum diffraction

To Detect Faint Sources You Need a Wide Aperture

1) Some objects in the sky are so distant and faint, only a tiny amount of radiation from them reaches us.
2) To collect enough of the radiation from these objects to see them, you need to use a telescope with a huge objective lens (or mirror). The diameter of the objective lens is called the aperture. The bigger the aperture, the more radiation can get into the telescope and the better the image formed.
3) Making large lenses is difficult and expensive, whereas big mirrors are much easier to make accurately. This is one of the reasons why many telescopes have a concave mirror instead of a lens (see p.75).

Aperture Size Must be Much Larger Than Wavelength

1) Because all waves can diffract when they pass through a gap, radiation entering a telescope spreads out at the edges of the aperture — causing the image to blur.
2) If you looked at radiation from a point source like a star when there was no diffraction, you'd see a bright dot. If you used too small an aperture to look at the star, the dot would be dimmer and surrounded by rings which get dimmer the further away from the image they are.
3) The only way round this problem is to have an aperture that's much wider than the wavelength of radiation you want to look at. This way the radiation passes through the aperture and into your telescope with very little diffraction and you get a sharp image.

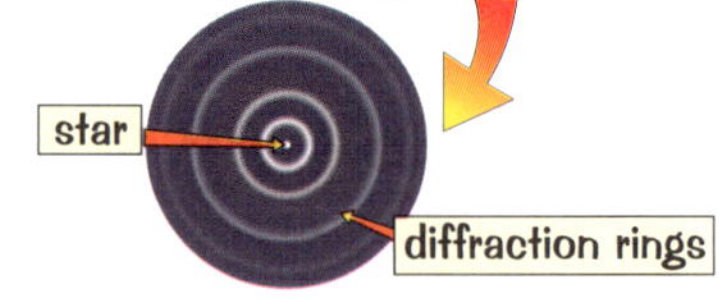

A Diffraction Grating Can Be Used To Make a Spectrum

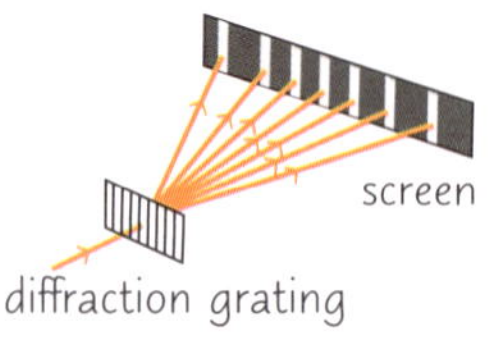

1) A diffraction grating has very narrow slits — small enough to diffract light.
2) When white light passes through the gaps in a diffraction grating, the different wavelengths of coloured light are all diffracted but by different amounts.
3) This creates a spectrum of different coloured light, as shown below.

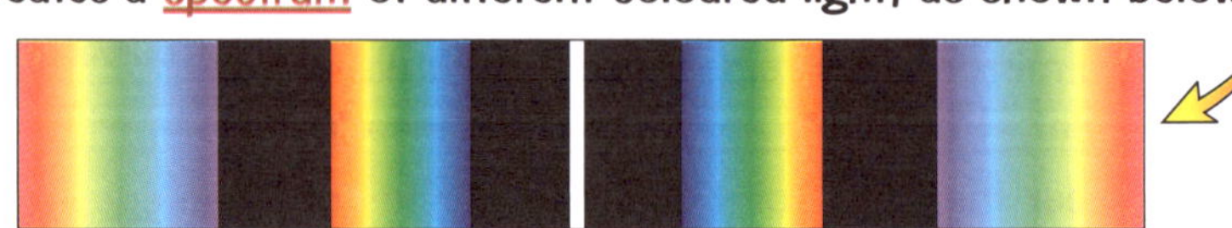

4) Astronomers can use these spectra to analyse the light coming from stars.

Mind the gap...

There's lots on this page, but it all boils down to "the bigger the gap, the less diffraction, the clearer the image." Sometimes diffraction is a good thing though — like when we want to split up light from stars to look at spectra.

Astronomical Distances and Brightness

Stars — they're bright and really far away. But are the brighter ones really brighter or just closer...

The Distance to Nearby Stars can be Measured by Parallax

1) Parallax is an apparent change in position of an object against a distant background. It makes closer stars appear to move relative to distant ones over the course of a year. In astronomy:

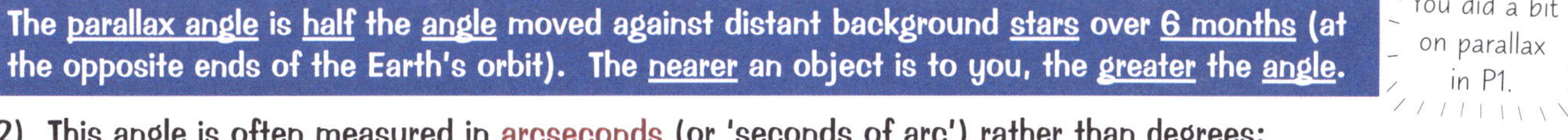

The parallax angle is half the angle moved against distant background stars over 6 months (at the opposite ends of the Earth's orbit). The nearer an object is to you, the greater the angle.

You did a bit on parallax in P1.

2) This angle is often measured in arcseconds (or 'seconds of arc') rather than degrees:

$$1 \text{ arcsecond} = 1'' = \left(\frac{1}{3600}\right)^{\circ}$$

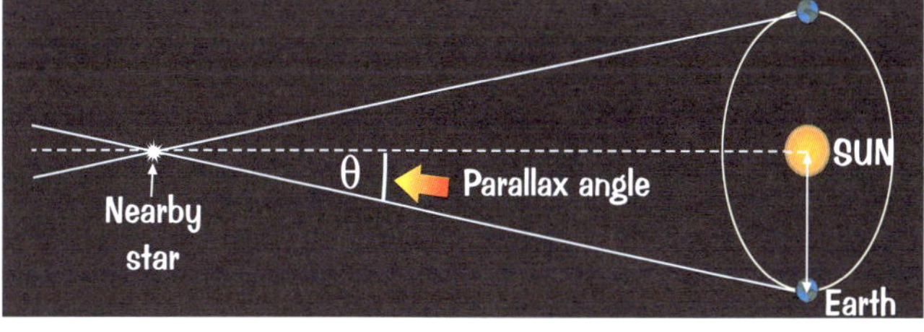

3) Parallax is useful for calculating the distance to nearby stars. The smaller the parallax angle, the more distant the star is.

4) Astronomers usually use a unit of distance called a parsec. It's a similar magnitude to a light year (1 parsec = about 3 light years) — a really long way. Distances between stars (interstellar distances) are normally a few parsecs.

A parsec (pc) is the distance to a star with a parallax angle of 1 arcsecond.

5) You can calculate the distance to a star (in parsecs) using this equation:

$$\text{distance (pc)} = \left(\frac{1}{\text{angle (arcsec)}}\right)$$

EXAMPLE: Mr Moore measures the parallax of a star to be 0.4". How far away is the star in parsecs?

ANSWER: $\text{distance (pc)} = \left(\frac{1}{0.4''}\right)$ = 2.5 pc

Observed Intensity Depends on the Distance to the Star

1) The luminosity, or intrinsic brightness, of a star (how bright it'd seem if you were right next to it) depends on it's size and temperature. The bigger and hotter it is, the more energy it gives out, so the brighter it is.

2) As you move away from a star, it looks dimmer — because the energy reaching you gets less (as it spreads out through space). So the observed intensity of the light (the observed brightness) of a star as seen on Earth depends on its luminosity and how far away it is from Earth.

3) So if you looked at two stars with the same luminosity but one was further away than the other, the more distant star would look dimmer.

Star 1 Star 2

Both stars have the same luminosity. Star 1 must be nearer than star 2.

A Cepheid Variable Star's Pulse Depends on Its Luminosity

1) A group of stars called Cepheid variables pulse in brightness — they get brighter and then dimmer over a period of several days.

2) How quickly they pulse is directly linked to their luminosity. The greater the luminosity, the longer the time between pulses (the pulse period).

3) So, if you see two Cepheid variable stars with the same observed brightness that pulse at different rates, you know that the star with the longer pulse period must have the higher luminosity. So the star with the longer pulse period must be further away.

4) Astronomers can work out the distance to a Cepheid variable by comparing the luminosity (worked out from the pulse period) and the observed brightness of the star.

I'm not dim — I'm just really far away...

Cepheid variables are really useful — you can use them to work out the distance to whatever big ball of gas they might be in. These cheeky chaps helped solve one of the most famous debates in astronomy... Next page...

The Scale of the Universe

We mightn't know exactly how big, but we know the Universe is biiiiiiiiiiiiiig.

Telescopes Showed That the Sun is a Star in the Milky Way

1) If you went out in the countryside on a clear night you could probably see about 1500 stars (if you've got good eyesight). If you looked with a small telescope, you could probably see over half a million.
2) The more stars you can see, the more you notice that they're not evenly dotted about the sky. Most of the stars appear to be concentrated in a bright strip across the sky — the Milky Way galaxy.
3) Away from this strip, the number of visible stars is much smaller.
4) Our Sun is just one of the approximately 10^{11} stars in the galaxy (this was worked out after a lot of peering through telescopes).
5) The Milky Way is actually a spiral galaxy. But because we're part of its disc, we see it edge on as a bright strip in the sky.

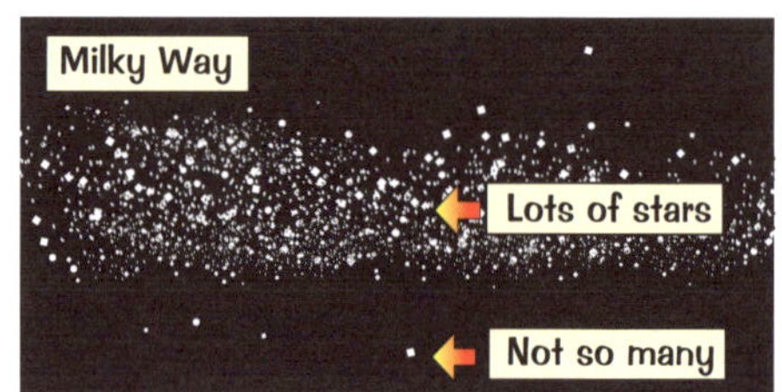

The Curtis-Shapley Debate

In the 1920s there was a debate about the size and structure of the Universe, led by two famous American astronomers — Harlow Shapley and Heber Curtis. Through telescopes, people had seen some faint, fuzzy objects that they called nebulae. Some of these objects looked spiral-shaped but some were just blobs. Shapley and Curtis argued about what these nebulae were and where they were:

Shapley's Argument

1) Shapley believed the Universe was just one gigantic galaxy about 100 000 parsecs across.
2) He reckoned our Sun and Solar System were far from the centre of the galaxy.
3) He believed that nebulae were huge clouds of gas and dust. These clouds were relatively nearby and actually part of the Milky Way.

Curtis' Argument

1) Curtis thought the Universe was made up of many galaxies.
2) He thought our galaxy was smaller than Shapley suggested — about 10 000 pc across, with the Sun at or very near the centre.
3) The spiral nebulae were other very distant galaxies, completely separate from the Milky Way.

And the winner is... well both of them really:

1) Shapley was right that the Solar System is far from the centre of our galaxy, but Curtis was right that there are many galaxies in the Universe (at least 100 000 000 000 of them).
2) Curtis was also right about spiral nebulae — Hubble used Cepheid variable stars to show that they're really far away (see next page). (The debate wasn't properly over until the 1930s, though, when better telescopes meant we could see the nebulae clearly, rather than just as blurry blobs.)

The Milky Way — not just a tasty snack...

At least it was all sorted in the end, and now it's a joy for you to learn instead... well, maybe not.

The Scale of the Universe

Edwin Hubble was possibly the most famous astronomer ever (apart from our Patrick with his xylophone).

Hubble Showed There Were Objects Outside the Galaxy

1) Hubble helped solve the Curtis-Shapley debate with his observations of the Andromeda nebula.
2) Using images taken using the largest telescope at the time, he found that this spiral-shaped fuzzy blob contained many stars, some of which were Cepheid variables (see p. 77).
3) Hubble calculated the distance to the Andromeda nebula by working out the distance to the Cepheid variables within it, using the relationship between their brightness and pulse frequency (see p. 77).
4) He found it was about 2.5 million light years away — much further than any stars in our galaxy.
5) He studied other spiral nebulae and found a similar result — they were all too far away to be part of the Milky Way, and so must be separate spiral galaxies themselves.

The distances to stuff in space are enormous. They're so big that astronomers tend to use units of megaparsecs when talking about distances to objects outside the Milky Way (intergalactic distances). 1 megaparsec (Mpc) is about 3×10^{19} km. The distance to the nearest spiral galaxy is just under 0.8 Mpc.

Distant Galaxies are Moving Away from Us

1) When a galaxy is moving away from us the wavelength of the light from it changes — the light becomes redder. This is called red shift.
2) By seeing how much the light has been red-shifted, you can work out the recession velocity of the galaxy (how quickly it's moving away). The greater the red shift, the greater the speed of recession.
3) Using red shift, Hubble compared the speed and the distances for many distant galaxies and found a pattern:

The more distant the galaxy, the faster it moves away from us.

4) This suggests that the whole Universe is expanding from a single point — which could be explained by an initial explosion millions of years ago that started off the expansion. The theory accepted by most scientists — the Big Bang theory — is that all the matter and energy in the Universe was compressed into a very small space, then it exploded 14 thousand million years ago and has been spreading out ever since.
5) Red shift is fairly easy to measure, so a galaxy's recession velocity can be calculated easily enough. The distance to a distant galaxy can be found from its recession velocity using Hubble's law.

Speed of recession	=	Hubble constant	×	distance
(km/s)		(s^{-1})		(km)
or (km/s)		(km/s per Mpc)		(Mpc)

6) The Hubble constant can have the units s^{-1} or km/s per Mpc (depending on the unit of distance you use). The value of the Hubble constant is roughly 2×10^{-18} s^{-1} or 70 km/s per Mpc.
7) You could be asked to use the equation in the exam to find any of the variables...

EXAMPLE: Find the distance to a galaxy that has a recession velocity of 475 km/s.

ANSWER: Rearrange the equation: Distance = Speed of recession / Hubble constant
$= 475 \div (2 \times 10^{-18}) = 2.375 \times 10^{20}$ km.

8) The value of the Hubble constant is still being researched and there are many different ways to calculate it, unfortunately the different methods all come up with slightly different answers.
9) Using data on Cepheid variable stars from distant galaxies has given us better values of Hubble's constant.

Hubble bubble toil and trouble...

Hubble was well clever — he sorted out the Curtis-Shapley squabble and made up a really useful law. He's so clever we named a jazzy space telescope after him (see page 87). So don't worry if this all seems a bit confusing — just keep trying and soon you'll be master of the Universe. Well, master of Hubble's law anyway.

Gas Behaviour

And now for two pages on gas. It may seem a little odd in the middle of all this Universe stuff but the Universe is made up of loads of balls of boiling gas. So you're just gonna have to live with it.

Kinetic Theory Says Gases are Randomly Moving Particles

1) Kinetic theory says that gases consist of very small particles. Which they do — oxygen consists of oxygen molecules, neon consists of neon atoms, etc.
2) These particles are constantly moving in completely random directions.
3) They constantly collide with each other and with the walls of their container. When they collide, they bounce off each other, or off the walls.
4) The particles hardly take up any space. Most of the gas is empty space.

Absolute Zero is as Cold as Stuff Can Get — 0 Kelvin

1) If you increase the temperature of something, you give its particles more kinetic energy — they move about more quickly or vibrate more. In the same way, if you cool a substance down, you're reducing the kinetic energy of the particles.
2) The coldest that anything can ever get is –273 °C — this temperature is known as absolute zero. At absolute zero, atoms have as little kinetic energy as it's possible to get.
3) Absolute zero is the start of the Kelvin scale of temperature.
4) A temperature change of 1 °C is also a change of 1 kelvin. The two scales are pretty similar — the only difference is where the zero is.
5) To convert from degrees Celsius to kelvins, just add 273. And to convert from kelvins to degrees Celsius, just subtract 273.

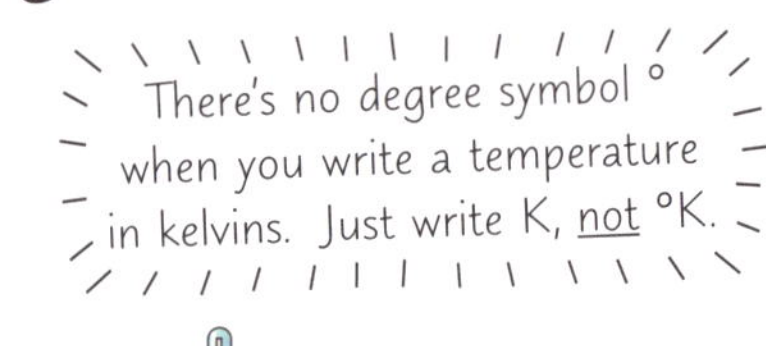

	Absolute zero	Freezing point of water	Boiling point of water
Celsius scale	–273 °C	0 °C	100 °C
Kelvin scale	0 K	273 K	373 K

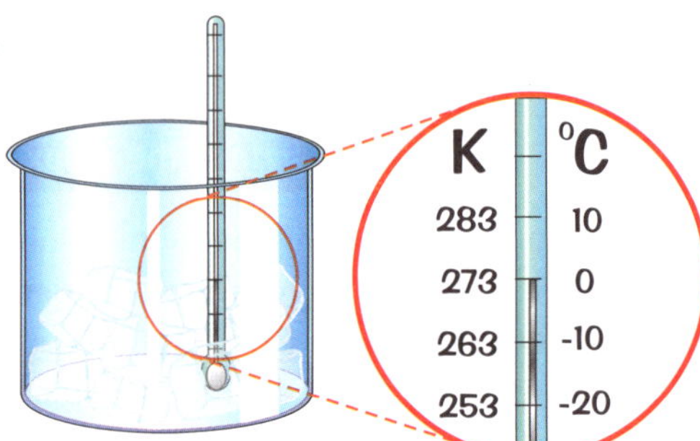

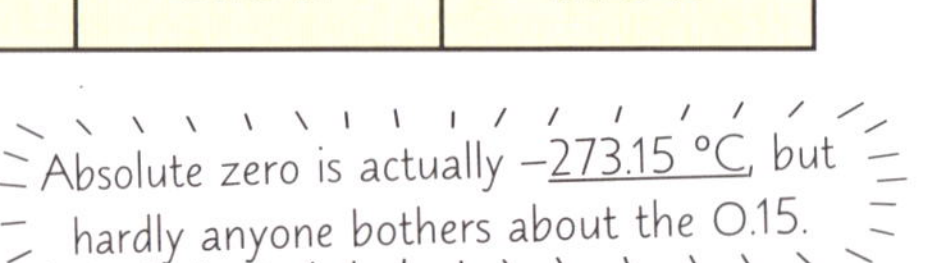

Kinetic Energy is Proportional to Temperature

1) Anything that's moving (e.g. a bunch of particles) has kinetic energy.
2) If you increase the temperature of a gas, you give its particles more energy, so as you heat up a gas the average speed of its particles increases.
3) In fact, if you double the absolute temperature (measured in kelvins), you double the average kinetic energy of the particles:

The temperature of a gas (in kelvins) is proportional to the average kinetic energy of its particles.

Absolute zero — nought, zilch, not a sausage...

Absolute temperature (the Kelvin scale) is handy because it means that temperatures can't be negative. Some equations (like those on the next page) only work using kelvin, so make sure you understand it. Confusingly, the guy who came up with the Kelvin scale was called William Thomson (who became Lord Kelvin).

More on Gas Behaviour

A Decrease in Volume Gives an Increase in Pressure

1) As gas particles move about, they bang into each other and whatever else happens to get in the way.
2) Gas particles have some mass, so when they collide with something, they exert a force on it. In a sealed container, gas particles smash against the container's walls — creating an outward pressure.
3) If you put the same amount of gas in a bigger container, the pressure will decrease, cos there'll be fewer collisions between the gas particles and the container's walls. When the volume's reduced, the particles get more squashed up and so they hit the walls more often, hence the pressure increases.
4) So the volume of a gas is inversely proportional to its pressure at a constant temperature — e.g. if you halve the volume, you double the pressure.
5) At constant temperature: **pressure × volume = constant**  **P × V = constant**

You can also write the equation as $P_1 \times V_1 = P_2 \times V_2$ (where P_1 and V_1 are your starting conditions and P_2 and V_2 are your final conditions). Writing it like that is much more useful a lot of the time.

EXAMPLE: A gas at a constant temperature in a 50 ml container has a pressure of 1.2 atm. Find the new pressure if the container volume is reduced to 40 ml.

ANSWER: $P_1 \times V_1 = P_2 \times V_2$ gives: $1.2 \times 50 = P_2 \times 40$ so $P_2 = 60 \div 40 =$ 1.5 atm

atm = atmosphere, a unit of pressure.

Increasing the Temperature Increases the Pressure

1) The pressure of a gas depends on how fast the particles are moving and how often they hit the walls of the container they're in.
2) If you heat a gas, the particles move faster and have more kinetic energy. This increase in kinetic energy means the particles hit the container walls harder and more often, creating more pressure.
3) Pressure is proportional to absolute temperature — doubling the temperature (in K), doubles the pressure.
4) At constant volume (i.e. in a sealed container):

$$\frac{\text{pressure}}{\text{temperature (in K)}} = \text{constant}$$

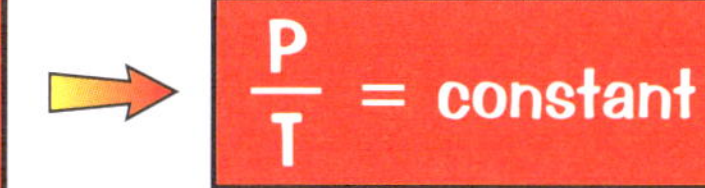

$$\frac{P}{T} = \text{constant}$$

You can also write the equation as: $P_1/T_1 = P_2/T_2$.

EXAMPLE: A container has a volume of 30 litres. It is filled with gas at a pressure of 1 bar and a temperature of 290 K. Find the new pressure if the temperature is increased to 315 K.

ANSWER: $P_1/T_1 = P_2/T_2$ gives: $1 \div 290 = P_2 \div 315$ so $P_2 = 315 \div 290 =$ 1.09 bar

1 bar is roughly the same as 1 atm.

Increasing the Temperature Increases the Volume

1) If a gas stays at a constant pressure, then heating it up increases its volume — the molecules are further apart so collisions happen less frequently, but with more force (because they have more kinetic energy).
2) Volume is proportional to absolute temperature. Doubling the temperature (in K), doubles the volume.
3) At constant pressure:

$$\frac{\text{volume}}{\text{temperature (in K)}} = \text{constant}$$

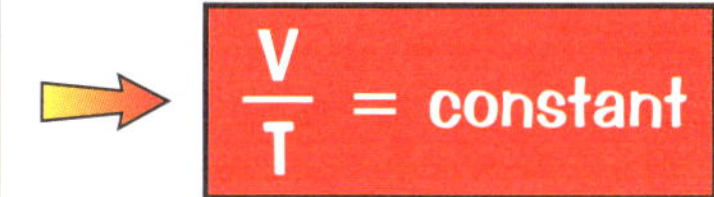

$$\frac{V}{T} = \text{constant}$$

You can also write the equation as: $V_1/T_1 = V_2/T_2$.

EXAMPLE: A gas at constant pressure, with a temperature of 270 K has a volume of 24 litres. Find the new volume if the temperature is increased to 315 K.

ANSWER: $V_1/T_1 = V_2/T_2$ gives: $24 \div 270 = V_2 \div 315$ so $V_2 = (24 \div 270) \times 315 =$ 28 litres

Less space, more collisions, more pressure — just like London...

These equations apply to so-called ideal gases. Ideal gases are those that are 'well behaved'. Nice gases. Stay.

Fusion

The Sun churns out vast amounts of energy because of nuclear fusion, which changes mass into energy.

Scientists Only 'Discovered' Fusion in the Early 20th Century

1) Scientists used to believe that the Sun just burned its own material. Then in the 19th century, they realised that the Sun would have needed an impossible amount of fuel to have kept burning for so long.
2) In the early 20th century, Einstein realised that mass could be converted to energy.
3) Lots of other clever people put the rest of the puzzle together. It was suggested that hydrogen is turned into helium inside the Sun, and that when this happens some mass gets 'lost' (they knew this by comparing the masses of hydrogen and helium atoms). Perhaps the missing mass was being changed into energy — and powering the Sun...
4) Hans Bethe did some hard sums to explain how fusion (see below) must be the power source of the Sun — and got a Nobel prize for his trouble.

Nuclei Have to be Brought Close Together to Fuse

1) Two nuclei can combine (fuse) to create a larger nucleus — this is nuclear fusion.
2) For example, in stars hydrogen nuclei fuse together to make helium nuclei.
3) Energy is liberated (released) when lighter (smaller) nuclei fuse to make heavier (larger) nuclei up to the size of an iron nucleus.
4) Nuclei can only fuse like this if they are brought close together.
5) For that you need lots of energy — high temperatures and pressures.

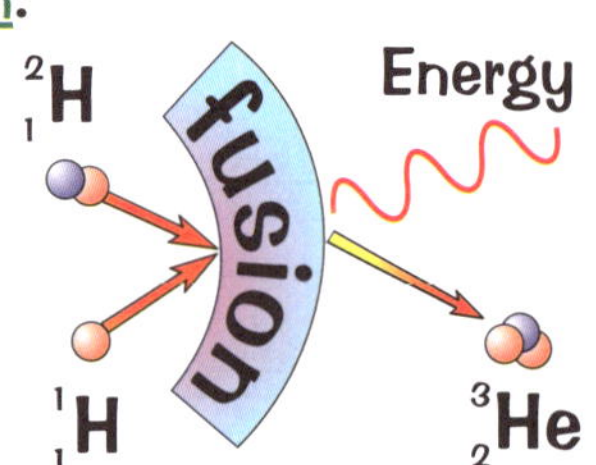

Nuclear Fusion Converts Mass into Energy

Fission is basically the opposite of fusion. Heavy atoms are split apart to release energy.

1) Albert Einstein reckoned that mass is a form of energy.
2) So, mass can be converted into other forms of energy.
3) This idea is summed up by his famous equation:
4) When nuclei undergo nuclear fusion (or fission) they lose mass and energy is released.
5) You can calculate how much energy is released during fusion (or fission) using $E = mc^2$.

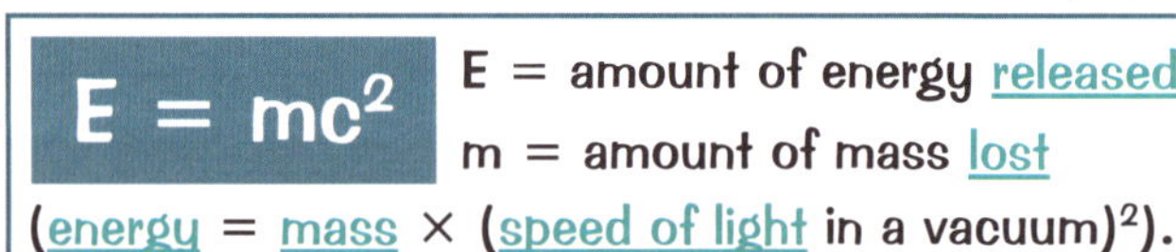

$E = mc^2$ E = amount of energy released, m = amount of mass lost
(energy = mass × (speed of light in a vacuum)^2).

Nuclear Equations — Make the Numbers Balance

Make sure the top (mass) numbers and the bottom (proton) numbers balance on both sides.

$^{0}_{1}e$ is a positron. It's a bit like a positive electron, and it conserves charge (makes the bottom number balance).

STEP 1: Two hydrogen nuclei combine to make a larger hydrogen nucleus:

$$^{1}_{1}H + ^{1}_{1}H \longrightarrow ^{2}_{1}H + ^{0}_{1}e + \text{energy}$$

top $1 + 1 = 2 \longrightarrow 2 + 0 = 2$
bottom $1 + 1 = 2 \longrightarrow 1 + 1 = 2$

STEP 2: A small hydrogen nucleus and a larger hydrogen nucleus combine to make a helium nucleus:

$$^{1}_{1}H + ^{2}_{1}H \longrightarrow ^{3}_{2}He + \text{energy}$$

top $1 + 2 = 3 \longrightarrow 3$
bottom $1 + 1 = 2 \longrightarrow 2$

STEP 3: Two helium nuclei combine to make a larger helium nucleus:

$$^{3}_{2}He + ^{3}_{2}He \longrightarrow ^{4}_{2}He + ^{1}_{1}H + ^{1}_{1}H + \text{energy}$$

top $3 + 3 = 6 \longrightarrow 4 + 1 + 1 = 6$
bottom $2 + 2 = 4 \longrightarrow 2 + 1 + 1 = 4$

In total: 6 Hydrogen ⟶ Helium + 2 Hydrogen + energy
So overall: 4 Hydrogen ⟶ Helium + energy

I'd have more energy if I found this massively interesting...

If a positron collides with an electron they both get annihilated (good word) and changed completely into energy.

Star Spectra

The light from stars doesn't just make the sky look pretty, it can actually tell you what stars are made of...

Continuous Spectra Contain All Possible Frequencies

1) All hot objects like stars emit radiation. Hot objects emit a continuous range of frequencies — a continuous spectrum (it doesn't have any gaps).
2) Hot objects always emit more of one frequency than any other. This wavelength is called the peak frequency.
3) The peak frequency emitted by an object depends on its temperature. The higher the temperature, the more energy the photons ('packets' of radiation) radiated will have, and so the higher the peak frequency.

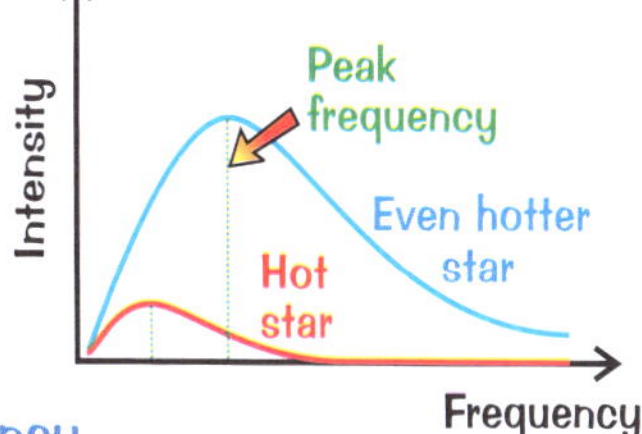

4) The luminosity (see p.77) or brightness also depends on temperature — hotter things glow more.
5) For example, we can tell how hot a star is by looking at its colour:
   red = has a low frequency = a cool star (well... still hot enough to cook you and your toast)
   blue = has a high frequency = scorchio (that's hot). The Sun's a fairly cool star — it looks yellowy.

Line Spectra — Electrons Moving Between Energy Levels

1) An atom contains electrons which move around a tiny positive nucleus.
2) Electrons can only be in certain energy levels (or shells) around the nucleus — with the lowest energy levels nearest the nucleus.
3) Electrons move between energy levels if they gain or lose energy.
4) Electrons can gain enough energy to be removed from the atom — this is called ionisation.

energy levels

ABSORPTION SPECTRA — At high temperatures, electrons become excited and jump into higher energy levels by absorbing radiation. Because there are only certain energy levels an electron can occupy, electrons absorb a particular frequency of radiation to get to a higher energy level.

You can 'see' this if a continuous spectrum of visible light shines through a gas — the electrons in the gas atoms absorb certain frequencies of the light, making gaps in the otherwise continuous spectrum. These gaps appear as dark lines.

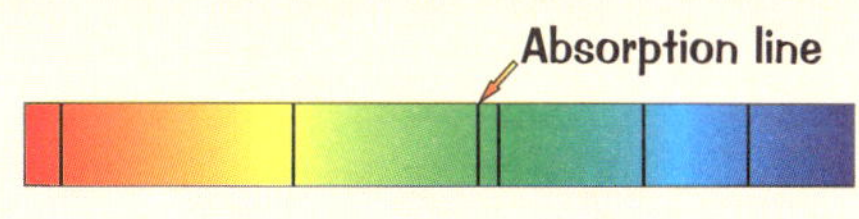

EMISSION SPECTRA — Electrons are unstable in the higher energy levels so they tend to fall from higher to lower levels, losing energy by emitting radiation of a particular frequency. This gives a series of bright lines formed by the emitted frequencies.

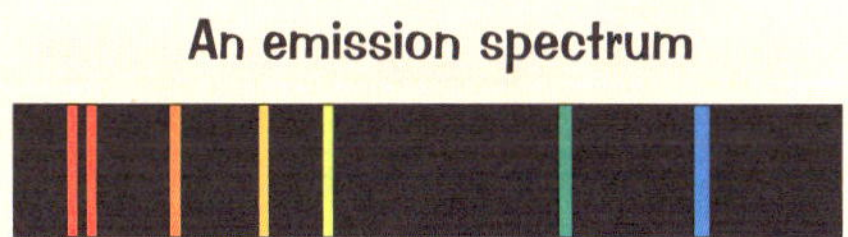

Astronomers Use Spectra to Work Out What Stars are Made Of

1) Energy levels in atoms are different for each element — so each element has its own line spectrum (corresponding to the energies needed for electrons to get from one energy level to another).
2) The photosphere (the surface) of a star emits a continuous spectrum of radiation. This radiation passes through the gases in a star's atmosphere, which produces emission and absorption lines in the spectrum.
3) By looking at the position of these lines in the star's spectrum, you can work out what chemical elements are present in the star's atmosphere — by comparing it with known spectra in the lab.

Stellar spectrum (containing H, He and Na)
Hydrogen
Helium
Sodium

What do you call a star detective? In-Spectra...

It's really useful stuff this line spectra business — it's as near as you can get to getting a spaceship, flying to a star, getting out your bucket and spade and having a good dig around to see what it's made of. Pretty neat, huh.

Stars

Stars — without them it would be really, really cold (and dark, and boring) in the Universe. Hooray for stars.

Stars Begin as Clouds of Dust and Gas

1) Stars are born in a cloud of dust and gas (which is mostly hydrogen and helium).
2) Gravity causes the denser regions of the cloud to contract very slowly into clumps.
3) When these clumps get dense enough, the cloud breaks up into protostars.
4) Protostars continue to collapse under gravity — reducing in volume. This makes the particles more squashed up, increasing pressure and temperature (if you're a bit lost have a look back at page 81).
5) Eventually the temperature at the centre of a protostar reaches a few million degrees, and hydrogen nuclei start to fuse together to form helium (see p.82).
6) This releases an enormous amount of energy and creates enough outward pressure (radiation pressure) to stop the gravitational collapse.
7) The star has now reached the MAIN SEQUENCE stage. It stays like that, relatively unchanging, while it fuses hydrogen into helium in the core...

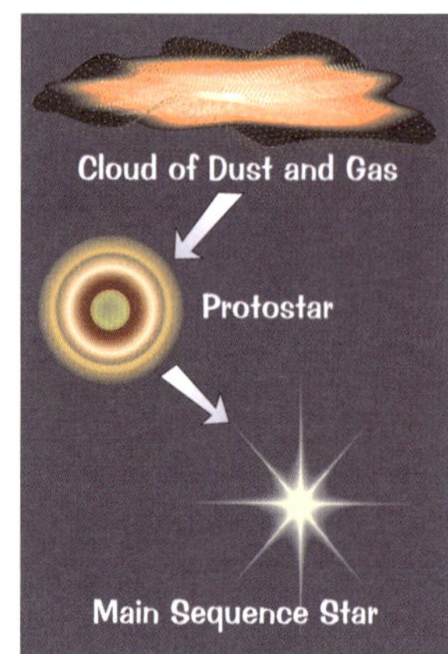

Fusion Happens in the Core of a Star

A star is made up of a core (centre) surrounded by different layers. The closer to the centre of the star, the hotter that bit will be, e.g. the core is hotter than the surface.

THE CORE — Most of the fusion in a star takes place in the centre. The pressure from the weight of the rest of the star makes the core hotter and denser than the rest of the star. So, the nuclei in the core are close enough (and have enough energy) to fuse together.

SURFACE (photosphere) — the outer region of the star, from where energy is radiated into space. Energy released from fusion in the core is transported by photons of radiation and convection currents to the surface of the star. This is the part of the Sun that we see from Earth.

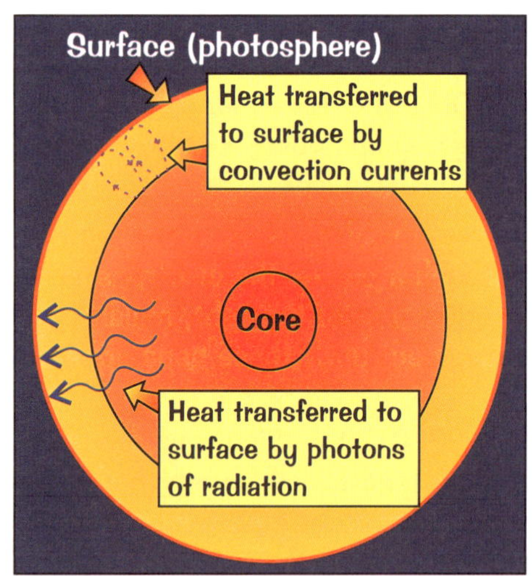

Main Sequence Stars have Hydrogen in their Core

1) A star stops being in the main sequence when it runs out of hydrogen in the core.
2) It then swells up to become a red giant or supergiant star.
3) In the process of swelling up, the star's photosphere cools down.

Check out the next page for more on the life cycle of stars.

More Massive Stars can Fuse Heavier Nuclei

1) The more massive (large) a star is the hotter the core is.
2) The hotter the core, the heavier the nuclei it can fuse together — so it can create even heavier nuclei.

Really massive stars can create iron (and demand higher wages)...

When a star runs out of hydrogen it starts to fuse helium nuclei together, then carbon, neon, oxygen, silicon... This is how most of the chemical elements in the Universe were made — and you're made of these bits of stars.

The Life Cycle of Stars

Stars — they're born, get middle aged (without feeling the need to buy a sports car) and then go bang.

Stars Fuse Other Elements When the Hydrogen Runs Out

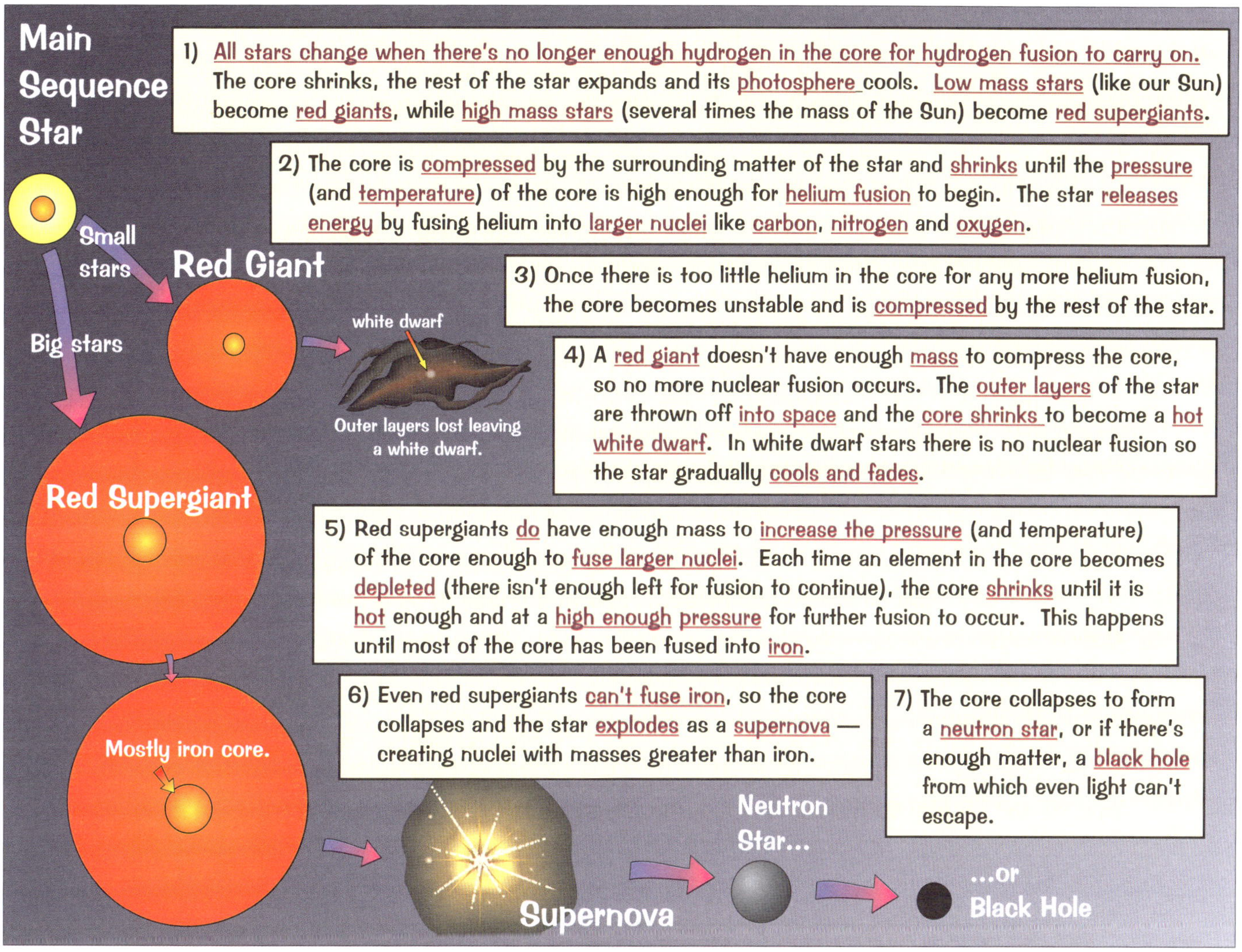

Main Sequence Star

1) All stars change when there's no longer enough hydrogen in the core for hydrogen fusion to carry on. The core shrinks, the rest of the star expands and its photosphere cools. Low mass stars (like our Sun) become red giants, while high mass stars (several times the mass of the Sun) become red supergiants.

2) The core is compressed by the surrounding matter of the star and shrinks until the pressure (and temperature) of the core is high enough for helium fusion to begin. The star releases energy by fusing helium into larger nuclei like carbon, nitrogen and oxygen.

Small stars

Red Giant

Big stars

3) Once there is too little helium in the core for any more helium fusion, the core becomes unstable and is compressed by the rest of the star.

white dwarf

Outer layers lost leaving a white dwarf.

4) A red giant doesn't have enough mass to compress the core, so no more nuclear fusion occurs. The outer layers of the star are thrown off into space and the core shrinks to become a hot white dwarf. In white dwarf stars there is no nuclear fusion so the star gradually cools and fades.

Red Supergiant

5) Red supergiants do have enough mass to increase the pressure (and temperature) of the core enough to fuse larger nuclei. Each time an element in the core becomes depleted (there isn't enough left for fusion to continue), the core shrinks until it is hot enough and at a high enough pressure for further fusion to occur. This happens until most of the core has been fused into iron.

Mostly iron core.

6) Even red supergiants can't fuse iron, so the core collapses and the star explodes as a supernova — creating nuclei with masses greater than iron.

7) The core collapses to form a neutron star, or if there's enough matter, a black hole from which even light can't escape.

Supernova

Neutron Star...

...or Black Hole

Luminosity vs Temperature — the Hertzsprung-Russell Diagram

1) If you plot luminosity (brightness) against temperature, you don't just get a random collection of stars. Different types of stars group together in distinct areas. This is called the Hertzsprung-Russell diagram:

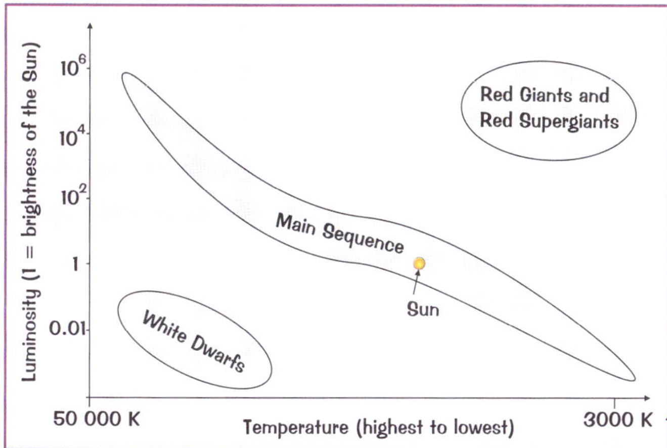

Temperature goes the "wrong way" along the x-axis — from hotter to cooler.

2) The different areas show the main stages of a star's life cycle: the main sequence, red giants and supergiants and white dwarfs.

3) The reason you can see these areas is because stars exist in these stable stages of their life cycle for long periods of time.

4) You don't see unstable phases, like supernovas, on the diagram because they happen too quickly.

Even stars die eventually — but at least they go out with a bang...

I'm going to name my dog after Ejnar Hertzsprung, because I like his diagram — and Ejnar is just a great name.

Observing with Telescopes

People have looked up at the sky for thousands of years, but about 400 years ago someone invented the telescope and made it a whole lot easier to work out what was going on up there...

Astronomers Use Local and Remote Telescopes

If you want to use a single local telescope (one nearby that you can easily get to), you can go to the telescope and point it at the object you want to look at. Easy. Most telescopes are now computer controlled — which has lots of advantages:

1) Instead of an astronomer having to always be there, they now just program the telescope to track an object in the sky, then go home for tea (or to bed).
2) Computer control is also very useful when astronomers are using a telescope to do a survey — scanning across large areas of the sky in search of particular objects. For this, the telescope needs to be constantly repositioned to look at different areas of sky. Thanks to computer control, this can just be programmed in too.
3) Computer control also allows telescopes to be positioned more precisely.
4) Astronomers like putting telescopes in remote locations, like on a hilltop in the middle of a desert (see p.88). Before computers, astronomers had to travel a long way to use these telescopes. Many telescopes can now be operated remotely via the internet. So astronomers can work from the comfort of their own offices, and don't have to spend time or money travelling.
5) Astronomers may need to have many telescopes pointing in the same direction at the same time. This happens a lot in radio astronomy, which uses information from many dishes spread across large distances. This can all be controlled ... you've guessed it, by a beautiful computer.
6) Optical astronomers can only observe during the night. Because the Earth's spinning, astronomers need a network of telescopes around the world — so it's always night for at least one telescope — if they want to observe an object continuously for longer than one night.
7) Computers are also used to record and process data from telescopes, which is handy.
8) And finally, without computer control we wouldn't be able to have space telescopes — you can't exactly just wander up there and nudge the telescope left a bit when you want to (see next page).

There Might be Other Life in the Universe

1) It's possible that life exists elsewhere in the Universe. After all, when you consider the how huge the Universe is, why should our planet be the only place with suitable conditions...
2) Scientists believe conditions necessary for life (e.g. water, nutrients...) are most likely to be found on other planets, or on moons. So they started a search for planets outside the Solar System.
3) There is evidence for planets orbiting around hundreds of nearby stars. And it's very likely there are a lot more, given how many stars there are out there.
4) Even if only a small proportion of stars have planets orbiting them, many scientists still think that there's probably life somewhere else in the Universe.
5) So far though, there's no evidence that any extraterrestrial (not from Earth) life exists, or has existed in the past.

Is there anybody out there — I'm listening.

Starry, starry night — I'll just get my telescope...

The first telescopes made objects in the sky look about 20 times closer and could be hand-held. The biggest telescopes today are huge and can see other galaxies clearly. The largest telescope ever built is used to detect radio waves (including ones that might be from other intelligent life forms) and is over 300 metres wide.

Space Telescopes

The atmosphere might be good for us (blocking out X-rays for instance), but it's a pain for astronomers...

The Atmosphere Can Mess Up Measurements

1) Astronomers need accurate measurements to be able to understand what's going on in space, but our atmosphere can muck up the results.
2) Our atmosphere only lets certain wavelengths of electromagnetic radiation through and blocks all the others. The graph shows how the transparency of the atmosphere varies with wavelength.
3) Some radiation, like radio waves, passes through the atmosphere without much trouble, but visible light can be badly affected.
4) Light gets refracted by water in the atmosphere, which blurs the images.

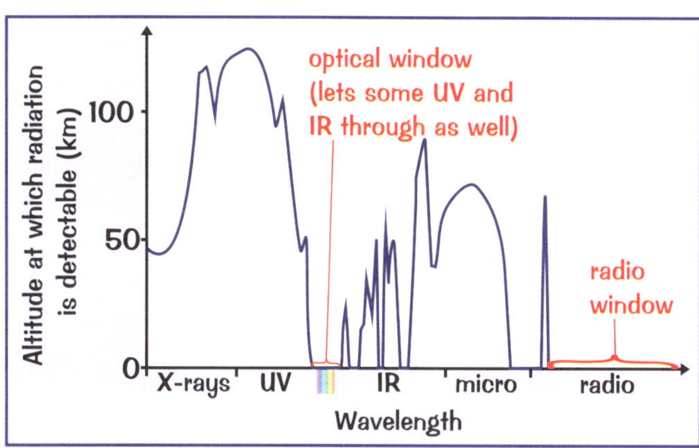

5) Light can also be absorbed by dust particles in the air. Boo hiss.
6) Sites for astronomical observatories on Earth are picked very carefully to try and minimise all these problems (see next page). Another solution is to take measurements from above the atmosphere...

Space Telescopes Have a Clearer View Than Those on Earth

1) If you're trying to look at EM radiation that's blocked or affected by the atmosphere, the thing to do is put your telescope in space, away from the mist and murk down here. The first space telescope (called Hubble) was launched by NASA in 1990. It can see objects that are about a billion times fainter than you can see just by standing in your back garden and looking up.

NASA/SCIENCE PHOTO LIBRARY

2) It's not all plain sailing though. Getting a telescope safely into space is hard. And when things go wrong, it's difficult to get the repair men out. Hubble's first pictures were all fuzzy, because the mirror was the wrong shape. NASA had to send some astronauts up there to fix it. D'oh.
3) Most astronomy is still done using Earth-based telescopes as they're a lot cheaper and easier to build and maintain. Hubble has cost over £3 billion to build, maintain and repair and people have to be sent to space to fix it.
4) Astronomers have also developed good techniques to remove the effects of the atmosphere from their measurements so the images are clearer.
5) It's also a lot easier to get a time slot to do your observing on Earth-based telescopes — there are lots more of them so there's much less demand for each one.

There are Many Uncertainties in Space Programmes

1) Space programmes are projects to send things like people, probes and telescopes into space. They're really expensive — the Apollo programme that ended with people walking on the Moon cost about $135 billion in today's money.
2) Governments have to balance paying these sums with other costly priorities like defence, healthcare and coping with natural disasters (which are unpredictable). The funding for space programmes is never guaranteed — there can be cut-backs at any time.
3) Many countries' space programmes are linked (see next page), so cut-backs in one country can have a knock-on effect on the others.

Telescope broken — we can't get the van up there, mate...

Space telescopes are so expensive because you've got to make a telescope that will be strong enough to withstand being blasted into space, but that's lightweight enough too. It's hard work being a boffin.

Observatories and Cooperation

It's just like primary school — astronomers have to learn to play together and share their toys.

Astronomers Need to Work Together

1) Whether it's building a new telescope on Earth or sending people into space, many science projects are too expensive for one country to do alone. These 'big science' projects are only possible if several countries cooperate and share the costs and resources.
2) By working together, you can get the best people and the best facilities for the job. E.g. scientists in the USA have expertise in launching components and equipment and so would probably be best to advise on getting a probe or object launched into space.
3) The International Space Station is a project led by the US but with the help of 15 other countries, including those in the European Space Agency. Each country is providing different parts of the Station and it's the largest and most expensive international science project in history.
4) The European Extremely Large Telescope is a project involving astronomers from across the whole of Europe, but based in Chile. It's too complex and expensive for a single country to build and operate.

Observatory Locations are Chosen for Astronomical Reasons...

1) Optical (visible light) observatories are often put in remote locations, e.g. Roque de los Muchachos in the Canary Islands. The idea is to avoid man-made light pollution (e.g. from street lamps) as well as dust and other particles (e.g. from car exhausts) affecting the observations.
2) Astronomers want as little atmosphere between the observatory and telescope as possible to minimise the distorting and blurring effects it has. So observatories are often built at high elevation (i.e. up mountains) where the atmosphere is thinner and so affects the light less. E.g. the Mauna Kea site in Hawaii is about 4200 m above sea level.

MAGRATH PHOTOGRAPHY/ SCIENCE PHOTO LIBRARY

3) Water in the atmosphere can cause problems by refracting light — so a dry location with low atmospheric pollution is good for a telescope. E.g. there are observatories in Australia and the Atacama desert in Chile.
4) Clouds block a telescope's view of the sky, so they're built in places that have loads of cloudless nights.

... But Other Factors Need to be Taken into Account

Scientists have to live in the real world. They can't just go building observatories in the most remote and awkward places, just because there's a nice view. There are other things to take into account...

1) **COST** — Observatories aren't cheap to build. Never mind carting all the stuff up a mountain in the middle of nowhere. There's the cost of building, running and eventually closing the observatory.

2) **ACCESS** — The site will have to have roads built to it (so you can get equipment and people there to build the telescopes) as well as electricity and other facilities. Some places are just too hard to get to.

3) **ENVIRONMENT** — Scientists have to be careful that building works, etc. will damage the surrounding environment as little as possible, e.g. by disturbance to wildlife or agriculture.

4) **SOCIAL** — Even with remotely controlled telescopes, there are always going to be a few people who need to work at the telescope site. They'll need facilities such as water, electricity, accommodation, shops, etc., which will be quite expensive to provide. In some areas observatories have benefited the local community — by providing jobs in building and maintaining the observatory.

Hawaii? — Sounds like a sneaky holiday to me...

Most of the big optical and infrared observatories on Earth are in Hawaii, Chile, Australia and the Canary Islands. Nice work if you can get it... Anyway folks, that is it — GCSE physics complete (apart from the next page).

Revision Summary for Module P7

There's a lot of tricky stuff to learn in this module, but at least there are lots of pretty pictures to help. Have a go at these questions, and if you get stuck have a sneaky peek back at the pages. Just keep going through them till you can do them all, cuz this is the last lot in the book. So once you're through these you're done. Huzzah.

1) Briefly explain what a sidereal day is.
2) State what a solar day is.
3) Describe how a lunar eclipse occurs.
4) Name the two angles which are used to measure the positions of stars in the sky.
5) Explain how a triangular prism can produce a spectrum of visible light.
6)* A lens has a focal length of f = 0.5 m. Calculate the power of the lens in dioptres.
7)* Ed Halley has a telescope with an f_o = 10.0 m and f_e = 0.25 m.
What is the magnification of Ed's telescope?
8) Draw a diagram to show what would happen if a wave passed through:
a) a gap much wider than its wavelength, b) a gap a bit wider than its wavelength,
c) a gap the same size as its wavelength.
9) State what the parallax angle is.
10) Briefly outline Curtis' argument in the Curtis-Shapley debate.
11)* The Tadpole galaxy is approximately 4×10^{21} km away from Earth. Calculate its speed of recession, if the Hubble constant is 2×10^{-18} s^{-1}.
12) What's absolute zero in °C? What does absolute zero mean in terms of kinetic energy of particles?
13)* Calculate the following temperature conversions:
a) –89 °C into K b) 120 °C into K c) 5 K into °C d) 312 K into °C
14) What two ways are there to increase the pressure of a gas?
15) What equation is used to calculate how much energy is released by nuclear fusion?
What does each letter in the equation represent?
16) What type of nuclei fuse together in the Sun to make $^{3}_{2}He$? What else is given out when this happens?
17) What is the 'peak frequency' of a star?
18) Explain how absorption line spectra can show what elements are present in a star's atmosphere.
19) Describe how a star is formed.
20) Give the two ways in which energy is transported to the surface of a star.
21) A star much larger than the Sun stops fusing hydrogen. Describe the phases the star will go through before becoming a neutron star or a black hole.
22) Give two advantages of computer-controlled telescopes.
23) Explain why many astronomers think there may be life elsewhere in the Universe.
Is there any evidence for extraterrestrial life so far?
24) Explain why astronomers can only detect certain wavelengths of radiation from space on Earth.
25) Give one advantage of using space telescopes.
Give two reasons why most astronomy is done with Earth-based telescopes.
26) Why do astronomers need to work together on 'big science projects'?
27) Write down two astronomical and two non-astronomical factors that have to be taken into account when choosing a site for an observatory.

* Answers on page 96.

Planning

Your controlled assessment is a practical investigation. To start with, you'll be given some material to get your head around. Here's what you'll need to do:

1) Come up with a hypothesis, then make a prediction based on your hypothesis that you can test.
2) Plan an experiment to test your prediction. You'll need to think about things like:
   - What you're going to measure and how you're going to do it (your method).
   - What equipment you're going to use (and why that equipment is right for the job).
   - How you're going to make sure your results are accurate and reliable.
   - The range of values and the interval (gap) between the values of the independent variable.
3) Write a risk assessment for the experiment.
4) Explain all the choices you made when planning the experiment.

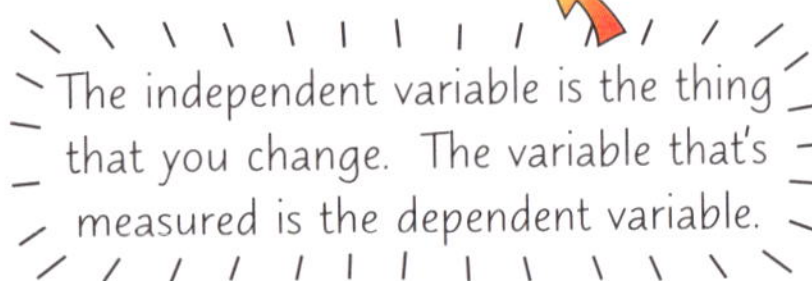

Here are a few tips to help you with the planning stage:

Think Carefully About the Method and Equipment You'll Use

1) You should test several different methods before you start — this will help you decide which is the best one to use. You'll need to be able to justify your choice of method when writing up your experiment.
2) You need to make sure your method produces reliable results, i.e. results that can be consistently reproduced each time you do an experiment. If your results are reliable they're more likely to be true.
3) Your results will end up being more reliable if you make sure your method is a fair test:
   - In a lab experiment you usually change one variable and measure how it affects the other variable.

     EXAMPLE: you might change only the angle of a slope and measure how it affects the time taken for a toy car to travel down it.

   - To make it a fair test everything else that could affect the results should stay the same (otherwise you can't tell if the thing that's being changed is causing the results or not).

     EXAMPLE continued: you need to keep the slope length the same, otherwise you won't know if any change in the time taken is caused by the change in angle, or the change in length.

4) Repeating the readings and calculating the mean (average) will also help your results to be more reliable.
5) You should also make sure that your results are accurate. This means that they're really close to the true answer. There are things you can do to make your results more accurate, such as using equipment that's sensitive enough to accurately measure the chemicals you're using. E.g. if you need to measure out 11 ml of a liquid, you'll need to use a measuring cylinder that can measure to 1 ml, not 5 or 10 ml.

Trial Runs Help Figure out the Range and Interval of Variable Values

1) A trial run is a quick version of your experiment.
2) Trial runs are used to figure out the range of variable values used (the upper and lower limit).
3) And they're used to figure out the interval (gap) between the values too.

EXAMPLE continued:
You might do trial runs at 20, 40, 60 and 80°. If the time taken is too short to accurately measure at 80°, you might narrow the range to 20-60°.
If using 20° intervals gives you a big change in time taken you might decide to use 10° intervals, e.g. 20, 30, 40, 50°...

Experiments Must be Safe

1) Part of planning an investigation is making sure that it'll be safe.
2) You should always make sure that you identify all the hazards that you might encounter.
3) You should also come up with ways of reducing the risks from the hazards you've identified.
4) Do this by carrying out a risk assessment. E.g. if you're using a Bunsen burner, there would be a fire risk — you'd need to take precautions such as keeping flammable chemicals away from the flame.

Processing the Data

Once you've planned your experiment you'll carry it out to collect your own data (called primary data). You'll then be given some secondary data (that's data collected by someone else). You'll also need to collect more secondary data yourself, e.g. from textbooks, websites or even from other people in your class. You'll need to process and analyse all the data you have. This might involve a few different things:

1) Displaying and organising the data using tables.
2) Carrying out mathematical calculations to process the data.
3) Drawing graphs or diagrams to display the data.
4) Looking for patterns in the now beautifully presented data.

Data Needs to be Organised

1) Data that's been collected needs to be organised so it can be processed — tables are dead useful for this.
2) Tables are also good for spotting any outliers (see page 3) — you'll need to have spotted these so you can account for them when you're concluding and evaluating later.
3) When drawing tables, make sure that each column has a heading and that you've included the units.

Data Can be Processed Using a Bit of Maths

1) Raw data generally just ain't that useful. You usually have to process it in some way.
2) A couple of the most simple calculations you can perform are the mean (average) and the range (how spread out the data is):
   - To calculate the mean ADD TOGETHER all the data values and DIVIDE by the total number of values. You usually do this to get a single value from several repeats of your experiment.
   - To calculate the range find the LARGEST number and SUBTRACT the SMALLEST number. You usually do this to check how precise your results are when you've taken repeated readings. Precise results are ones where the data is all really close to the mean (i.e. not spread out). The greater the spread of the data, the lower the reliability of the results.

Different Types of Data Should be Presented in Different Ways

1) You'll need to present your data so that it's easier to see patterns and relationships in the data.
2) Different types of investigations give you different types of data, so you'll always have to choose what the best way to present your data is.

Bar Charts

If the independent variable is categoric (comes in distinct categories, e.g. blood types, metals) you should use a bar chart to display the data. You also use them if the independent variable is discrete (the data can be counted in chunks, where there's no in-between value, e.g. number of people is discrete because you can't have half a person).

There are some golden rules you need to follow for drawing bar charts:

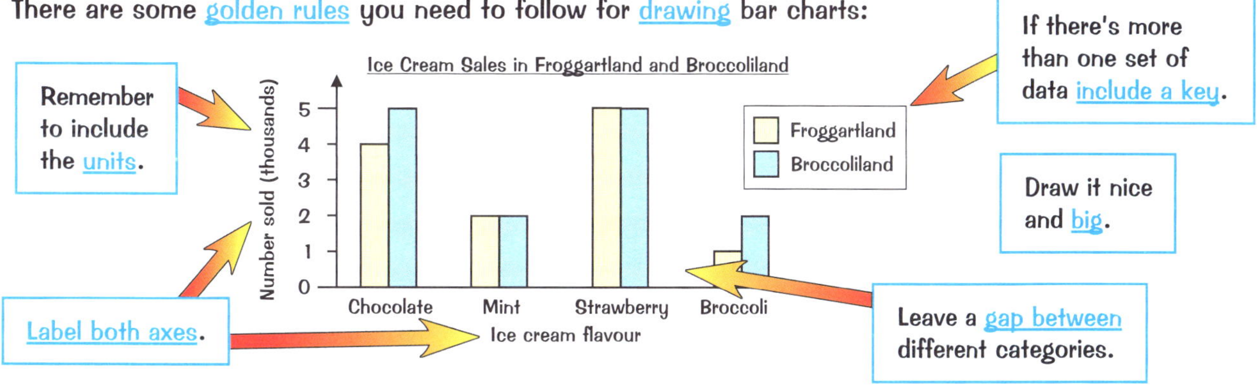

Processing the Data

Hold up, you haven't finished with data processing yet, and there's still the analysis to think about. Sheesh.

Line Graphs

If the independent variable is continuous (numerical data that can have any value within a range, e.g. length, volume, temperature) you should use a line graph to display the data.

Use the biggest data values you've got to draw a sensible scale on your axes. For example, the highest compression is 8.8 mm, so it makes sense to label the y-axis up to 10 mm.

The dependent variable goes on the y-axis (the vertical one).

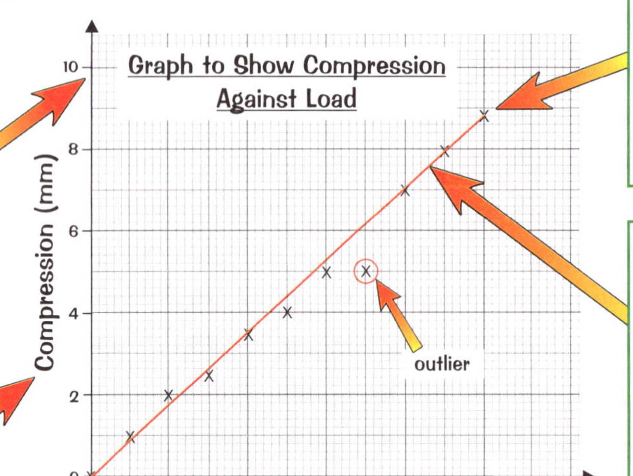

The independent variable goes on the x-axis (the horizontal one).

When plotting points, use a sharp pencil and make a neat little cross (don't do blobs).

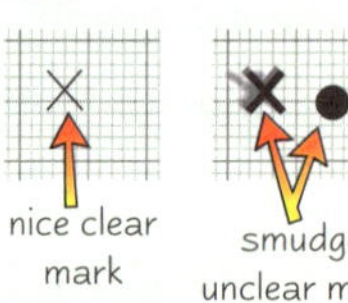

Don't join the dots up. You should draw a line of best fit (or a curve of best fit if your points make a curve). When drawing a line (or curve), try to draw the line through or as near to as many points as possible, ignoring any outliers.

Remember to include the units.

Graphs Can Give You a Lot of Information About Your Data

If you've presented your data in a graph, you can use it to show a bit more about the data or even do some calculations. For example, if 'time' is on the x-axis, you can calculate the gradient (slope) of the line to find the rate of reaction:

1) Gradient = y ÷ x
2) You can calculate the gradient of the whole line or a section of it.
3) The rate would be in cm^3/s.

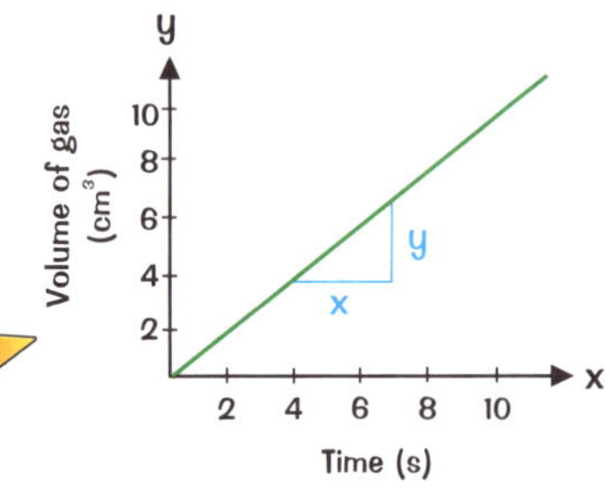

Line Graphs Can Show Relationships in Data

Before you can make any conclusions, you need to look for patterns or relationships between variables.

1) Line graphs are great for showing relationships between two variables.
2) Here are the three different types of correlation (relationship) shown on line graphs:

There's more on correlation on page 4.

POSITIVE correlation — as one variable increases the other increases.

INVERSE (negative) correlation — as one variable increases the other decreases.

NO correlation — there's no relationship between the two variables.

3) Remember, don't confuse correlation with cause — there might be other factors involved (see page 4).

Conclusion and Evaluation

At the end of your practical investigation, the conclusion and evaluation will be waiting. Don't worry, they won't bite. Here's what you'll need to do:

1) Draw a conclusion from your primary data.
2) Compare the secondary data with the primary data. Say whether the secondary data agrees or disagrees with your conclusion from the primary data.
3) Look back at the hypothesis and say how well it's supported by your conclusion and secondary data.
4) Look critically at your method and your results and write an evaluation of your investigation.

I know, I know, the suspense is killing me too. So, without any further ado, here are the finer details...

A Conclusion is a Summary of What You've Learnt

1) Drawing a conclusion can be quite straightforward — just look at your data and say what pattern you see.

EXAMPLE: The table on the right shows the decrease in temperature of a beaker of hot water insulated with different materials over 10 minutes.

Material	Mean temperature decrease (°C)
A	4
B	2
No insulation	20

CONCLUSION: Material B reduces heat loss from the beaker more over a 10 minute period than material A.

2) However, you also need to use the data that's been collected to justify the conclusion (back it up).

EXAMPLE continued: Material B reduced heat loss from the beaker by 2 °C more on average than material A.

3) There are some things to watch out for too — it's important that the conclusion matches the data it's based on and doesn't go any further.

EXAMPLE continued: You can't conclude that material B would reduce heat loss by the same amount for any other type of container — the results could be totally different.

4) You then need to look back at the hypothesis and use your scientific knowledge to explain how well your conclusion supports the hypothesis.
5) If the conclusion agrees with the hypothesis, then it increases confidence in the hypothesis (makes us more sure that it's right). If the conclusion doesn't agree with the hypothesis, then it decreases confidence in the hypothesis (makes us less sure that it's right).

Evaluation — Weigh Up How Well Things Went

An evaluation is a critical analysis — be honest and point out the problems with your investigation.

1) Comment on the method — you should say if there were any problems with the method (e.g. with the techniques or apparatus you used), then you should say how it could be improved.
2) Comment on the quality of the results — was there enough evidence to reach a valid conclusion? Were the results reliable, accurate and precise?
3) Were there any outliers in the results — if there were none then say so.
4) If there were any outliers, try to explain them — were they caused by errors in measurement? Were there any other variables that could have affected the results?

After you've done the evaluation, you'll know what you could have done better. So, you should explain in detail how you would collect more data to increase confidence in the hypothesis.

If you couldn't find any problems with the investigation, but your conclusion just doesn't match the hypothesis, then you should suggest alterations you could make to the hypothesis so that it matches your conclusion. You could then suggest ways to test the new hypothesis with further experiments.

Index

Index

Answers

Waves — The Basics (page 16)

Speed = Frequency × Wavelength,
so speed = 19 000 Hz × 0.125 m
= 2375 m/s

Revision Summary for Module P1 (page 17)

26) Speed = Frequency × Wavelength,
so frequency = speed ÷ wavelength
= 3×10^8 m/s ÷ 3 m = 1×10^8 Hz = 100 MHz

27) Speed = Frequency × Wavelength. In one second, half a wave passes so frequency is 0.5 Hz, and speed = 0.5 Hz × 0.9 m = 0.45 m/s

Revision Summary for Module P3 (page 39)

2) Power in kW, so 5 W = 0.005 kW.
Energy = Power × Time,
so energy = 0.005 kW × 3 h = 0.015 kWh.
Cost = kWh × cost per kWh,
so cost = 0.015 kWh × 10p = 0.15p.

3) Power = Voltage × Current,
so Power = 230 V × 5 A = 1150 W = 1.15 kW

Work (page 47)

Work done = force × distance
Want to work out force, so use:
Force = work done ÷ distance
Force = 1050 J ÷ 3 m
Force = 350 N

Revision Summary for Module P4 (page 50)

2) a) Speed = distance ÷ time
Speed = 3.2 m ÷ 35 s = 0.091 m/s
b) There are 60 seconds in a minute so:
Time = 25 × 60 = 1500 s
Rearrange formula to get one for distance:
Distance = speed × time
Distance = 0.091 m/s × 1500 s = 137 m

3) Speed = distance ÷ time
Speed = 6.3 m ÷ 0.5 s = 12.6 m/s
This is less than 13.3 m/s so no, the car wasn't breaking the speed limit.

15) Momentum = mass × velocity
Momentum = 78 kg × 5 m/s = 390 kgm/s

18) Work done = force × distance
Work done = 535 N × 12 m = 6420 J

20) G.P.E. = weight × height
G.P.E. = 120 N × 4.5 N = 540 J

21) K.E. gained = G.P.E. lost
K.E. gained = 150 kJ

22) K.E. = $\frac{1}{2}mv^2$
K.E. = ½ × 600 × 40^2 = 480 000 J
K.E. = G.P.E. = weight × height
Rearranging to get formula for height
Height = G.P.E. ÷ weight
Height = 480 000 J ÷ 6000 N = 80 m

23) G.P.E. = weight × height
G.P.E. = 200 N × 50 m = 10 000 J
K.E. gained = G.P.E. lost = 10 000 J
K.E. = $\frac{1}{2}mv^2$
Rearranging to find formula for v^2:
$\frac{1}{2}mv^2$ = 10 000 J
v^2 = 10 000 J ÷ (½ × 20 kg) = 1000 $[m/s]^2$
v = $\sqrt{1000}$ = 31.6 m/s

Revision Summary for Module P5 (page 61)

13) Resistance = voltage ÷ current
Resistance = 12 V ÷ 2.5 A = 4.8 Ω

15) The circuit is wired in series, so the current is the same everywhere: A_1 = 0.2 A
Resistance = voltage ÷ current, rearrange to get voltage = resistance × current, and find the voltage across each resistor:
V_1 = 7 Ω × 0.2 A = 1.4 V
V_2 = 2 Ω × 0.2 A = 0.4 V
Total voltage in series = $V_1 + V_2 + V_3$ = 12 V,
so, V_3 = 12 V – (1.4 V + 0.4 V) = 12 V – 1.8 = 10.2 V
Resistance = voltage ÷ current,
so, R_1 = 10.2 V ÷ 0.2 A = 51 Ω

19) 0.4 A

25) $V_p/V_s = N_p/N_s$ so V_s = (500 ÷ 20) × 9
= 25 × 9 = 225 V

Revision Summary for Module P6 (page 69)

7) a) $^{131}_{53}I \rightarrow ^{131}_{54}Xe + ^{0}_{-1}\beta$
b) $^{148}_{64}Gd \rightarrow ^{144}_{62}Sm + ^{4}_{2}\alpha$

9) After one half-life the activity will be 840 ÷ 2 = 420 Bq. After 2 half-lives, it will be 420 ÷ 2 = 210 Bq. After 3 half-lives, it will be 210 ÷ 2 = 105 Bq. This takes 4 hours. i.e. 3 half-lives = 4 hours.
So 1 half-life = 4÷3 = $1\frac{1}{3}$ hours = <u>1 hr 20 minutes</u>.

Revision Summary for Module P7 (page 89)

6) Power = 1 ÷ Focal length = 1 ÷ 0.5 = 2 D

7) Magnification = $F_o \div F_e$ = 10.0 ÷ 0.25 = 40

11) Speed of recession = Hubble constant × distance
= $2 \times 10^{-18} \times 4 \times 10^{21}$ = 8000 km/s

13) a) – 89 + 273 = 184 K
b) 120 + 273 = 393 K
c) 5 – 273 = – 268 °C
d) 312 – 273 = 39 °C